What You Need to Know about ADHD

What You Need to Know about ADHD

Victor B. Stolberg

Inside Diseases and Disorders

GREENWOOD

An Imprint of ABC-CLIO, LLC
Santa Barbara, California • Denver, Colorado

Library of Congress Cataloging-in-Publication Data

Names: Stolberg, Victor B., author.
Title: What you need to know about ADHD / Victor B. Stolberg.
Description: Santa Barbara, California : Greenwood, an imprint of ABC-CLIO, LLC, [2019] | Series: Inside diseases and disorders | Includes bibliographical references and index.
Identifiers: LCCN 2019018617 (print) | LCCN 2019019177 (ebook) | ISBN 9781440861826 (eBook) | ISBN 9781440861819 (hardcopy : alk. paper)
Subjects: LCSH: Attention-deficit hyperactivity disorder. | Attention-deficit hyperactivity disorder—Treatment. | Attention-deficit hyperactivity disorder—Family relationships. | Attention-deficit hyperactivity disorder—Case studies.
Classification: LCC RJ506.H9 (ebook) | LCC RJ506.H9 S76 2019 (print) | DDC 618.92/8589—dc23
LC record available at https://lccn.loc.gov/2019018617

ISBN: 978-1-4408-6181-9 (print)
      978-1-4408-6182-6 (ebook)

23 22 21 20 19   1 2 3 4 5

This book is also available as an eBook.

Greenwood
An Imprint of ABC-CLIO, LLC

ABC-CLIO, LLC
147 Castilian Drive
Santa Barbara, California 93117
www.abc-clio.com

This book is printed on acid-free paper ∞

Manufactured in the United States of America

*In thinking about and contending with ways to convey
what we need to know about ADHD,
it has been my pleasure to ruminate on this
sublimely intriguing brain-based condition.
In the process, I have been reminded about a phrase penned by
Alexander Pope: "All our knowledge is ourselves to know."
In reading this work,
I hope it challenges you to wrestle with this sort of perspective.
To this end,
I dedicate this book to all those I've met who have ADHD and
to my family for allowing me to muddle through its preparation.*

Contents

Series Foreword

Disease is as old as humanity itself, and it has been the leading cause of death and disability throughout history. From the Black Death in the Middle Ages to smallpox outbreaks among Native Americans to the modern-day epidemics of diabetes and heart disease, humans have lived with—and died from—all manner of ailments, whether caused by infectious agents, environmental and lifestyle factors, or genetic abnormalities. The field of medicine has been driven forward by our desire to combat and prevent disease and to improve the lives of those living with debilitating disorders. And while we have made great strides forward, particularly in the last hundred years, it is doubtful that mankind will ever be completely free of the burden of disease.

Greenwood's Inside Diseases and Disorders series examines some of the key diseases and disorders, both physical and psychological, affecting the world today. Some (such as diabetes, cardiovascular disease, and ADHD) have been selected because of their prominence within the modern United States. Others (such as Ebola, celiac disease, and autism) have been chosen because they are often discussed in the media and, in some cases, are controversial or the subject of scientific or cultural debate.

Because this series covers so many different diseases and disorders, we have striven to create uniformity across all books. To maximize clarity and consistency, each book in the series follows the same format. Each begins with a collection of ten frequently asked questions about the disease or disorder, followed by clear, concise answers. Chapter 1 provides a general introduction to the disease or disorder, including statistical information, such as prevalence rates and demographic trends. The history of the disease or disorder, including how our understanding of it has evolved over time, is addressed in chapter 2. Chapter 3 examines causes and risk factors, whether genetic, microbial, or environmental, while chapter 4 discusses signs and symptoms. Chapter 5 covers the issues of diagnosis (and misdiagnosis), treatment, and management (whether with drugs, medical procedures, or lifestyle changes). How such treatment, or the lack thereof, affects a patient's long-term prognosis, as well as the risk of complications, are the subject of chapter 6. Chapter 7 explores the disease or disorder's effects on the friends and family of a patient—a dimension often overlooked in discussions of physical and psychological ailments. Chapter 8 discusses prevention strategies, while chapter 9 explores key issues or controversies, whether medical or sociocultural. Finally, chapter 10 profiles cutting-edge research and speculates on how things might change in the next few decades.

Each volume also features five fictional case illustrations that exemplify different aspects of the book's subject matter, highlighting key concepts and themes that have been explored throughout the text. The reader will also find a glossary of terms and a collection of print and electronic resources for additional information and further study.

As a final caveat, please be aware that the information presented in these books is no substitute for consultation with a licensed health care professional. These books do not claim to provide medical advice or guidance.

Acknowledgments

I would like to take this opportunity to acknowledge my family, particularly my wife and our two young sons, for their ongoing support and forbearance during my time on this project. I would like to wholeheartedly thank all the staff and consultants behind the scenes at ABC-CLIO for bringing this work to completion. Chiefly, I would like to thank Maxine Taylor, senior acquisitions editor for Health/Wellness and Psychology at ABC-CLIO, for steering me through this journey.

Most importantly, I would like to sincerely acknowledge all of those individuals who are struggling with ADHD, particularly those with whom I have had the pleasure of interacting, both professionally and personally. Further, the hard work and dedication of so many individuals working with individuals with ADHD and their families established a platform upon which I could build this project.

Introduction

This book provides an overview of the essentials of what one needs to know about attention deficit hyperactivity disorder (ADHD). It covers its history; causes and risk factors; signs and symptoms; major variants; potential complications; effects on family and friends; prevention; usefulness of various treatments, including pharmacological and supportive approaches; and future directions.

This book opens with ten essential questions that introduce and briefly answer some of the key misperceptions about ADHD. The points explored here are more fully explained in the subsequent chapters. Nevertheless, they provide the reader with the basics of what one really needs to know about ADHD.

The initial chapter discusses what the disorder of ADHD is. Issues of incidence and prevalence rates are surveyed, and the neurobiological background is broken down. A quick look is made into various domains of personal, educational, and workplace issues impacted by ADHD. The second chapter covers the historical background of ADHD and the development of respective ADHD medications.

Causes and risk factors of ADHD are examined, and common signs and symptoms summarized. Diagnosis, treatment, and management of the disorder are critiqued. While treatment with ADHD medications produces substantial benefits for over two-thirds of those with ADHD, other approaches are also useful. Taken as prescribed, these medications don't tend to result in dependence, rather significantly decreasing such likelihood. Treatment doesn't cure ADHD but, rather, reduces the occurrence of negative symptoms. Family and friendship concerns are covered, and prevention strategies reviewed, as are other associated controversies. The final full chapter explores current research and future directions. What the future holds for ADHD is difficult to predict, but increasing evidence is accumulating, with promises of a brighter future for understanding and addressing ADHD.

Case illustrations present selected case histories of ADHD in the lives individuals and those around them, principally family members. These are intended to present more intimate pictures of how ADHD can play out in the lives and experiences of individuals with ADHD and their families and close associates. ADHD often persists into adolescence and adulthood, as our case studies indicate. Without diagnosis and treatment, individuals with ADHD are likely to experience serious difficulties in school and other life areas. Earlier initiation of treatment helps individuals perform better in academics and work and also helps avoid feelings of anxiety and depression, commonly associated with the difficulties experienced with ADHD, including peer rejection and conflicts with parents, teachers, and other authority figures.

The basic tenet of this book is to expand general understanding related to the disorder of ADHD. This isn't intended to dismiss or negate prevailing views but rather to sit alongside positivist perspectives and contribute to a more comprehensive and nuanced understanding of the myriad phenomena around ADHD.

Essential Questions

1. WHAT IS ADHD?

ADHD is recognized to be a neurobiological behavioral disorder that is characterized by developmentally inappropriate and chronic problems related to issues of impulsivity, inattention, and sometimes hyperactivity. ADHD is fundamentally the result of the inability of the brain to release enough of the appropriate neurotransmitter substances, particularly dopamine and norepinephrine, which results in the characteristic symptoms of inattention, hyperactivity, and impulsiveness.

2. IS ADHD AN ACTUAL MEDICAL CONDITION?

The American Psychiatric Association defines ADHD as a medical disorder in its *Diagnostic and Statistical Manual of Mental Disorders, Fifth Edition* (DSM-5). The U.S. Department of Education, the National Institutes of Health, the American Academy of Pediatrics, and many others recognize ADHD as a legitimate medical diagnosis.

3. WHAT CAUSES ADHD?

The exact causes of ADHD are not fully known, but there are many risk factors that have been identified as increasing an individual's risk. ADHD tends to run in families, and there is clearly a strong genetic component to ADHD, but it does not appear to be caused by a single gene. Children who are born prematurely and/or at a low birth weight, for instance, have an increased risk of having ADHD. Maternal cigarette or alcohol consumption during pregnancy, as well as exposure to pesticides, lead, or other toxins, is also associated with higher risks for developing ADHD.

4. HOW IS ADHD DIAGNOSED?

ADHD is a relatively common diagnosis; in fact, it is the most common psychiatric diagnosis among children in the United States. A comprehensive evaluation is necessary to make an accurate diagnosis of ADHD. A skilled clinician, such as a general practitioner, psychiatrist, psychologist, or therapist, will typically use multiple assessments, interviews, and evaluations to help make a diagnosis. This process will commonly include a lengthy clinical interview, the taking of a complete medical history, and completion of standardized assessment instruments, usually behavioral rating scales completed by parents and by teachers. The symptoms of ADHD must have started by the age of twelve, and they must be present in two or more settings, like in home, school, or work.

5. WHAT CAN CONFUSE A DIAGNOSIS OF ADHD?

Many conditions are recognized to frequently occur along with ADHD, and these can confuse the diagnosing of ADHD. For example, up to 50 percent of individuals with ADHD also have a comorbid specific learning disability, usually a language-based one. About 70 percent of individuals with ADHD will be treated at some time during their life for depression. Around 30 percent of children and up to 40 percent of adults with ADHD also have a comorbid anxiety disorder. Sleep problems are more common among individuals with ADHD than among those without.

6. IS ADHD REALLY MORE COMMON AMONG CHILDREN, PARTICULARLY BOYS?

ADHD affects individuals of every age, gender, racial, religious, and socio-economic background. It is a nondiscriminatory disorder, diagnosed in about 9.5 percent of U.S. children, and it is believed that 4.4 percent of U.S. adults experience symptoms of ADHD. Females and males are as likely to have ADHD, but it tends to be diagnosed more frequently in males, who are more likely to be perceived as disruptive, than in females. Consequently, females are less likely to get appropriate treatment. Males seem to be more likely to be hyperactive, while females are more likely to present with symptoms of inattention.

7. CAN AN INDIVIDUAL WHO IS NOT HYPERACTIVE HAVE ADHD?

Yes. According to the DSM-5, there are three major types of ADHD, but only two of these contain diagnostic criteria for symptoms of hyperactivity.

There is the primarily hyperactive-impulsive type of ADHD and the combined type of ADHD, both of which require the presence of symptoms of hyperactivity and impulsivity for a diagnosis. However, there is a third variant, the primarily inattentive type of ADHD, formerly referred to by some as Attention Deficit Disorder (ADD), for those individuals who have ADHD but are not hyperactive.

8. CAN WE CURE ADHD?

While there is no cure for ADHD, it is a highly treatable and manageable disorder. Except for in very young individuals, the most commonly recommended first line of treatment for ADHD is pharmacological, along with some form of behavioral therapy. The most typical initial treatment approach begins with a prescription for a psychostimulant medication, like Ritalin or Adderall, but there are several nonstimulant medications available as well.

9. ARE THERE LIFESTYLE CHANGES THAT CAN HELP MANAGE ADHD?

There are many nonpharmacological approaches that can effectively treat individuals with ADHD. These include various behavioral and cognitive treatments that can be implemented either by parents, teachers, or therapists. There are many alternative therapeutic approaches that have been found to help individuals with ADHD, such as acupuncture, biofeedback, chiropractic, hypnosis, massage, and relaxation exercises. There are also many healthy lifestyle choices that can help reduce ADHD symptoms. Regular physical exercise, for example, has been demonstrated to significantly help individuals with ADHD stay more focused, ignore distractions, and improve their academic performance. Appropriate nutrition can not only reduce the incidence of ADHD symptoms but also lessen their severity. Extra sleep can also help reduce restlessness and improve behavior.

10. CAN SOMEONE GROW OUT OF ADHD?

While it used to be a widely held belief that most individuals would grow out of ADHD, this is no longer the generally accepted understanding. Although some children with ADHD may appear to outgrow the condition, most will continue to grow up to be adults with ADHD. As individuals develop, mature, and adjust, they usually learn how to better cope with things, including the symptoms of ADHD. These symptoms certainly may present themselves differently at different stages of an individual's life.

Older adolescents and young adults may learn to be less disruptive than they were as children; on the other hand, other adolescents and young adults who are predominantly inattentive may begin to experience more difficulties as the expectations of sustained attention increase as they age. Symptoms in adults may be less overt, but they can still be impairing, such as failed relationships or lost jobs. At any rate, one does not actually grow out of ADHD, but the impact of ADHD symptoms may often lessen.

1

What Is ADHD?

To understand ADHD, we must review its incidence and prevalence in children and adults, as these impact diagnosing and related issues. More generally, an overview of neurotransmission helps us better understand ADHD and how it impacts personal, educational, and workplace domains.

UNDERSTANDING ADHD

ADHD is a neurobiological behavioral disorder characterized by developmentally inappropriate and chronic problems with inattention, impulsivity, and sometimes hyperactivity. Most people with ADHD aren't overtly hyperactive but have internal restlessness or hyperactivity. Many don't have deficits of attention but focus too much attention on certain things. ADHD is understood to be brain based. Someone with an ADHD brain may have more difficulty than others without the disorder, known as neurotypicals, in getting motivated and focused on tasks. Understanding the brain, particularly as related to executive functions, including regulation or dysfunction of attention, is essential. The prefrontal cortex is the site of executive control, particularly regulation of attention and emotions. ADHD is the consequence of insufficient activity—rather than hyperarousal—in the neural circuits that are responsible for modulating attention and controlling behavior. Frontal cortex signal transmission to other brain regions allows processing and task performance. If signals are weak, as with ADHD, the individual's attention can be directed elsewhere. This lack of attention leads to performance problems. Neurotransmitters are implicated in ADHD, but no single neurotransmitter is responsible.

A behavioral disorder like ADHD is understood to be a persistent condition, characterized by patterns of abnormal behaviors manifesting as attributes, such as unusual and contextually inappropriate actions or words and inappropriate responses. Behavioral disorders like ADHD can result in severe and continual disruptions in activities of daily living, leading to problems at home, school, and work. In children, ADHD usually results in behaviors that interfere with academic and social success; in adults, work and intimate personal relations are more often affected.

ADHD can impact personal, familial, academic, vocational, and societal functioning, including relationships with family, friends, teachers, and colleagues. ADHD presents as a diverse disorder, manifesting differently at different ages and in variable ways. Distinguishing features are chronic repeated inattention or impulsivity or hyperactivity interfering with normal development and age-appropriate functioning.

There are levels of how ADHD affects people. Some may have mild levels, while others may experience more severe symptomology. Those experiencing predominantly mild symptoms may only exhibit minor problems within areas such as organization or risk initiation, while others may suffer more pervasive dysfunctionality. Those mildly impacted can still experience situations of greater impairment, like high-stakes examinations.

There are different ADHD subtypes. This isn't surprising when we recognize that not all experience ADHD the same way; nevertheless, common symptom clusters suggest subtypes. There is no consensus as to what the specific subtypes are. Although many believe there are three major subtypes, others assert there are more. For example, one well-respected psychiatrist, Daniel Amen (1995, 2013), described more than seven subtypes. These include the classic ADHD subtype, with symptoms including easily distracted and difficulty sustaining attention, which Amen suggests result from low dopamine; inattentive subtype, with trouble focusing attention, introverted, not hyperactive, appearing more in females; the overfocused subtype, with difficulty changing focus of attention, excessive worrying, and being argumentative, may be associated with low dopamine and serotonin and high anterior cingulate activity; the limbic subtype, which seems to be a combination of classic with depression and is associated with low dopamine and serotonin levels and overly active limbic systems; the temporal lobe subtype, with symptoms of classic and temporal lobe issues, such as difficulties with learning, memory, and temper outbursts, low GABA (gamma-amino butyric acid) is suspected; the anxious subtype, characterized by symptoms of classic, with high levels of anxiety and difficulties focusing, with suspected low dopamine and GABA levels and prefrontal cortex activity; and, finally, the ring-of-fire subtype, with mood swings and easy distractibility, low serotonin and GABA levels and an overly active brain suspected.

There are other subtype systems. Most widely accepted are the three subtypes presented in the *Diagnostic and Statistical Manual of Mental Disorders,* Fifth Edition (DSM-5) of the American Psychiatric Association (2013). These are predominantly inattentive, predominantly hyperactive/ impulsive, and combined presentation. Predominantly inattentive is considered most prevalent among children, adolescents, and adults. The subtypes differ on variables, including demographics, comorbidities, and functional impairments. It is speculated that the inattentive subtype may be an entirely different disorder with qualitatively different kinds of inattention.

DSM-5 offers a common nomenclature with standardized diagnostic criteria. The second-most used system is the *International Statistical Classification of Diseases and Related Health Problems* (ICD), produced by the World Health Organization (WHO), and there are other systems. In France, they use *Classification Francaise des Troubles Mentaux de L'Enfant et de L'Adolescent* (CFTMEA), first released in 1983 and updated in 1988, and again in 2000. CFTMEA focuses on identifying and addressing underlying psychosocial causes of symptomatic behaviors more than DSM-5 or ICD do.

ATTENTION

It is important to understand attention to better examine ADHD. Etymologically, our word "attention" comes from Latin *attentio,* meaning "stretch" (in Old French, *atendre* conveyed a similar meaning). During the fifteenth through seventeenth centuries, it came to its present meaning of stretching the mind toward an object.

Most information coming into and out of the brain goes through the reticular formation, an area within the medulla and brain stem that acts as a central clearinghouse. It gives priority to select incoming messages and filters out others—what we call attention. Human brains have fixed attention capacity. Anesthesiologists understand this and use distraction to shift focus from painful situations, such as injections.

Attention involves our entire bodies. Watching something requires focusing eyes and depends on coordination of nerves and muscles; we might have to position our bodies differently to see certain things. Establishing states of alertness for attention requires psychological and physiological focus, and coordination is necessary between body areas, including the central nervous system, muscles, and heart.

Many factors influence attention, but motivation or interest is crucial. Motivation prepares us to be attentive. Anything generating expectant attitudes arouses us to be more attentive by preparing focus. Motives, like sex and anxiety, help direct attention. We focus on very intense stimuli while becoming habituated to repetitious stimuli. Attention can be voluntarily directed, but individuals with ADHD often have difficulties doing this.

We pay more attention to novel or different things. Stimuli that are colorful, unusually shaped, loud, or unusually large or that change position will more likely elicit involuntary attention; repetition also helps. Unfortunately, someone with ADHD may move things out of attention more rapidly than neurotypicals.

Attention is essential for learning. Learning is an interconnected process, typically beginning with information retrieval. It requires understanding of what is seen, discussed, or experienced—prior knowledge is crucial. The brain seeks novel stimuli, and stimuli are constantly devalued. This is more pronounced in ADHD. Uncertainty heightens awareness and prompts attention. It follows that we must enhance the abilities of individuals with ADHD to arouse their attention to learn. Whether we accomplish this through behavioral, environmental structuring, pharmaceutical approaches, or other techniques, is of little difference, but it cannot be ignored.

RATE-DEPENDENCY THEORY

Rate-dependency theory explains why medicines are so commonly used to treat ADHD and how they work. It suggests that drug effects are dependent upon dose and are rate-dependent. Clinical research supports this. Most psychostimulants, such as amphetamines and methylphenidate, affect activity rates and attention differentially when administered under varying reinforcement schedules. Studies show that the effects of the same dosage of psychostimulants differ if the subject experiences high, rather than low, responding rates. This is because the pharmacological effects of psychostimulants are inversely related in direction and magnitude to both baseline activity and the distractions presented to subjects with ADHD. More specifically, small doses of psychostimulants increase very low rates of response while decreasing high rates. Most people with ADHD, who respond at relatively high rates, would have lowered response rates when using psychostimulants. Under such conditions, they would generally behave in routinely accepted ways, like waiting to be called upon by raising their hands, rather than blurting out responses and interrupting the conversations or activities of others. An inverse relationship between severity of ADHD symptoms and the degree of therapeutic response has been observed for psychostimulants, supporting the rate-dependency theory.

INCIDENCE AND PREVALENCE

Incidence and prevalence of ADHD are closely related. Increases in incidence are reflected by increases in prevalence. However, no direct linear relationship exists between one and the other. Intervening variables affect the associations. Effective prevention—particularly effective secondary and tertiary prevention—management, and treatment modify correlations between incidence and prevalence. Incidence refers to the total number of new cases of ADHD that are diagnosed during specific time, usually one year, for a specified population, and prevalence refers to the total number of cases in a specified population at a point in time.

Incidence of ADHD impacts over three million individuals in the United States annually. While incidence of ADHD is only somewhat common among young children aged three to five. It is very common among children aged six to eighteen and young adults aged nineteen to forty and less common among adults aged forty-one and older.

ADHD prevalence varies along several variables, such as age, cultural background, gender, trauma, substance use, and comorbidities. It is estimated there are 6.4 million U.S. children aged four to seventeen diagnosed with ADHD, equaling 11.4 percent of the population. Estimated prevalence of diagnosed cases increased from 6.1 percent in 1997–1998 to 10.2 percent in 2015–2016. The true rate of diagnosis is about 7.8 percent in the United States. Differences are attributed to misdiagnosis, thought to be greater among younger children and adults. Different subpopulations with different issues are expected to have variable prevalence. Around 25 percent of adults in substance-use treatment programs could be diagnosed with ADHD.

Prevalence varies across the world. While rates are highest in North America, South America, and Africa, they are lower in Asia, Australia, Europe, and the Middle East. Within a particular country, rates in different subpopulations can differ considerably. In the United Kingdom, where stricter diagnostic criteria are used, prevalence among grade-schoolers is less than 1 percent, substantially lower than in the United States. Environmental factors, population variables, and other reasons may also account for these differences. Similarly, in France less than 0.5 percent of children and adolescents are diagnosed and medicated for ADHD.

ADHD prevalence for respective countries can be calculated through the extrapolation of prevalence in well-studied countries like the United States, United Kingdom, Canada, and Australia against the total population. This method doesn't account for environmental, sociocultural, genetic, racial, or other differences. Extrapolations can be helpful in considering the scale of ADHD worldwide. It can be extrapolated that the prevalence of ADHD could be 12.922 million for India, 2.893 million for Indonesia, 2.234 million for Brazil, 1.931 million for Pakistan, 1.747 million for Russia, 1.715 million for Bangladesh, 1.273 million for Mexico,

1.046 million for the Philippines, 1.003 million for Vietnam, and 1 million for Germany.

It is difficult to make exact comparisons between countries with estimated prevalence, since assessment methods and samples are not uniform. Prevalence for other countries seems to generally fall within U.S. rates. When standardized diagnostic procedures are followed, there is no evidence of significant differences over decades in ADHD prevalence globally. Variability seems to be explained by methodological differences, like impairment and diagnostic criteria and data sources.

Children and Youth

Worldwide, average prevalence for ADHD among children and adolescents is 5.3–7.1 percent. According to Centers for Disease Control and Prevention (CDC), in 2015, 9.5 percent of U.S. children aged three to seventeen were diagnosed with ADHD. Many of these six million U.S. children and youth need treatment and professional support sometime in their lives. In the United States, ADHD is the most common behavioral disorder and the most common psychiatric diagnosis for children and youth. ADHD symptoms differ with age and other demographics. U.S. preschool and younger elementary students commonly exhibit hyperactivity, while for upper-elementary- and middle-school-aged children, inattention is more common. Boys are two to three times more likely than girls to receive an ADHD diagnosis; and it is most common among firstborn boys. Girls with ADHD are more likely to be overtalkative than hyperactive, they frequently daydream, and they can be overemotional and anxious. Adolescents of both sexes exhibit symptoms of hyperactivity, such as fidgeting, jitteriness, and impatience. Young adults with ADHD are less likely to be hyperactive, but often experience difficulties fulfilling complex responsibilities.

ADHD prevalence varies by family structure and income. In U.S. families, when both mother and father are present, eleven million children (7.3 percent) are diagnosed with ADHD. In those with a mother but no father present, 1.7 million children (11.1 percent) have ADHD. In those with a father but no mother present, 178,000 children (8.7 percent) have ADHD. In U.S. families where there is neither father nor mother, 316,000 children (15.37 percent) have ADHD. More four- to seventeen-year-olds whose family income was below the federal poverty level in 2015–2016 were diagnosed with ADHD (12.9 percent) than those at or above it (around 10 percent).

Adults

Professionals used to think that children and adolescents with ADHD would age out of the disorder. This is no longer the consensus, as research indicates that it usually continues into and through adulthood, appearing to be a lifelong disorder. Although estimates vary and what criteria to use for diagnosis at older ages is questioned, 15–65 percent of children and adolescents diagnosed with ADHD report symptoms into young adulthood and beyond. About 80 percent of adolescents administered ADHD medicines as children continue to need them at least through adolescence, and 50 percent or more will continue to need them as adults. Clinicians report that about half of diagnosed children have symptoms throughout adulthood. The average worldwide prevalence is 2.5–3.4 percent of all adults. In the United States, 4.4 percent of adults aged eighteen and older have already been diagnosed with ADHD. The National Institute of Mental Health (NIMH) estimates that 8.1 percent of adults experience ADHD at some time.

In adults, ADHD affects individuals at work, home, and in social or other settings. Symptoms affect adults differently than children and youth. For most people, symptoms of impulsivity and hyperactivity taper off as they age. Adults with ADHD exhibit more inattentive symptoms, such as difficulties planning, completing tasks, and time management, along with other problems, including disorganization, forgetfulness, and unreliability. Among middle-aged and older adults, symptoms of depression and anxiety typically increase as ADHD symptoms increase. Adults with ADHD experience greater difficulties in critical life areas, such as employment, education, arrests, and relationships, than neurotypicals. Much of this has only recently been recognized.

DIFFERENCES IN RATES OF ADHD

Differences in prevalence rates of ADHD can be explained by many factors. These include diagnostic concerns and differences due to societal factors, gender, race, ethnicity, and special populations.

Diagnostic

Substantial increases are observed in those around the world who are diagnosed and treated for ADHD. In the United States, diagnostic prevalence has risen dramatically. In 1995, there were 2,357,833 children diagnosed with ADHD in the United States, twice the number in 1990. From 1997 to 2006, diagnoses among children and adolescents between four and seventeen years old increased about 3 percent per year; from 2003 to 2011, diagnoses increased around 5 percent annually. Over the last decade, the number of U.S. children and adolescents aged four to seventeen diagnosed with ADHD rose about 40 percent. This gives the United States the highest prevalence of ADHD diagnosis globally. In 2003, prevalence in the United States among children and adolescents aged four to seventeen was 7.8 percent. It was 9.5 percent in 2007, and 11 percent in 2011. Presently, more than 10 percent, or more than one out of every ten children and adolescents in the United States under the age of seventeen is diagnosed with ADHD.

While ADHD is usually diagnosed in children, symptoms can persist into adulthood. There are also many adults who were children when ADHD wasn't as widely diagnosed, and, consequently, they likely were never diagnosed. Symptoms appear in children as young as three to six and can continue throughout adolescence and adulthood. The majority of children with ADHD are diagnosed in elementary school. For adolescents or adults to receive a diagnosis under DSM-5 criteria, symptoms must have been observed before the age of twelve.

Social Issues

Different societies have different cultural expectations and values pertaining to what is or isn't a disorder, affecting how diagnoses are made and what treatments may be considered. Social factors influence us as well. In the early 1990s, after reauthorization of the Individuals with Disabilities Education Act (IDEA), ADHD was added as a specific diagnostic category, making children eligible for special education services. After its passage, rates of ADHD diagnoses increased 30–40 percent at U.S. public schools. That does not mean that there were suddenly more individuals with ADHD, but more were diagnosed and eligible for services.

Another policy change that fueled diagnosing was the No Child Left Behind Act, signed by George W. Bush in 2002. This gave schools incentives to raise standardized-test scores. Educators know that when more students are diagnosed with ADHD and receive accommodations, such as extended test times, scores will improve.

Diagnosis of ADHD varies by regions, as do prescribing rates. The highest prevalence is in southeastern United States, while southwestern and Western regions have the lowest. From 1998 to 2009, diagnoses increased about 10 percent in Southern and Midwestern regions. Prevalence also varies between states and even by counties within states. For example, in 2011, diagnostic prevalence among four- to seventeen-year-olds in Colorado was 5.6 percent, while in Kentucky, it was 14.8 percent. Similarly, in 2011, those four- to seventeen-year-olds diagnosed and prescribed psychostimulants was 47 percent in Nevada, but 86.2 percent in Nebraska. The proportion of four- to seventeen-year-olds in the United States taking prescribed medicines for ADHD increased 28 percent from 2007 to 2011. In 2007, 4.8 percent of four- to seventeen-year-olds were taking ADHD medicines, and by 2011, this increased to 6.1 percent. This represents an average of approximately 7 percent annual increases in prescribed ADHD medicines.

ADHD, if untreated or treated ineffectively, can become a serious problem. About 52 percent of untreated adolescents and adults with ADHD use alcohol or other drugs. Nearly one-fifth (19 percent) of adults with ADHD smoke tobacco, compared to one-tenth of the U.S. adult population. Around 46 percent of young adolescent males with untreated hyperactive subtype are arrested for a felony before reaching the age of sixteen, and 21 percent of adults with untreated ADHD will be arrested for felonies. Individuals with untreated ADHD have more emergency-room and medical visits and get injured more often than neurotypicals or those with properly treated ADHD.

Gender

Boys are more likely diagnosed with ADHD than girls, at least during childhood and adolescence. Although the percentage of five- to seventeen-year-olds diagnosed with ADHD has been increasing, it remains higher among boys. Boys, at 13.3 percent, are more than twice as likely as girls, at 5.6 percent, to get an ADHD diagnosis. Around one-fifth of U.S. high school male students have been told they have symptoms. Diagnostic prevalence of ADHD has been increasing; between 1998 and 2000, it was 9.9 percent for boys, increasing in 2007–2009 to 12.3 percent, while for girls, it was 3.6 percent in 1998–2000, increasing to 5.5 percent in 2007–2009. Female children and adolescents are more likely than males to be diagnosed with predominantly inattentive subtype; further, they are more likely than neurotypical females to be diagnosed with comorbid anxiety, mood, and conduct disorders and to have lower IQ and achievement scores. Young females with ADHD are five times more likely than males to be diagnosed with depressive disorders and three times more likely to be treated for depression before receiving their ADHD diagnosis. This unbalanced sex ratio for diagnosis among children and adolescents seems to be remedied by higher rates of self-referrals by adult women. At some point, about 4.9 percent of females and 12.9 percent of males will receive an ADHD diagnosis. Whatever gender differences there are, it seems that females and males with ADHD are more similar than different. There are no essentially sex-specific differences with respect to ADHD.

It is agreed that ADHD is underdiagnosed among females. It is estimated that one-half to three-quarters of females with ADHD are undiagnosed. This is attributed to the formulation of diagnostic criteria that are based on studies of young white males who were treated at specialized behavioral clinics. Women with ADHD tend to be less hyperactive and impulsive than males, while being more disorganized, forgetful, introverted, and scatterbrained. Skewing of diagnostic criteria toward symptoms that are characteristic of males while minimizing those common among females would result in female underrepresentation.

Findings suggest that treatments for ADHD, including pharmacological-based treatments, are equally effective for females and males. There is referral bias, as more males are referred to treatment than females, at least at younger ages. Gender differences seem to reverse as we age.

Racial/Ethnic Groups

Racial and ethnic differences underlie ADHD and prescribing of medicines. White children were once more likely than Hispanics to be diagnosed with ADHD. Differences in diagnoses narrowed between racial and ethnic groups from 1998 to 2009. There are substantial differences within ethnic groups. Among primarily Hispanic countries, there are significant differences in diagnostic rates; for instance, Mexican children are about five times more likely than those in Puerto Rico to be diagnosed with ADHD and 10 times more likely than those in Cuba. Racial and ethnic variation with respect to diagnostic rates within the United States is highly variable. While 9.6 percent of Caucasians are diagnosed with ADHD at some point in their lives, prevalence among African Americans is 10.5 percent, Native American/Alaskan natives is 6.4 percent, Hispanics is 4.9 percent, and Asians is 1.4 percent. From 2001 to 2010, diagnoses of ADHD among African American girls increased 90 percent. Diagnostic prevalence is highest, at 11.6 percent, among those identified as multiracial. Overall diagnostic prevalence for ADHD among all Americans is 9.4 percent.

Racial and ethnic differences are reflected in the use of ADHD medicines. It is estimated that 76 percent of U.S. Caucasian children with ADHD take ADHD medicines, while only 56 percent of diagnosed African American and 53 percent of Hispanic children do.

Special Populations

Special populations vary in diagnostic prevalence of ADHD. There are gender differences. Males tend to be diagnosed more with comorbid conditions like conduct disorder (CD) or oppositional defiant disorder (ODD), while females are more likely to be diagnosed with a condition like separation anxiety disorder. Adult men with ADHD are more likely to be incarcerated than women with ADHD.

Those diagnosed with disabilities other than ADHD are more likely than neurotypicals to be diagnosed with ADHD. About 20–30 percent of school-aged children with ADHD also have a specific learning disability. It is known that 20–40 percent of all children diagnosed with ADHD will eventually develop CD. Similarly, one-third to one-half of all children with ADHD also receives a diagnosis of ODD. Between 25 and 40 percent of all individuals with ADHD also have anxiety disorder. Likewise, 25–40 percent of those with ADHD have bipolar disorder. Depression is three times more common among those with ADHD; up to 70 percent of individuals with ADHD will be treated for depression at some time.

One study found that for five- to eleven-year-olds who committed suicide, 59.3 percent had received an ADHD diagnosis; on the other hand, twelve- to fourteen-year-olds who completed suicide were less likely to experience symptoms or be diagnosed with dysthymia or depression, and less than one-third (29.0 percent) also received an ADHD diagnosis.

The socio-economic status of the family of origin influences the probability of receiving an ADHD diagnosis. From 1998 to 2009, ADHD diagnostic prevalence rates increased faster among children and adolescents from families with household incomes below poverty levels. From 2008 to 2011, two- to five-year-olds who were covered by Medicaid were twice as likely to receive clinical care for ADHD, typically medications, than those with employer-sponsored health insurance.

OVERVIEW OF NEUROTRANSMISSION

ADHD, being brain based, results from neurotransmitter imbalances. Understanding brain structure and function in those with and without ADHD helps understand ADHD and how to address it. Our brain consists primarily of neurons, cells that communicate through chemical and electrical messages, or neurotransmission. The average adult brain weighs 3.09 pounds (about 1.4 kilograms), has an average volume of 97.6 cubic inches (1,600 cubic centimeters), and is composed of one hundred billion neurons arranged in complex ways to transmit and receive electrochemical messages across trillions of synapses. Messages get to the brain with electrochemical signals, are processed, and sent out.

Each neuron has several components. Dendrites can be considered the beginning of each neuron. Dendrites extend outward in branch-like extensions and contain receptors, where chemical signals from adjacent neurons bind, along their edges. Small extensions are dispersed outward in all directions from the dendrites. Single dendrites can have up to thirty thousand small extensions spreading out to receive chemical messages from neighboring neurons. Dendrites are continuously involved in creating new links and breaking old links. This process of forming connections, or neural pathways, is how learning and memory occur.

The cell body of a neuron is called the soma. The area between the soma and axon is the axon hillock. Most of the length of a neuron consists of the axon, functioning as a highway, along which electrical signals of action potentials are sent. Axons extend outward from the soma and terminate at synaptic terminals. Each neuron generally has one axon, ranging from 0.05 inches (0.127 centimeters) to 3 feet (nearly one meter) or more in length. Bundles of axons in the peripheral nervous system are called nerves, while those in the brain and spinal cord are called neural tracts.

Synaptic terminals are specialized protuberances that contain neurotransmitters, which are held in vesicles. As electrical impulses reach the axon terminal, they stimulate synaptic knobs to open, allowing an influx of positively charged sodium ions. Action potentials last for less than one-thousandth of a second. Some neurons transmit action potentials nearly continually, while others do so only occasionally. Action potentials translate electrical signals within neurons into chemical messages to be transmitted to the next neuron, stimulating the neurotransmitter for release, called exocytosis. Synaptic vesicles are specialized sacks holding neurotransmitters that are waiting to be released near or at the synapses.

Electrical messages travel down the length of neurons to open calcium ion channels within the synaptic terminals at the other end. This causes vesicles to move closer to neuronal membranes and fuse with them. Neurotransmitters can then be released into the synapses.

The surfaces of the receptive regions of most brain neurons can be exposed to thousands of synapses. Synapses are the spaces between neurons that don't touch each other. A synapse is only about an eighteen-millionth of an inch wide, or fifty nanometers, across. A healthy human brain is estimated to contain over one hundred trillion synapses. Synaptic connections create numerous potential links, through which messages can be sent.

There are different kinds of neurons. There are specialized neurons that have short axons, or some that have none. These are interneurons, which coordinate activity within particular brain regions, rather than transmitting signals from one region to another. There are nearly one-thousand different types of specialized neurons. No single neuron is exactly the same as any other; they differ in shape, firing threshold, or other variables. They are dynamic, continually extending or deleting connections with other neurons.

Individual neurons communicate with each other through release and uptake of neurotransmitters. Neurotransmitters are constantly made, released, and broken down or recaptured as transmission occurs. More than sixty different neurotransmitters have been identified, with more to be discovered—it is estimated that there may be two thousand or more different neurotransmitters.

There are two different groups of neurotransmitters, excitatory and inhibitory. Excitatory neurotransmitters, such as epinephrine and glutamate, create localized increases in permeability of cell membranes, leading to depolarization, while inhibitory neurotransmitters, such as gamma-aminobutyric acid (GABA), block neuronal firing. ADHD medicines can inhibit or increase synthesis, release, action, and deactivation of neurotransmitters.

After travelling across a synapse, neurotransmitters attempt to bind to receptors, located along postsynaptic membranes. There is around a one-millisecond delay for messages transmitted by neurotransmitter release to be sent to adjacent neurons. Each receptor is composed of proteins, to which only specific neurotransmitters can bind. Neurotransmitters that don't bind to receptors must be eliminated. Some are removed by reuptake and recycled, while others are degraded by enzymes, the products of which can be reused.

Neurons monitor neurotransmitter levels. When levels of excitatory neurotransmitters exceed the inhibitory ones, neurons can successfully send messages on to adjacent neurons along neural pathways. Neurotransmitter systems have complex interactions with each other, and ADHD may be the result of imbalances in any number of known, or even as of yet unknown, neurotransmitter systems. When neurotransmitters that are conveying incoming messages get to the brain, neurons in various parts of the brain must be activated in order for signals to be perceived. While there is a close association between brain neurons firing and the perception of signals, cognitive factors influence what meanings will be attributed to particular stimuli. Nearly all brain parts are constantly accessed by the dynamic firing of neurons. Cognitive centers must filter through this mass of signals to make sense of them.

MONOAMINES

ADHD results from neurotransmitter imbalances. Monoamine neurotransmitters, including dopamine, epinephrine, norepinephrine, and serotonin, are derived from amino acids. There are two primary types of monoamines: indolamines and catecholamines. Indolamines, represented by serotonin, function in many tissues, including in the gastrointestinal tract, where most serotonin is produced. Catecholamines, as norepinephrine and dopamine, work primarily within sympathetic and central nervous systems. Psychostimulants act as analogues of catecholamines. Monoamines regulate processes like emotion, arousal, and cognition.

Many ADHD medicines target actions to increase or decrease effects of monoamines.

Norepinephrine

Norepinephrine is formed primarily in the locus coeruleus, located in the pons of the brain stem. Its activity is correlated with reaction speed, vigilance, mood control, and satisfaction. Norepinephrine increases alertness and attention, processing sensory inputs, feeling happy, formation and retrieval of memories, and ability to react to stimuli. Low norepinephrine levels are associated with issues like memory problems and loss of alertness.

Dopamine

Dopamine is found mainly in the substantia nigra of basal ganglia and the ventral tegmental region of the brain, as well as in the midbrain, helping to regulate emotions such as arousal and pleasure. Dopamine serves as a neuromodulator within our reward system, and is significant in compulsive conditions, such as eating disorders, gambling, and substance use. However, when dopamine is persistently elevated, sensitivity decreases. In the dorsolateral prefrontal cortex, this is associated with executive functioning and cognition, while within the ventromedial prefrontal cortex, it is associated with emotions and affect.

Dopamine is associated with attention and arousal within the forebrain. It is crucial, as it rewards actions, making them easier to evoke again, and also lowers the threshold to evoke behaviors by enhancing happiness. Deficiencies of dopamine are believed to be responsible for many ADHD symptoms, such as difficulties inhibiting behaviors, regulating attention, and remembering specific things.

Serotonin

Serotonin is crucial to cognitive functioning, such as learning and memory, in ADHD, and with feeling happy and full. In the brain, serotonin is not usually degraded but is more often removed through reuptake by serotonin transporters.

DOMAINS OF LIFE IMPACTED BY ADHD

Domains impacted by ADHD include personal, educational, and workplace issues. These are the major domains considered by clinicians.

Personal Issues

Personal issues are a greater concern for individuals with ADHD compared to neurotypicals. These include difficulties with interpersonal relationships, including with friends and family, to more intrapersonal concerns.

Individuals with ADHD commonly have difficulties making and keeping friends. They are often unaware that their behavior affects others. Children with ADHD often have trouble reading social cues. Those with ADHD may routinely interrupt others and have difficulties filtering out what others say. This makes others less willing to befriend them. Many with ADHD can be demanding and intense, often without realizing it. They have trouble taking turns and cooperating with others. Some easily lose their train of thought, become distracted, and struggle to maintain conversations. It isn't uncommon for them to overreact and have self-control problems. Children with ADHD may react physically when frustrated or upset, striking others. Age-inappropriate emotional meltdowns are common.

Many with ADHD have problems planning and following through with tasks. This makes them seem unreliable and interferes with forming strong friendships. Strained parent-child relationships are common. Repeated negative interpersonal outcomes, such as persistent rejection, leads to emotional pain and suffering for those with ADHD and those around them.

Low self-esteem, combined with chronic emotional stress and tension, is common and causes myriad health-related problems. Associated issues include higher incidences of conditions such as anxiety, compulsive eating, criminal behavior, depression, sexual dysfunction, and substance use.

Educational Issues

Educators acknowledge that 10–20 percent of any school-age sample will have academic difficulties. In any elementary- or secondary-school classroom, there are likely at least two children seriously affected by ADHD, to the point of causing problems. Reasons for these difficulties are manifold, including maintaining attention, sitting still, and responding before thinking.

Poor academic performance is common with ADHD. Academic issues include complications such as likelihood of retention, failing grades, lower standardized-achievement test scores, and increased prevalence of learning disabilities. Writing difficulties in spelling and expression are common, as are weaknesses in grammar, linguistic adequacy, lexicon, and structure; reading deficiencies are also typical. Deficiencies are reported for other issues, such as integrating multiple cognitive operations, such as planning and working memory, and visuospatial tasks.

ADHD can make school more challenging than for neurotypicals. Around one-third of individuals with ADHD never finish high school, compared with a national average of 8.7 percent. Adults with ADHD complete less formal education than neurotypicals do.

Workplace Issues

Employers report that employees with ADHD have lowered work performance and impaired task completion, lack independent skills, and have poor relationships with coworkers and supervisors. These and related issues lead to higher rates of unemployment, job changes, and lower socioeconomic status of adults with ADHD. Adults with ADHD often develop coping skills, allowing workplace survival. For example, someone with the hyperactive subtype might appear to be overworking or more competitive. Adults with ADHD often acquire coping mechanisms that permit adjustments to work environments, such as relying on coworkers for assistance and selecting careers and work environments that are accommodating their needs.

A recent study estimated that 83 percent of annual costs of ADHD are incurred by adults, totaling $105–$194 billion per year. Workplace issues, primarily productivity and income losses, represent the largest costs of adult ADHD, amounting to $87–$138 billion per year in the United States. For example, workers with ADHD are more likely to have at least one more sick-day per month compared to neurotypicals. WHO estimates that untreated adults lose an average of twenty-two days of job productivity each year. We know that adults with ADHD are eighteen times more likely to be disciplined at work for perceived behavior problems and are 60 percent more likely to lose their jobs. Adults with ADHD, on average, earn $5,000–$10,000 less per year than neurotypicals. These factors contribute to ADHD societal costs, estimated at $12,005–$17,454 per year per individual in this country.

2

The History of ADHD

The history of ADHD helps us better understand the disorder and its varied treatments. Earlier conceptions of what we now recognize as ADHD significantly affect how we see and deal with it today.

HISTORY OF ADHD

ADHD has a considerable history. Our understanding of it is influenced by earlier views, and particularly by the nineteenth-century concepts of children's mental health. Early descriptions exist for what we now call ADHD, including hyperkinetic disorder, and for the development of diagnostic standards.

Children's Mental Health in the Nineteenth Century

In the early nineteenth century, children's mental health was rarely considered. The minds of children were seen as soft, vulnerable, and susceptible to external influences. This was better than earlier notions, which asserted that children couldn't experience mental problems like adults did.

In the nineteenth century, mental health care consisted mainly of institutionalization, usually in hospitals or asylums. Placing mentally ill patients in asylums was considered a rational approach to madness.

Several nineteenth-century British laws, like the 1800 Criminal Lunatics Act, 1808 County Asylums Act, 1828 Madhouses Act, and 1898 Defective and Epileptic Children's Act, increased the number of asylums. Laws establishing asylums in the United States were usually enacted by states rather than federally. The Boston Prison Discipline Society, founded in 1825, pressured the Massachusetts legislature to form a committee to examine jail conditions, which it did in 1827. The first Massachusetts asylum was the Worcester Lunatic Asylum, opened in 1833 as a 120-bed hospital. Mentally ill people were then generally incarcerated. Many U.S. and European asylums were built during the nineteenth century, usually in rural locales far from fast-paced, industrialized, urban settings, and were considered compassionate institutions of social reform. Early asylums were custodial and used physical restraints and other less enlightened measures. By the mid-nineteenth century, social reformers, like Dorothea Dix, were concerned that large proportions of inmates in almshouses, asylums, prisons, jails, workhouses, and related institutions were children. In 1841, Dix advocated for better mental illness services in Massachusetts and subsequently along the East coast. Her activities resulted in at least thirty-two state psychiatric hospitals. There were then seventy-five public psychiatric hospitals in the United States, and many private ones. By the late nineteenth century, these were replaced by reformatories, which were essentially warehouses for troubled and difficult youth, terms applied to children with ADHD. By the late nineteenth century, social Darwinism held sway, and insanity, including of children, was considered incurable, degenerative, and largely inherited, fueling eugenics movements.

Early Descriptions of ADHD-Like Conditions

People recognized that the behaviors of certain children were inappropriate and differed from expectations. Since prehistory, individuals with mental illness were ostracized, stigmatized, tortured, persecuted, and even killed. They were considered cursed, possessed by demons, or engaged in witchcraft.

There were early references to behaviors that are now recognized as suggestive of ADHD. Melchior Adam Weikard, a German physician, in 1775 published *Der Philosophische Artz*, containing the first recorded description in medical literature of behaviors that is now attributed to ADHD. He described these children "are mostly reckless, often copious considering imprudent projects, but they are also most inconstant in execution." (Barkley & Peters, 2012, p. 628). Sir Alexander Crichton, a Scottish physician, in his 1798 *An Inquiry into the Nature and Origin of Mental*

Derangement, reported that for some, "Attention is so little under control, that it cannot be strongly directed to any subject, except for a very short time" (Crichton, 1798, p. 5). William James, in his 1890 *Principles of Psychology*, discussed what he regarded as a normal variant of behavior, where some tend to be "overflowing with animation, and fizzling with talk" (James, 1890, p. 800). Sir George Frederic Still, a British pediatrician, reported in 1902 to the Royal College of Physicians (later published in *Lancet*) on forty-three children who had severe difficulties sustaining attention and self-regulating and who, although of normal intelligence, didn't learn from negative results of actions but were aggressive, defiant, and excessively emotional and resisted discipline. They would appear to meet DSM-5 criteria for ADHD combined type. Still and others considered these symptoms came from a "defect in moral control" (Still, 1902, p. 1009).

Many nineteenth-century writers examined relationships between creativity and madness. Some, like John Clare, were thought to be insane, and many spent time in asylums. Many writers described those we would now say had ADHD. Several centuries earlier, William Shakespeare described a character in *King Henry VIII* who had a malady of attention. In 1844, Heinrich Hoffmann, a German physician, created illustrated children's stories for his family, including one later published about *Zappelphilipp* (Fidgety Philip), a boy who was unable to sit still at the dinner table (Hoffmann, 2015). Hoffman's descriptions of Philip's hyperactivity and inattention seem to fulfill ADHD diagnostic criteria.

In the late nineteenth century, there was an epidemic of neurasthenia, a vague, and now essentially obsolete (at least in the United States), disease of "weak" nerves that was considered hereditary and characterized by inattention, memory loss, lack of motivation, and chronic weakness. The term "neurasthenia" was introduced in 1869 by George Miller Beard, a Boston neurologist. Childhood neurasthenia soon became a popular diagnosis, including so-called "nervous children," many of whom would now meet ADHD criteria. Dr. John Harvey Kellogg, of corn flakes fame, observed in 1915 that the proportion of neurasthenic "children to the total school population is unquestionably increasing" (Kellogg, 1915, p. 49). Kellogg advocated a vegetarian diet, regular physical activity, open-air sleeping, and abstinence from "condiments, tea, coffee, pastry, and confectionery" (Kellogg, 1915, p. 50).

The term "minimal brain dysfunction" (MBD) came into use during the early 1940s. This concept held that for some all brain mechanisms might be present and functioning but that brain wiring was different and didn't work customarily. Children with MBD were considered to have dysfunctional nervous systems, causing difficulties with learning and substantial problems with hyperactivity and distractibility, manifested in academic, emotional, and family problems.

Hyperkinetic Disorder

A notion that was popular before ADHD was hyperactivity, specifically hyperkinetic disorder or hyperkinesis. Professionals explained behaviors of hyperactive children in terms of their academic backgrounds. Many psychoanalysts referred to them as acting out. This psychoanalytical perspective was reflected in descriptors used in the 1968 second edition of *Diagnostic and Statistical Manual* (DSM-II) of the American Psychiatric Association for what was then called hyperkinetic reaction of childhood. From the psychoanalytical perspective, a child who would now be considered to have ADHD would be described as reacting against early experiences or simply acting out. The term "hyperkinetic impulse disorder" was introduced in 1957 by physicians who emphasized a neurological basis and asserted "dysfunction of the diencephalon exposes the cortex to unusually intense storms of stimuli" (Laufer, Denhoff, & Solomons, 1957, p. 38). For the remainder of the 1950s and into the 1960s, professionals wrote about children with hyperkinetic impulse disorder, attributing it to overstimulation of the cortex, resulting from inadequate filtering of incoming stimuli by the thalamus. The term hyperactive child syndrome was used during the 1960s to describe developmentally excessive motor activity. From the 1960s to 1980s, competing educators, physicians, therapists, and others debated whether it was more experiential and dynamic or more brain based, with metabolic irregularities and probably genetically influenced, with hyperkinetic terminology preferred by the former (e.g., Freeman, 1976; Berger, 1981) and MBD by the latter (e.g., Knights & Hinton, 1969; Edwards et al., 1971). Representatives from both groups advocated psychostimulants (e.g., Freeman, 1976; Shaywitz et al., 1978) and nonmedication treatments (e.g., Conners & Delamater, 1980; Berger, 1981). Released in 1980, the third edition of *Diagnostic and Statistical Manual* (DSM-III) largely superseded the hyperkinetic versus MBD debate, placing greater emphasis on inattentiveness and inability to focus and using the term "attention deficit disorder" (ADD). ADD is a term still used by some.

Development of Diagnostic Standards

Development of criteria for diagnosing ADHD evolved. In 1952, when the first edition of *Diagnostic and Statistical Manual* (DSM-I) was released, there was no mention of any condition that would now be recognized as ADHD. DSM is intended to provide an agreed-upon nomenclature and standardized diagnostic criteria for defining and classifying mental disorders. By the release of DSM-II, the agreed nomenclature was hyperkinetic reaction of childhood, "characterized by overactivity, restlessness, distractibility, and short attention span" (American Psychiatric Association, 1968, p. 50). DSM-II focused on high levels of motor activity.

This disorder was thought to be outgrown during adolescence and early adulthood.

DSM-III, released in 1980, listed ADD according to three specific subtypes: ADD with hyperactivity, without hyperactivity, and residual. DSM-III specified that the initial appearance of symptoms had to be before the age of seven and had to last for at least six months. Evidence indicated that some symptoms persisted into adulthood. By 1987, it was thought necessary to issue a new nomenclature, with a revised third edition of *Diagnostic and Statistical Manual* (DSM-III-R). It was DSM-III-R that introduced the now accepted term "attention deficit hyperactivity disorder, or ADHD, but without subtypes.

The fourth edition of *Diagnostic and Statistical Manual* (DSM-IV), released in 1994, specified that symptoms must not only have been present but also resulted in impairment before the age of seven. The symptoms must have existed in two or more settings and caused substantial impairment in two or more life areas, persisting for six months or longer. Further, DSM-IV included subtypes of inattentive, hyperactive, and combined, and added ADHD not otherwise specified for those demonstrating symptoms but not meeting the full diagnostic criteria for specific subtypes. The fourth edition, text-revision (DSM-IV-TR), seemed necessary in 2000, and listed ADHD combined, predominantly inattentive, and predominantly hyperactive impulsive, as well as ADHD not otherwise specified for those not meeting the full diagnostic criteria but demonstrating daydreaming, sluggishness, and hyperactivity, even if the age of onset was after the age of seven.

The fifth edition of *Diagnostic and Statistical Manual* (DSM-5), published in 2013, lists ADHD combined, predominantly inattentive, predominantly hyperactive/impulsive, other specified ADHD, and unspecified ADHD. The major difference from DSM-IV in DSM-5 is the symptom list, followed by clinical examples of how symptoms can present.

After DSM, the second most commonly used nomenclature is *International Statistical Classification of Diseases and Related Health Problems* (ICD), produced by World Health Organization (WHO). Since October 1, 2014, ICD-10-CM codes have been used for coding purposes. The ICD classification of mental disorders is harmonized with DSM-5. With respect to ICD-10-CM codes for various ADHDA subtypes are F90.0 for predominantly inattentive, F90.1 for predominantly hyperactive/impulsive, F90.2 for combined, F90.8 for other-specified, and F90.9 for unspecified.

DISABILITY LAWS

Neuropsychiatric disorders, including ADHD, are the most common cause of disability in the United States, and, since 2010, mental and substance-use disorders are among the leading causes of disability globally. Now and in the future, disability laws will shape how we respond to and serve individuals with ADHD and other disabilities.

The rights of individuals with ADHD are legally protected, particularly by the American with Disabilities Act (ADA) and Section 504. Other federal laws also protect the rights of individuals with disabilities, like the Fair Housing Act and Individuals with Disabilities Education Act (IDEA). Additionally state, county, and local laws extend protections to individuals with disabilities and their families.

Americans with Disabilities Act

The Americans with Disabilities Act (ADA) was signed by George H. W. Bush on July 26, 1990. ADA and ADA Amendments Act of 2008 (ADAAA) are broad laws that prohibit discrimination of physical or mental disabilities, including ADHD. ADAAA remedied the Supreme Court's misinterpretation of who is protected under ADA. ADA and amendments also expands types of institutional and service-provider responsibilities beyond earlier laws that required reasonable accommodations. ADA is a comprehensive antidiscrimination law for individuals with disabilities.

ADA protects individuals against discrimination in employment, state and local government, public accommodations, commercial facilities, telecommunications, and transportation. It covers almost all sectors of society and aspects of daily living. To be protected by ADA, one must have, or be perceived to have, a disability or have association or relationship with an individual with a disability. An individual with a disability is defined as having a physical or mental impairment or both that substantially limits one or more major life activities or a person who has history or record of such impairment or be perceived by others as having such, including ADHD. However, ADA does not specifically name all the impairments that are covered. The original text of ADA didn't specifically mention ADHD—it is covered as a "mental or psychological disorder." The severity of ADHD is assessed by limiting impairment without potential for alleviation following treatment.

Freedom to seek employment is the first right protected under ADA. It bans discrimination based on disability in hiring, promotions, and wages. Employers must accommodate the workplace needs and limitations of employees with disabilities. Minor adjustments or assistance can make someone with ADHD a more valuable employee.

Right to equal access to primary, secondary, and postsecondary education is covered. However, educational institutions are not required to accept or accommodate everyone who has disabilities. Students with a disability such as ADHD must satisfy all standards that are required by educational institutions. Individuals with a disability must perform all "essential academic and technical standards of the program," either with or without accommodations.

Section 504

Section 504 of the 1973 Rehabilitation Act is a federal civil rights law. The Rehabilitation Act was signed on September 26, 1973, by Richard Nixon. From 1973 to 1977, there were no regulations directing implementation of Section 504. Joseph Califano, the secretary of health, education, and welfare, signed such regulations on April 28, 1977. Section 504 mandates "no qualified individual with a disability in the United States shall be excluded from, denied the benefits of, or be subjected to discrimination under" any program or activity receiving federal funds. Requirements under Section 504 include reasonable accommodations for employees with disabilities, accessible new construction and alterations, program accessibility, and effective communication for people with hearing or visual disabilities. Individuals with disabilities may, if needed, receive accommodations under Section 504 within academic or employment settings.

Section 504 requires that no individual with a disability be excluded from programs or services due to lack of appropriate aids; however, it doesn't require employers and educational institutions to have all aids available at all times. Although architectural accessibility for individuals with disabilities is a component of Section 504, completely barrier-free environments aren't required. Nondiscriminatory placement in the "most integrated setting appropriate" is mandated, and, for most with ADHD, this would be within regular classrooms and work environments, although a reasonable accommodation for testing could be in separate, quiet rooms without distractions.

U.S. Department of Education's Office for Civil Rights on July 26, 2016, issued guidance in clarifying the obligations of schools to provide students with ADHD equal educational opportunities. Schools must provide parents due-process rights, including allowing parents to appeal decisions concerning identification, evaluation, or educational placement of students with ADHD.

Fair Housing Act

The Fair Housing Act was Title VII of the Civil Rights Act of 1968, signed by Lyndon Johnson. The Fair Housing Act initially prohibited housing discrimination on the basis of race, color, religion, sex, and national origin; in 1988, disability and familial status were added as additional protected classes. Coverage includes private housing, housing receiving federal funds, and state and local government housing. It is unlawful to discriminate in any aspect of selling or renting housing or to deny a dwelling to a renter or buyer because of a disability, an individual associated with the renter or buyer or intending to live in the residence.

Individuals with Disabilities Education Act

The Individuals with Disabilities Education Act (IDEA) requires public schools to make themselves available to all eligible children with disabilities for a free, appropriate public education in the least restrictive environment that is appropriate to individual needs. From 1975 to 1990, IDEA was known as the Education for All Handicapped Children Act. IDEA was signed by George H. W. Bush on October 30, 1990, and major amendments include the No Child Left Behind Act of 2001 and Individuals with Disabilities Education Improvement Act of 2004, signed by George W. Bush on January 23, 2001, and on December 3, 2004, respectively. IDEA guarantees that each student with a disability, including ADHD, must get a culturally unbiased and valid assessment of needs. It is under this provision that most children in the United States receive an ADHD diagnosis. However, IDEA more narrowly defines individuals with a disability than either ADA or Section 504. Most, if not all, individuals eligible under IDEA are also covered by ADA and Section 504. When IDEA was reauthorized, and after ADHD was added as an approved category for services, diagnostic prevalence escalated 30–40 percent.

IDEA requires that public schools develop appropriate individualized education programs (IEPs) for each child with special needs. However, IDEA does not directly apply to students in higher education, nor do IEPs. Specific special education and related services outlined in each IEP reflect individualized needs of each student in public schools and may not be appropriate in college. IDEA asserts that students must be placed in the least restrictive environment (LRE). Many children with ADHD who are not eligible for an IEP under IDEA may qualify for an educational plan under Section 504.

DEVELOPMENT OF ADHD MEDICATIONS

The development of medicines for ADHD presents a paradox. On one side, strong and even possibly dangerous drugs offer relief for a sometimes perplexing disorder. On the other, many of these substances can and are sometimes misused or abused. Many suffering from substance-use disorders can be overwhelmed and lose their abilities to act and think rationally.

Millions struggle daily with ADHD. Identification of ADHD as a treatable disorder is relatively recent. For millennia, those with what we now identify as ADHD had no systematic relief. Certainly, some people experimented with varied naturally occurring substances that had psychotropic effects. Some proto-experimenters discovered that they could enhance their abilities to function under the influence of these substances.

Use of medicines to treat what we now refer to as ADHD has a short history. Charles Bradley reported in 1937 on the use of Benzedrine (amphetamine) to improve behavior of "difficult" children. Bradley discovered that when amphetamine was administered to children at the Emma Pendleton Bradley Home, their hyperactive and impulsive behaviors diminished. Herbert Freed and Charles Peifer reported in 1957 on the use of chlorpromazine to treat those who were then called hyperkinetic, emotionally disturbed children. Chlorpromazine was the first antidepressant; it was initially used on depressed patients at Saint Anne Hospital in Paris, who demonstrated remarkable improvements. In 1963, C. Keith Conners reported using methylphenidate to reduce the inappropriate symptomology of emotionally disturbed children and to improve their focus and learning.

More recently, there has been an explosion of medicines for treating ADHD. Prescriptions written annually in the United States for ADHD in ten- to nineteen-year-olds increased 26 percent from 2007 and 2012. By 2012, the number reached twenty-one million. A need for treating adults with ADHD fueled expansion of these trends. In this regard, Express Scripts, the largest U.S. prescription processing company, reported prescriptions for medicines for adults with ADHD doubled in the last four years. Half were for amphetamine-based drugs.

Central Nervous System Psychostimulants

The use of stimulating substances found in plants goes back millennia. Many psychostimulants occur naturally as alkaloidal substances that people inadvertently stumbled upon. For example, tobacco contains nicotine and has been used for at least eight thousand years in the Americas. Khat has been chewed in Africa since Neolithic times, continued in ancient Egypt, and is used today for the stimulating effects of cathinone. Tea leaves containing theophylline were used to make a mild stimulating drink in China over five thousand years ago. Coca leaves were chewed at least four thousand years ago in South America. Cacao beans were used to brew a warm chocolate drink containing theobromine at least since 1900 BCE in Mesoamerica. Coffee beans were used since the fourth century BCE to make a caffeinated beverage in what is now Ethiopia. Kola nuts were chewed in Africa long before Western contact, and kava roots were steeped across Polynesia to make a drink. Many mildly stimulating, naturally occurring substances were consumed for a long time in nearly all corners of the world.

The recognition and identification of substances with stimulating properties is largely the result of nineteenth-century science. In 1819, Friedlieb Runge, a German physician, isolated and purified caffeine.

Wilhelm Posselt and Ludwig Reimann, students at Heidelberg in 1828, isolated and refined a volatile and active alkaloid from tobacco that they called nicotine, in tribute to Jean Nicot, the sixteenth-century French ambassador to Portugal who introduced tobacco to the French court. Nicot learned about the purported curative properties of tobacco while in Portugal and returned to France in 1560, promoting its medicinal uses. He used tobacco to treat the migraine headaches of Catherine de Medici, queen-consort of Henry II of France. She popularized snuff, which others imitated.

In 1855, a German chemist, Friedrich Gaedcke, separated the alkaloidal extract, which he referred to as erythroxyline, from coca plants. Albert Niemann, doing graduate studies in 1859 at Gottingen University in Germany, developed a process separating and refining what he called "cocaine" from coca leaves. In 1862, Wilhelm Lossen, a colleague of Niemann's, identified the chemical formula for cocaine.

Amphetamines

Amphetamines refers to a group of psychostimulants. They include amphetamine, methamphetamine, dextroamphetamine, and lisdextroamphetamine.

Formulation and Original Uses. Amphetamine was synthesized in 1887 by Lazar Edeleanu, a Romanian chemist in Berlin. Nagai Nagayoshi, a Japanese chemist, synthesized methamphetamine from ephedrine in 1893. Akira Ogata, a Japanese pharmacologist, synthesized methamphetamine in 1919 by reducing ephedrine, using red phosphorous and iodine. Gordon Alles, an American chemist and pharmacologist, independently synthesized amphetamine in 1927 and reported on its stimulating effects; his research led to production and use of amphetamines. Amphetamine was marketed beginning in 1932 by Smith, Kline, and French (SKF), later GlaxoSmithKline, under the trade name Benzedrine, a liquid free-base amphetamine used as a bronchodilator. Fred Nabenhauer of SKF developed the Benzedrine inhaler, marketed beginning in 1933 for relief of congestion associated with colds and related conditions. People discovered that they could open inhalers and swallow the paper strips inside to get high. Benzedrine tablets were soon manufactured to try to prevent illicit use. U.S. college students were using amphetamine "pep" pills as early as 1936 for all-night studying or partying. SKF began marketing dextroamphetamine tablets in 1937 as Dexedrine.

During World War II, amphetamines were used for their stimulating and performance-enhancing effects by military forces and those in war industries. U.S. military forces, particularly bomber crews and jungle fighters, were issued 180 million amphetamine tablets and pills during World War II, and British forces were supplied with 72 million amphetamine tablets. Japanese and Nazi pilots and soldiers, including kamikaze pilots, were routinely using amphetamines, which were referred to as *Senryoka Zokyo Zai* (literally, drug to inspire fighting) in wartime Japan. During World War II, methamphetamine was marketed by Temmler Pharmaceutical in Berlin as Pervitin and used by Nazi troops, particularly Luftwaffe pilots, who called it *Hermann-Goring-Pillen* (literally, Herman Goring pills). Adolf Hitler was given daily injections of methamphetamine by his doctor Theodor Morell. Other Nazi leaders, including General Erwin "Desert Fox" Rommel, were also frequent users of psychostimulants.

Amphetamines were previously used to treat conditions like depression, nasal congestion, and obesity. SKF was manufacturing 1 million amphetamine pills daily in 1945, and there were other companies producing as well. Approximately 750 million amphetamine pills were made in the United States in 1945—enough for half a million Americans to have 2 pills every day. By 1946, amphetamine was indicated for at least thirty-nine different conditions, including caffeine dependence, low blood pressure, chronic hiccups, and seasickness. The U.S. patent expired in 1949, and generic manufacturing began. In 1949, sixteen thousand pounds of amphetamines were produced in the United States, and production increased to seventy-five thousand pounds, equaling 3.5 million tablets, by 1958.

U.S. pilots fighting in the Korean Conflict were given high dosages of amphetamines. Amphetamines were widely administered during the Vietnam War, as they had been in World War II. U.S. military continues to use amphetamines for troops, including those in Iraq and Afghanistan. Amphetamines were widely used among Beatniks in the 1950s and early 1960s and commonly mentioned in Beat literature, like Jack Kerouac's *On the Road*, Allen Ginsberg's poem "Howl," and other literary works and song lyrics. Estimated production of amphetamine pills in the United States is estimated to have reached eight billion annually by 1962. By 1971, twelve billion amphetamine pills were manufactured in the United States annually.

Use in Treating ADHD. There was an outbreak of pediatric viral encephalitis in the United States in 1937. Some of these children, as they recuperated, demonstrated hyperkinetic and distractible behaviors. Bradley gave some of these children Benzedrine and observed that it helped them become less hyperactive and distractible. The report that this medication helped problem children become better behaved, quiet, and studious led to its use for ADHD.

Use of psychostimulants to treat ADHD subsequently increased dramatically. By 1970, approximately 150,000 U.S. children were prescribed psychostimulants. This number rose to between 270,000 and 541,000 by 1980, and, by 1988, between 750,000 and 1.6 million school-aged children were prescribed psychostimulants, mainly for ADHD. Richwood Pharmaceuticals introduced a combination instant-release amphetamine tablet formulation in 1996 marketed as Adderall, which led to a rise in prescriptions. By 1999, 3.4 percent of U.S. children were prescribed psychostimulants for ADHD; today that number is closer to 10 percent. By 2000, over 2 million U.S. children were taking psychostimulants. Various ADHD psychostimulants have been introduced: Vyvanse, trade name for lisdextroamphetamine, in 2007; ProCentra, a liquid formulation of dextroamphetamine, in 2008 by Independence Pharmaceuticals; and Adzenys XR-ODT, an amphetamine oral-disintegrating tablet, in 2016 by Neos Therapeutics.

Since the early 1970s, the main approach to treating ADHD is psychostimulants. Today, approximately 8 percent of four- to seventeen-year-olds have an ADHD diagnosis. Of these, 4.5 percent take psychostimulants, usually Ritalin or Adderall, while many trade and generic versions are also available.

Restrictions on Availability. Due to addictive liability, restrictions on the availability of psychostimulants were imposed around the mid-twentieth century. Japan initiated restrictions on methamphetamine as a dangerous substance in 1948. Japan enacted the Pharmaceutical Affairs Law in 1949 regulating amphetamines, requiring prescriptions, and pharmaceutical companies had to limit production. Japanese authorities thought limiting oral medicines while increasing intravenous-formulations would restrict use to hospitals, but illicit injection exploded. In Japan, illicit psychostimulant use escalated among young ethnic minorities, particularly Chinese and Koreans. Japan enacted the Awakening Drug Control Law in 1951, restricting the manufacture, possession, and sale of psychostimulants; importing precursors was prohibited. Despite restrictions, psychostimulant use rose dramatically, peaking in 1954, when an estimated 2 million Japanese in a population of 88.5 million were using psychostimulants.

A similar epidemic occurred in the United States and Europe, particularly in Great Britain, France, and Sweden, as efforts to rebuild after World

War II necessitated hardships. In the 1950s, U.S. truck drivers, shift workers, returning veterans, students, inmates, celebrities, and others were regularly using amphetamines. In 1959, the FDA made amphetamine only available by prescription; nevertheless, production increased.

Psychostimulant use peaked in Sweden during 1966 and 1967, when one out of three persons who were arrested in Stockholm was because of amphetamine injection. Broad societal approaches, including public campaigns, stricter controls, and increased treatment led to declines in Sweden. Passage in 1970 of the Controlled Substances Act (CSA) of the Comprehensive Drug Abuse Prevention and Control Act listed amphetamines as schedule-III drugs, but they were moved to Schedule-II in 1971, meaning users needed new prescriptions for each refill, and physicians and pharmacies had to keep detailed records. After enactment, amphetamine sales declined by 60 percent. Similar efforts were developed in other countries. There was a fivefold increase in the number of psychostimulants covered under international controls from 1971 to 1995.

Pharmaceutical preparations of amphetamines and related substances evolved. Since psychostimulants are fast-acting, they have short durations, so combination medicines and extended-release formulations were created. For instance, SKF marketed a combination of dextroamphetamine and amobarbital, a barbiturate, as marketed as Dexamyl. In the 1950s, SKF introduced an extended-release dextroamphetamine capsule, marketed as Dexedrine Spansule. New River Pharmaceuticals developed lisdextroamphetamine as a longer acting and supposedly less easily abused alternative to dextroamphetamine. New River was taken over by Shire Pharmaceuticals, which released lisdextroamphetamine as Vyvanse after FDA approval on February 23, 2007. A U.S. patent was filed on June 1, 2004, by Travis Mickle et al. of New River for synthesis of lisdextroamphetamine as an abuse-resistant substance that was useful for ADHD. GlaxoSmithKline sold the rights to Dexedrine Spansule to Amedra, a subsidiary of CorePharma in October 2010.

Methylphenidate

Methylphenidate is a psychostimulant that stimulates the arousal system in the brain stem and activates regions of the cerebral cortex. In clinical settings, it appears to improve cognitive function.

Formulation and Original Uses. Leandro Panizzon, a researcher at CIBA, synthesized methylphenidate in 1944. Compared to amphetamines, methylphenidate is a relatively mild psychostimulant, but abuse and dependence are possible. Panizzon and Max Hartmann patented a process for synthesizing methylphenidate in 1950. CIBA was granted a patent in

1954 for use of methylphenidate as an antidepressant. FDA granted approval in 1955 for methylphenidate to treat several conditions, including depression, fatigue, narcolepsy, obesity, schizophrenia, and what was then called either hyperactivity or MBD but is now known as ADHD. It is used for other purposes, such as helping patients with drug-induced comas, typically from anesthesia. The trade name, Ritalin, was a tribute to Panizzon's wife Marguerite, nicknamed Rita. FDA granted approval in 1961 for methylphenidate to treat children with behavioral problems.

Use in Treating ADHD. Treating ADHD with methylphenidate has a relatively long history. It was used since the 1950s, progressively increasing from the 1960s onward. FDA granted approval in 1955 to CIBA, now Novartis, for methylphenidate. FDA approval was granted in 2008 for the use of methylphenidate in treating adults with ADHD. It is used around the world for ADHD.

Dramatic Increase in Use. In the 1990s, there were dramatic increases in the use of methylphenidate. Around two hundred thousand children aged two to four were prescribed methylphenidate (Ritalin) from 1991 to 1995. Methylphenidate became the ADHD medicine of choice in the United States by the late 1990s, as it was prescribed to about 90 percent of those with ADHD. Production of methylphenidate increased sixfold from 1990 to 2005. From 2007 to 2012, prescriptions for methylphenidate in Great Britain increased 50 percent, and, by 2013, consumption of methylphenidate reached 2.4 billion, representing a 66 percent increase over 2012. The ALZA Corporation received FDA approval in 2000 to market an extended-release methylphenidate-formulation as Concerta. Methylin ER, the trade name of another extended-release methylphenidate-formulation, was also introduced in 2000. Trade names for other extended-release methylphenidate pill formulations include Biphentin, Equasym XL, Medikinet XL, and Rubifen SR, and extended-release capsules are marketed under names such as Metadate CD and Ritalin LA. Pfizer introduced an extended-release oral suspension, marketed as Quillivant XR, in 2012 and a chewable methylphenidate-formulation, marketed as Quillichew ER, in 2016. Today, the United States alone accounts for over 80 percent of methylphenidate consumption globally.

Nonstimulant Medications

Many nonstimulants have been found to help with ADHD. Nonstimulant ADHD medicines include amantadine, atomoxetine, antihypertensives, anticonvulsants, eugeroics, cholinergic agents, and others. Each has its own history and associated issues.

Amantadine

W. Haaf of Germany synthesized amantadine and received a patent on October 6, 1964. Marvin Paulshock and John Watts of E. I. du Pont de Nemours and Company filed a U.S. patent on May 5, 1966. In October 1966, the FDA approved the use of amantadine as a prophylactic for Asian influenza and for treating influenza-A virus. In 1969, amantadine was accidently discovered to help reduce symptoms of Parkinson's disease, akathisia, and drug-related extrapyramidal symptoms. Kathleen Clarence-Smith of Prestwick Pharmaceuticals filed a patent on November 8, 2005, for amantadine to treat hyperkinetic disorders. Amantadine manufactured by Endo Pharmaceuticals is marketed as Symmetrel.

Atomoxetine

On February 27, 1985, Jerry Misner of Eli Lilly applied for a patent for a racemization process to produce atomoxetine. Atomoxetine was initially called tomoxetine, but FDA requested a name change, as the original name sounded similar to tamoxifen, a breast-cancer medicine. Eli Lilly initially explored atomoxetine as an antidepressant, but it did not have satisfactory benefit-to-risk ratios, so development for depression was halted. Eli Lilly then began exploring use of atomoxetine as an ADHD medicine, since it does not have the side effects associated with methylphenidate and similar medicines. John Heiligenstein and Gary Tollefson of Eli Lilly filed a U.S. patent for atomoxetine to treat ADHD was filed on July 17, 1996, and it was granted on August 19, 1997. Atomoxetine is marketed by Eli Lilly as Strattera. In the United States, generic production of atomoxetine began in 2017, when it lost patent protection.

Other Medications

Other medicines are used off-label for ADHD, including antihypertensives, anticonvulsants, eugeroics, and anticholinergics. Another example is a substance that has been around for a long time—nicotine. Many herbal treatments, nutritional approaches, and other medicinal cures have been tried to manage ADHD. Off-label prescribing occurs whenever a medicine is used outside its area of marketing authorization with respect to factors like disorder treated, demographics, particularly age of patient, dose, route-of-administration, and duration-of-treatment. Off-label use is use of licensed medicines for unlicensed purposes; it is common, and shouldn't be assumed inappropriate or reckless. Health care providers use professional judgment in developing treatments for ADHD or related conditions.

Medicines that previously had other uses and new substances yet to be approved will continue to be tried to individualize ADHD treatments. This is how medical knowledge advances and is how many substances that are now recognized as ADHD medicines were developed.

Clonidine and guanfacine are two antihypertensives that are used for ADHD. These were initially developed for hypertension and later found helpful for ADHD. FDA approved clonidine, manufactured by Boehringer Ingelheim and marketed as Catapres, for hypertension on September 3, 1974. FDA approved guanfacine, manufactured by Promius Pharma and marketed as Tenex, for hypertension on October 27, 1986. In the late 2000s, use of antihypertensives for ADHD was explored. Evidence suggests that selective alpha-2 adrenergic receptor agonists act directly on the prefrontal cortex to enhance executive functioning, which could help with ADHD. Guanfacine (Tenex) and clonidine (Catapres) were reformulated for treating ADHD. Guanfacine, manufactured by Shire and marketed as Intuniv, was FDA approved on September 1, 2009.

Clonidine, when used orally, is almost entirely absorbed in the gastrointestinal tract, but it is subject to rapid liver metabolism, creating a short biological half-life with interindividual variability. It was recognized that having extended-release formulations would be desirable. A transdermal clonidine patch was developed for more stable serum levels. H. Joseph Horacek filed a patent on October 13, 1993, for extended-release clonidine tablets, and on September 28, 2010, the FDA approved use of extended-release clonidine alone or in combination with stimulants for treating six- to seventeen-year-olds with ADHD. Initially manufactured by Shionogi Pharma and now by Concordia Pharmaceuticals and marketed as Kapvay, extended-release clonidine tablets were later approved for treating adults with ADHD.

Carbamazepine and valproate are the main anticonvulsants used for ADHD. The initial formulations and application were for seizure control. Beverly Burton synthesized valproate in 1882 as an analogue of valeric acid, which naturally occurs in valerian. Valproate, considered to be metabolically inert, was used in laboratory experiments as a solvent for organic compounds. Pierre Eymard, a French scientist, accidently discovered in 1962 that valproate prevented chemically induced seizures in rats. It was approved in France in 1967 as an antiepileptic and is still used for such in many places.

Walter Schindler, a chemist in Switzerland at J. R. Geigy, now Novartis, discovered carbamazepine in 1953. In 1963, carbamazepine was marketed in Switzerland as Tegretol for anticonvulsant use and for trigeminal neuralgia. It was first used in 1965 in the United Kingdom, and the FDA approved it in 1968 for U.S. use.

After their original formulation and use, it was suspected anticonvulsants might be useful for ADHD. This was reasonable, since they alter brain neuronal firing rates, which is how they control seizures. Some with ADHD have outbursts of aggression and anger, and anticonvulsants have calming effects. These two anticonvulsants seem to also be helpful in controlling impulsivity. By the 1990s, they were used with many children and adolescents with ADHD around the world. Some with ADHD found that the use of an anticonvulsant with a psychostimulant was effective.

In the late 1970s, Michel Jouvet of Lafon Laboratories in France created modafinil while working on benzhydryl-sufinyl compounds, including adrafinil, which was experimented with for narcolepsy in 1968. The primary metabolite of adrafinil is modafinil, which is used clinically. Modafinil was originally designed to help fighter pilots stay awake on long missions. It became available by prescription in France in 1986 and FDA approved on December 24, 1998, for narcolepsy and for shift-work sleep disorder and obstructive sleep apnea in 2003. It was approved in December of 2002 for use in the United Kingdom. In the U.S., modafinil is marketed as Provigil and is manufactured by Cephalon, which originally leased rights from Lafon Laboratories and later purchased the company. Modafinil is marketed under other trade names and, since 2012, has been available in generic formulations. Modafinil also has stimulant effects, which helps individuals stay awake and increases alertness, but, for some, it does not improve focus. FDA denied approval for modafinil for ADHD in children in 2006 over concerns of nonfatal toxic epidermal necrolysis, or Stevens-Johnson syndrome rashes.

Armodafinil is another closely related eugeroic that has been marketed in the United States since June 15, 2007, when it was granted FDA approval. Armodafinil is sold as Nuvigil and is also manufactured by Cephalon.

There is evidence that neuronal nicotinic acetylcholine receptors may be involved in ADHD pathophysiology. Nicotine demonstrates positive effects on cognition in human and animal subjects, including clinical trials on adults with ADHD. In 1828, Wilhelm Posselt and Karl Reimann isolated nicotine from tobacco. Its chemical structure was discovered by Adolf Pinner and Richard Wolffenstein in 1893, and it was first synthesized in 1904 by Amé Pictet and A. Rotschy. Unfortunately, undesired side effects from nicotine (Nicorette) preclude use as a general therapeutic agent, other than for smoking cessation.

Other cholinergic agents have been examined for safety and efficacy in treating ADHD. For example, ABT-089, or pozanicline, a weak partial neuronal nicotinic receptor agonist, has been shown effective and safe for treating ADHD. ABT-418, another cholinergic, is a nicotinic analog that has been demonstrated safe and efficacious in treating ADHD in children and adults.

3

Causes and Risk Factors

Causes of ADHD are multifactorial, and associations work in complex interplays of genetic and environmental risks. While exact causes aren't entirely known, many specific risk factors have been identified. ADHD clearly runs in families and is highly inheritable; accordingly, we must discuss its genetic basis. Whatever the causes, it is clear ADHD is fundamentally brain based, and, thus, we need to understand how neurotransmission is different in brains of those with ADHD, and in what ways their brain development is different. Many risk factors are known to increase one's risk of having ADHD, including diet, substance use, metabolic deficiencies, excessive screen time, and tendencies to crave stimulation.

GENETIC BASIS OF ADHD

ADHD is currently understood to be a highly heritable disorder, with genetic alterations in neural pathways that produce neurotransmitters, such as norepinephrine and dopamine. However, it must be understood that no one simply inherits ADHD—one only inherits genetic predispositions to disorders such as ADHD. This predisposition, which is highly inheritable, only gives one a greater probability for having symptoms. Whether they are ever expressed or not is a different matter, which is influenced by many variables. This is in accord with epigenetic theory, as postulated by Bruce Lipton, asserting that environments in and around cells significantly affects how genetic coding in DNA (deoxyribonucleic acid) is or isn't expressed. Epigenetics refers to chromosome changes that activate or deactivate the activity and expression of genes, which can result in certain disorders and diseases, including how emotions can alter electromagnetic frequencies to control gene activities. It is the complex interaction between variables, including genetic, biological, and psychosocial factors that sometimes interact and combine to produce ADHD. Environmental risk factors, including life experiences and exposure to numerous substances, ultimately determine whether a genetic tendency for ADHD is or isn't expressed. For instance, it has been speculated that if an individual plays computer games too often, there may be greater probability that genetic proneness to ADHD will be expressed. On the other hand, it is suspected that if that same individual didn't play computer games excessively, then the ADHD might never actually develop, even though the genetic predisposition was inherited. However, there is insufficient research supporting this commonly held belief.

Multiple research supports the genetic basis of ADHD. At least three specific gene sites have been implicated as having probable roles in the genetic foundations of ADHD. Identified sites include dopamine transporter gene (DAT1), situated on chromosome r, D2 gene, which is a dopamine receptor gene, and D4 receptor gene (DRD4), situated on chromosome 11. Additional genes that are indicated as likely involved in the heritability of ADHD include HTR1B, SLC6A3, and SNAP25. Glutamate receptor genes GRM1, GRM5, GRM7, and GRM8 have also been implicated in the etiology of ADHD. Other gene sites are also likely involved, including some that influence serotonin production and reuptake. However, it must be recognized that there are more than one dozen specific subtypes of receptors for serotonin, each with different genetic factors. Other genes that are also suspected of having associations with ADHD include CHRNA4, GIT1, NOS1, SLC6A2, SLC6A4, and TPH-2. Although evidence is currently sparse and inconsistent, in the future, we will hopefully have a better understanding of the complex heritable basis of ADHD. Interestingly, with respect to adults with ADHD, it appears that, at least sometimes, different alleles of the same genes associated with childhood ADHD are involved, while in other cases, different genes may be. Two genes identified as unique to adult ADHD are LPHN3 and CDH13.

Studies suggest the genetic architecture of ADHD is complex. Genome-wide linkage analysis is being used to identify novel candidate genes. Additional approaches, such as epigenetic studies or neuroimaging genetics, are being explored to gain better understanding of the etiologic complexity of ADHD.

Deficiency or excess of one or more neurotransmitters can lead to various psychiatric disorders, such as bipolar depression and schizophrenia, as well as, of course, ADHD. Twin studies further support the genetic basis for ADHD, with greater concordance observed among monozygotic compared to dizygotic twins. If one fraternal twin has ADHD, around 29 percent of twin siblings will also, while if one monozygotic twin has ADHD, around 81 percent of identical twin siblings, who have the same genes, also will. It is understood that the biological parents of individuals with ADHD have higher incidences of children with ADHD than adoptive parents do. For example, at least one-third of biological fathers who either have or had ADHD will have children who are also diagnosed.

It is recognized if one biological parent has ADHD, there is around a 30 percent chance that their children will. If both biological parents have ADHD, odds rise to more than a 50-percent likelihood (with estimates as high as 85–90 percent). Despite these probabilities, it is possible that either all or none of the children in a particular family will inherit ADHD. Similarly, if one child has ADHD, there is around a 30 percent chance that all siblings also would. However, if the sibling in question is an adult with ADHD, the probability of another adult sibling also having it rises to over 40 percent. It is evident that ADHD runs in families.

As ADHD impacts the regulation of specific brain functions, particularly those related to executive functioning, it can result in myriad impairments to related behaviors. This neurodevelopmental condition can make it challenging for some children to sit still, focus, and sustain attention. Highly genetic-driven influences foster chemical differences in the brains of individuals with ADHD, contributing to behavioral challenges. Challenges include executive functions such as maintaining attention, concentration, and effort; learning from mistakes; memory; motivation; and organizational and social skills.

Only a relatively low percentage of phenotypic variance of ADHD is explained by genetic variants that have presently been identified. As with most similar conditions, genes alone don't determine the incidence of ADHD phenotypes. Many environmental risk factors interact in complex ways with an individual's repertoires of genetic risk factors to determine whether or not ADHD will be expressed.

Genes don't directly control complex human behaviors, such as attention or hyperactivity. Rather, genes act primarily on the expression of proteins that can alter physiological functioning, particularly within the brain. Two major neurotransmitter systems seem to be involved most directly with ADHD—those associated with dopamine and norepinephrine, both with their synthesis and release, as well as their subsequent reuptake. Inadequate levels of these neurotransmitters for only brief milliseconds in numerous synapses of myriad neural circuits is largely what impairs the ability of someone with ADHD to momentarily address the task at hand. This is basically the underlying mechanism of ADHD.

Additional research is required to gain more comprehensive and detailed understanding of the actual mechanisms involved in the expression of the respective genes that are involved in ADHD.

WEAK NEURAL NETWORKS

Research suggests that ADHD is comprised of several important subgroups, each of which appears to be related to inherent weaknesses in connections within various brain neural networks. These networks consist of myelinated neurons, generally referred to as white matter, which connect respective brain circuits. While growth of myelin sheathing usually peaks in the twenties, in those with ADHD, it can continue well into the thirties. The immature deposition of myelin fibers makes neural transmission slower and less efficient. Electrical signals travel as ripples down the axon as an altering of hyperpolarizations, followed within a millisecond by depolarizations. Insufficient myelination slows down the transmission speed and appears to play a major role in the symptomology of ADHD.

Differences have been observed among individuals with ADHD compared to those without white-matter neural tracts connecting different brain parts and serving as communication links between them. Individuals with ADHD appear to exhibit variable patterns of functional connectivity, with patterns of oscillations in brain activity that permit different parts of the brain to communicate with each other to exchange information.

Brain neural networks are numerous and complicated. Individual neurons transmit messages and make connections to other neurons and, often, to different brain regions. The brains of many with ADHD tend to be smaller and have fewer connections than those of neurotypicals. Underdeveloped connections, typical of ADHD, create varied problems with quantity and quality of neural networks, resulting in slower processing of information and greater difficulties filtering out unimportant signals. Varying patterns of brain-network maturation impact the nature of the presentation of ADHD symptoms. Further, production, release, and removal of neurotransmitters affect different neural networks differently. Appropriate dopamine levels are essential to maintaining alertness and energy. Appropriate norepinephrine levels are essential to maintaining attention and motivation. Appropriate serotonin levels are essential to avoiding obsessions and compulsions. Neural imbalances help to explain why some have more difficulties than others with regulating attention, impulsivity, and emotions.

Underdeveloped neural networks help to partially explain many of the inattention, impulsivity, and emotional regulatory problems frequently observed with ADHD. Inattention might stem from the weaknesses of networks that run outward from frontal-parietal areas and elsewhere to remind us to ignore distracting stimuli and maintain focus on desired goals. Weaknesses in neural networks that run from the thalamus through the limbic-hippocampal regions to the frontal cortex can manifest as impulsivity, since signal transmission to stop inappropriate behaviors can be impaired. Weaknesses in the neural networks running from the cerebral cortex down to the amygdala can manifest as poor emotional control, caused by the ineffectiveness of signals to regulate negative emotions. Similarly, overexcitement, anger, frustration, and inability to respond to delayed rewards could stem from reduced activation of the networks between the prefrontal cortex and nucleus accumbens and the rest of the reward system.

Some have referred to these weak neural networks, typical in ADHD, as the default mode network (DMN). Dysfunction of the DMN in individuals with ADHD can result in poor performance and necessitates more effort to maintain focus and engagement. Weak neural networks result from a relative lack of synaptic connectivity between neurons, but there are still numerous connections formed in all brains. Around sixty trillion connections are estimated between neurons in the cerebral cortex alone.

BRAIN DEVELOPMENT

While an embryo, the brain forms and develops more rapidly than other internal organs or limbs. The brains of newborn humans are far from fully developed. The brain of a typical newborn weighs less than one pound (0.5 kilograms). The brain of a neonate is dominated, for survival purposes, by activity in the lower "reptilian" brain, where much control of basic life functions, like respiration and heart rate, is situated. The brain of a newborn grows about three times its size during the first year. Although 90 percent of brain development happens before the age of five, brain growth and development continues throughout the remainder of childhood and into early adulthood.

The human brain is the only organ that is not fully developed at birth. While every human brain is somewhat unique, it attains its full weight at around six years of age. Most increase in brain weight comes from the growth of neurons and supporting cells, principally glia, and the development of new synaptic connections. Later developmental changes have been observed in the caudate, cingulate, and insula brain regions. Emerging findings about brain development indicate that critical regions, like those involved in decision-making and attention, aren't fully developed until around the age of twenty-five.

Neonate brains actually contain many more neurons than adult brains, but synaptic matrices are far less refined. The cerebral cortex of a healthy, adult human contains between fifteen and thirty-three billion neurons, not all of which were present at birth. New neurons continue to be generated, particularly in the olfactory center and dentate gyrus of hippocampus, where newly acquired memories are thought to be stored, and connectivity between them is a dynamic, lifelong process.

Some brain areas appear to take three to five years longer to mature in those with ADHD compared to neurotypicals. This is complicated by atypical development of white-matter connections across brain regions and by global reductions of gray matter. There also seem to be decreases in cortical thickness in those with ADHD.

Brain-imaging studies indicate that individuals with ADHD have prefrontal lobe asymmetry indices, which are significantly negatively associated with age, suggesting prefrontal regional cerebral blood flow lateralization increases from right to left side with increasing age. These observations are consistent with findings that suggest left-hemisphere dominance in the prefrontal cortex significantly increases with age in ADHD.

Research suggests that difficulties for individuals with ADHD can be attributed to deficiencies in brain circuits, particularly those in the prefrontal cortex. However, there may also be alterations in the circuitry of other brain regions, particularly in the cerebellum, parietal, and temporal lobes. Cortices in the parietal and temporal lobes interconnect with the prefrontal cortex to mediate aspects of attention. Parietal cortices are crucial for orienting attentional resources in time and space, while temporal cortices help to analyze visual data. Collectively, these areas help evaluate stimulus salience. The prefrontal cortex is critical to attributing meaning to stimuli and screening out distractions, as well as for inhibiting inappropriate emotions and impulses. Underactivity in these, with weakened connections to other regions, is common in ADHD brains, which becomes more problematic when too little or too much of the respective neurotransmitters, particularly dopamine or norepinephrine, is available.

We know that deformations in basal ganglia nuclei, specifically in the caudate, globus pallidus, and putamen, have been observed in the brains of individuals with ADHD. Generally, the more pronounced the deformations are, the more severe the extent of ADHD symptoms. Evidence further suggests that psychostimulant medications can help to normalize these brain deformations.

Many things that impair normal brain development or harm the brain can potentially increase the risks for development of ADHD. One significant consequence of such harm can be traumatic brain injury (TBI). TBI is caused by a broad array of incidents that are implicated as possible causes of ADHD. This concept has roots in earlier notions of ADHD, regarded as minimal brain dysfunction. While that idea has been largely discarded as a general cause, there is still the possibility that TBI may be associated with ADHD, particularly as it could make someone with a genetic predisposition for ADHD become more susceptible. Although most discussion around relationship between TBI and ADHD deals with prenatal and perinatal causes, TBI can happen at any point in life.

Most cases of TBI among children from infancy to age fourteen are from unintentional falls and being struck by objects, while most common reasons for TBI among those aged fifteen to twenty-four are motor vehicle accidents and falls. Mild TBI is common, accounting for 70–80 percent of emergency department visits among children. Mild TBI accounted for 2 million outpatient visits and almost 3 million emergency department visits for children from 2005 to 2009. CDC reports that in 2013, there were about 640,000 emergency department visits related to TBI in children aged fourteen and younger, while 1,500 children died of TBI. Moderate to severe TBI is associated with higher rates of not advancing in school and being placed in special education, which are all too common for many children with ADHD. In the United States, there are 1.7 million incidents of TBI annually among individuals of all ages. These result in 1.4 million visits annually to hospital emergency departments, 275,000 hospitalizations, and 52,000 deaths.

One particular subpopulation with higher risk for TBI is military veterans. While TBI is largely a disorder of organic origin with psychological consequences, post-traumatic stress disorder (PTSD) is another condition that is largely of psychological origin, with some organic sequelae that may also be, in some cases at least, associated with ADHD. PTSD, while frequently associated with veterans, is another disorder that can occur at any age. Projected lifetime risk for PTSD in the United States at the age of seventy-five is 8.7 percent, and annual prevalence in the United States among adults is around 3.5 percent.

OTHER RISK FACTORS

Numerous other risk factors are associated with a higher probability of having ADHD. Many pregnancy complications are linked to an increased risk of ADHD. Certainly good prenatal care reduces chances of having children with ADHD. Regular prenatal medical visits; healthy eating; and avoiding substance use and exposure to other harmful substances, such as lead and mercury, are all advisable for preventing ADHD. For example, the offspring of women who smoked while pregnant are twice as likely to develop ADHD. Low infant birth weight is another factor identified as increasing risk for ADHD, and that is directly associated with maternal weight before and during early gestation. Maternal weight gain in the first half of pregnancy results mainly from the deposition and expansion of fat and other tissues, while later weight gain is more related to placental and fetal growth. Early- and midpregnancy weight gain may affect infant birth weight by increasing the availability of maternal resources, such as amino acids, free fatty acids, and glucose, which aid in fetal development and reduce the probabilities of ADHD.

Prenatal exposure to various pollutants can affect later development due to alterations of cells that are developing into organs, including the brain. For instance, prenatal exposure to diesel exhaust particles is thought to modify immune microglia cells in the brain, thereby influencing neuronal connections and associated behaviors. Exposure to myriad pollutants could alter susceptibility to ADHD.

Maternal diseases present a range of possible risk factors for ADHD. Maternal gestational diabetes, particularly when combined with low socioeconomic status, as well as maternal type-2 diabetes requiring antidiabetic medication, appears to increase risks for ADHD in offspring. Many conditions identified as ADHD risk factors are related to maternal health, including several autoimmune diseases, which are associated with significantly greater risk for ADHD in offspring, including autoimmune hepatitis, ankylosing spondylitis, psoriasis, and type-1 diabetes. Mechanisms that may underlie various autoimmune diseases with psychiatric disorders like ADHD may include an altered immune response and shared genetic and environmental exposure factors, such as infections and alcohol, tobacco, and other drug use, including the consumption of acetaminophen (Tylenol). Major histocompatibility genes, such as HLA (human leukocyte antigen)-DR4, HLA-DRB1, and the complementary C4B gene, have been linked to ADHD and to various autoimmune diseases, such as autoimmune hepatitis, juvenile arthritis, and type-1 diabetes.

Birth complications are another area recognized as possibly contributing to risk for ADHD. For example, oxygen deprivation or lack of blood flow to the baby's brain near the time of birth, such as experienced in hypoxic ischemic encephalopathy, or birth asphyxia, has been recognized as having a high risk for ADHD. Several conditions can cause this, including delayed emergency C-section, umbilical cord prolapse, nuchal cord, placental abruption, and preeclampsia (high maternal blood pressure). Breech presentation at birth, premature birth, transverse-lie (shoulder-first) presentation, and umbilical cord problems are all other recognized conditions that increase the chances of the child later developing ADHD.

Health problems experienced by individuals—not their mothers—have also been found to increase risks for ADHD. This is particularly true in illnesses affecting the brain and nervous system, such as encephalitis, meningitis, or fetal alcohol syndrome. However, most individuals with

ADHD never had any of these illnesses, and most individuals with such don't develop ADHD. Having many other illnesses also seems to increase risks for ADHD. Children and adolescents with atopic dermatitis, for instance, are at greater risk for ADHD, as well as for other related behavioral disorders, including CD and ODD, both of which have high ADHD comorbidity.

Dietary Habits

The dietary patterns of mothers during pregnancy and those of children, particularly during the first five years of life, have important effects on later mental health. Dietary habits of mothers during pregnancy are recognized as influencing the likelihood that their offspring will experience behavioral problems, including ADHD, later in life. Unhealthy prenatal diets, generally considered higher in foodstuffs such as refined breads and cereals, processed meats, and sweetened beverages, have been identified as increasing risks for children later developing common mental problems, including anxiety and depression. Adequate intake of folic acid has especially been shown to reduce the risk of certain birth defects.

Diets that are low in nutrition have been implicated as increasing risks for ADHD and related disorders. Omega-3 fatty acids are regarded as essential fats that we cannot make but that we must get from our diets. Omega-3s are important in the formation of fatty myelin sheaths around neurons and for other aspects of fetal development. Docosahexaenoic acid (DHA), an omega-3 fatty acid, accumulates in fetal brains and eyes, particularly during the third trimester. It is important for normal development that maternal diets include other fatty acids, such as arachidonic acid (ARA), eicosapentaenoic acid (EPA), linoleic acid (LA), and gamma-linoleic acid (GLA). ARA plays important roles in regulating blood pressure and our immune response.

Consumption of certain food additives is recognized as a potential risk factor for ADHD. Brominated vegetable oil (BVO), for instance, is FDA approved for foods, but dozens of other countries have banned its use over concerns with endocrine disruption. BVO was initially developed as a flame retardant, but is now used as emulsifier in products like citrus-based sodas. Propyl gallate is an FDA-approved preservative in fats, like those in lard and sausages, including pepperoni pizza, but is suspected of causing tumors in rats. Butylated hydroxytoluene (BHT) is an FDA-approved additive that is included in several breakfast cereals but is recognized as a possible carcinogen.

Young children who eat more unhealthy foods are at greater risk for ADHD and related disorders. In fact, individuals of any age who have poor diets have a greater risk for ADHD symptoms. Diets providing insufficient amounts of certain amino acids, which operate as precursors for many neurotransmitters, can result in diminished neurotransmitter levels; conversely, excessive amino acid levels can result in elevated neurotransmitter levels. Consumption of aspartame, an artificial sweetener, has been associated with high amino acid levels, implicated in increasing hyperactivity. Eating excessive carbohydrates can trigger a dopamine rush in the brain. Certain food additives, such as preservatives, such sodium benzoate and benzoic acid, and colorings, such as allura red, azorubine, sunset yellow, quinoline yellow, and tartrazine, have all been suggested as causing hyperactivity. Poor dietary habits contribute to assorted health-related problems, many of which are thought to increase ADHD risks. Obesity, for example, is known to be directly related to cognitive decline. On the other hand, there is no conclusive evidence that an elimination diet actually prevents or alleviates ADHD. Nevertheless, many parents have felt that restricting items from diets, most typically sugars, helps improve behavior. Others suggest it could be the increased parental attention that is typically paid to children on elimination diets that helps promote better behaviors. Certain common food allergens, such as corn, nuts, chocolate, and wheat, have also been implicated as possible dietary offenders.

Substance Use

There is good and bad associated with most things in life, and such is certainly the case with substance use. For example, moderate alcohol consumption, generally defined as no more than one drink a day for women and two drinks a day for men, is associated with certain health benefits. Moderate alcohol consumption increases levels of high density lipoprotein (HDL), our good cholesterol, which keeps arteries open and clear of plaque. Moderate drinking also makes it less likely that blood platelets will stick together, which can lead to clot formation that could block blood flow, ultimately causing strokes or heart attacks. Low alcohol consumption is associated with larger hippocampal volumes. On the other hand, excessive use of alcohol or other substances can be problematic. About one in six (17 percent) U.S. adults (roughly thirty-eight million) binge drink, defined as four or more drinks at one time for females and five or more for males. In addition, one in twelve (8 percent) U.S. adults meets the diagnostic criteria for alcohol abuse or dependence. Withdrawal symptoms for alcohol use include anxiety, depression, extreme agitation with others, difficulty making decisions, confusion, mood swings, hand tremors, and involuntary movements, all of which could be confused as signs of ADHD. Prescription drug misuse is also widespread. More than 7 percent of individuals aged twelve or older in the United States (over twelve million) misused prescription drugs in the past year. There is no safe level of alcohol consumption during pregnancy, and high levels, such as associated with fetal alcohol syndrome, are clear risks for having offspring with ADHD and other related neurodevelopmental disorders. Certainly no one needs to drink alcoholic beverages to be healthy.

Many forms of psychoactive substance use are recognized as increasing the risk of ADHD and related disorders and for exacerbating symptoms. Individuals who consume excessive alcohol at any time can experience neuronal loss and decreased brain volume. Compared to adolescent light drinkers, adolescent heavy drinkers, those consuming six to nine or more drinks at least once a week have smaller gray matter volumes in their bilateral anterior cingulate cortex, right frontopolar and orbitofrontal cortices, right insular cortex, and right superior temporal gyrus. These differences are troubling, as we recognize the human brain continues to develop into the mid-twenties, and interfering with normal brain maturation by repeated bouts of heavy drinking can cause long-term negative effects. Tobacco consumption and use of marijuana and other drugs can accelerate brain function declines as we mature, resulting in memory loss. Further, the growing brain will not fully develop when deprived of regular flow of oxygenated blood, as associated with smoking marijuana and tobacco. These substance-use patterns can increase the risks of developing ADHD and also exacerbate symptom severity.

Metabolic Deficiencies

We all have different metabolisms, and some of us react to and process respective nutrients differently. Several metabolic irregularities contribute to a greater likelihood that someone will experience ADHD. A few individuals with ADHD might actually suffer from various metabolic disorders that deplete the body of essential nutrients, like calcium or iron. Hypoglycemia, or low blood sugar, can cause symptoms that look similar to ADHD. Certain food allergies or sensitivities may be causative in certain ADHD cases. Food allergies include those to chocolate, citrus, corn, dairy, peanuts, soy, and wheat. Myriad environmental allergens may contribute to the onset of ADHD. Some may experience heavy-metal toxicity from exposure to substances such as aluminum, lead, or mercury, which may lead to ADHD.

Screen Time

Screen time is part of the daily life of many. It has more than doubled for children under two since 1997. The average two- to five-year-old U.S. child spends thirty-two hours in front of a television, DVR, video screen, or game console each week. Studies report strong relationships between more screen time and developmental delays among very young children. U.S. children aged six to eleven spend about twenty-eight hours per week in front of screens. By the time U.S. children are in school, nearly one-third have televisions in their bedrooms.

The American Academy of Pediatrics recommends no use of screens until after eighteen months of age and limiting screen time to occasional video-chatting until the age of two. After twenty-four months of age, children can learn from interactive touch-screens, where answers must be selected or from live video-chatting with responsive adults, such as grandparents. For children older than six, it is recommended that family guidelines be established around healthy lifestyles, including adequate physical activity, diet, and sleep, with around one to two hours per day of screen time as general rule of thumb.

There was a limited study indicating that the more television watching by children one to three years old, the greater the likelihood of developing problems with attention by age seven. There was a direct relationship for each extra hour per day of television viewing. Risks of difficulty concentrating increased by 10 percent compared to children who watched no television. Excessive television viewing was associated with a 28 percent increase in attention problems. However, that study didn't assess whether any of the children had ADHD or not, nor did it consider the types of programs, whether educational or noneducational, watched. No study has confirmed that excessive screen time causes ADHD, but it seems prudent to limit screen time so not to exacerbate underlying problems. Excessive screen time is associated with cognitive deficits, behavioral problems, and even changes in brain structure. Further, more than two hours of screen time per day increases the risk of being overweight.

It is recommended that parents or guardians supervise children when they view any media. Young children cannot adequately differentiate between fantasy and reality, and it is the parents' responsibility to help them learn this distinction. Parental education must focus on teaching children that the characters portrayed on screen are playing imaginary roles; that violence as depicted on screens is "make-believe"; and that if the violence depicted were real, the characters would be severely injured. This is important for all children, but more so for a child with ADHD, who may lack impulse control and could more easily hurt someone by imitating violent acts seen on the screen.

Digital Media

The common use of digital interactive and social media is increasing heavily and has been implicated with risks and health consequences pertaining to ADHD. In 2016, the American Academy of Pediatrics issued guidelines on the potential benefits and risks of electronic media use by young children. Benefits of digital-electronic media, supported by research, include opportunities for early learning; introduction of new ideas and knowledge; increased social support and contact; and availability of up-to-date, appropriate information for health education, prevention, and maintenance. However, possible risks of too much early exposure include negative effects on learning and attention; increased prevalence of health problems such as depression and obesity; less sleep; privacy and confidentiality concerns; and exposure to inaccurate, inappropriate, or unsafe content and contacts. Young children, beginning around eighteen-months old—long before they can safely begin to use ADHD medicines—can learn from digital-electronic media, including high-quality media programming. Brain-training theory suggests that specialized video games, like those designed around algorithms that are based on principles, such as response inhibition or cognitive flexibility, can be helpful.

The widespread proliferation and use of smartphones is an aspect of digital technology that is suspected of leading to impaired cognitive resources related to attentional control, mainly for older children, adolescents, and adults. Constant connectivity related to consumer interaction with smartphones could lead to cognitive deficits, even when off-line. The cognitive resources dedicated to automatic attention to cell phones isn't available for other activities, even when individuals successfully control the conscious orientation of attention performance on other tasks. Sustained attention, working memory, and fluid intelligence are constrained by the availability of attentional resources and of moment-to-moment availability of resources, especially smartphones. A direct relationship was observed between dependence on digital media and the extent of cognitive decrease, particularly if denied access to smartphones, as the process of requiring ourselves to not think about something actually uses some of our finite cognitive resources. Anxiety experienced by not being able to check devices creates difficulties in processing information effectively. Deficiencies from denial of access to digital media would be expected to have more severe impacts in someone with ADHD, who would have constraints on cognitive resources. Individuals are encouraged to experience defined and protected periods of separation from devices to increase available cognitive capacities. Engaging in healthier behaviors and less recreational screen time is associated with improved global cognition. The significance of these findings is underscored by observations that the average U.S. child today spends about fifteen times more time connected to technology than they do with parents or caregivers.

4

Signs and Symptoms

Diverse signs and symptoms are associated with the neurodevelopmental disorder of ADHD. The three major symptoms, identified as characteristic hallmarks of ADHD, are inattention, hyperactivity, and impulsivity. More recent discussion on the nature of ADHD has focused primarily on executive function issues. Difficulties arising from exaggerated emotions has been recognized as a highly problematic sign of ADHD for some time, and there are, not surprisingly, many other signs commonly associated with ADHD.

CLASSIC SYMPTOMS OF ADHD

Several behavioral symptoms are customarily associated with the neurodevelopmental disorder of ADHD, but ADHD affects different individuals in varied ways. One person with ADHD may exhibit inattentiveness but may not be generally either hyperactive or impulsive, while another might present with clear indications of hyperactivity yet not be easily distracted. Most who are hyperactive will also usually tend to be somewhat impulsive, but, of course, this isn't always true. Dominant symptoms of ADHD very often change as people grow, mature, and develop. Certain symptoms, depending on how the disorder impacts them, may get progressively worse with increasing age, while others frequently get better and sometimes even disappear. Many children with the predominantly hyperactive/impulsive subtype of ADHD or with the combined subtype may

49

find that as they become adolescents, their symptoms of excessive locomotor activity tend to diminish, but they are often replaced with a pervasive internal sense of restlessness. Nevertheless, the three core symptoms of ADHD, at least as codified under current DSM-5 subtypes, are inattention, hyperactivity, and impulsivity. According to DSM-5, children up to and including sixteen years of age must demonstrate at least six or more of the nine specific diagnostic criteria of inattention and/or hyperactivity and impulsivity, consistent with their developmental level, for a period of six months or longer, to the extent that these behaviors negatively impact social and academic activities, while those individuals aged seventeen and older (i.e., adolescents and adults) must exhibit at least five of the same list of symptoms of inattention.

Inattention

Inattention, usually considered to be inability to attend to specific tasks in developmentally appropriate ways, is one of three core characteristic symptoms of ADHD. Individuals with the predominantly inattentive kind of ADHD experience symptoms characterized being unable to sufficiently pay attention to or appropriately concentrate on specific tasks in developmentally appropriate ways. These individuals may frequently appear to not be listening, but sometimes they actually are. There are, of course, considerably different expectations as to the degree of attention relative to age and other individual characteristics. The very act of paying attention requires energy expenditure but might not necessarily give rise to subjective conscious experiences; this sort of attention would operate largely unconsciously. Similarly, withdrawal of attention necessitates a certain degree of repression, as our attentional capacity is somewhat limited. Disorganization, such as regularly losing things, is another somewhat common attribute of this mixture of ADHD symptoms. Specific examples of inattentive symptoms include often being easily distracted, lacking persistence, often seeming to not be listening when spoken directly to, and generally having difficulties organizing activities and other tasks.

Primary and secondary school-age students with these sorts of inattentive symptoms commonly don't finish homework or assigned household chores, and they regularly hastily complete assignments, and, thus, they typically tend to make many careless mistakes. Girls with ADHD generally tend to present with more of the predominantly inattentive sort of symptoms, while boys tend to demonstrate either the predominantly hyperactive/impulsive diagnostic variant or the combined symptoms subtype cluster.

Selective attention is a concept that is closely related to inattention. If the volume of incoming stimuli exceeds one's span of attention, there must be some sort of filtering or selection process, since one cannot bear the costs of attending to all items. One's attention may be rather transitory and diffuse under such conditions so that focusing selectively on some stimuli, while not paying attention to others, allows conscious recognition. This selectivity of stimuli can happen somewhat automatically. It isn't unreasonable to assume that such selective attention is, at least to some extent, a skill that is acquired as part of normal development. As those with ADHD can be assumed to sometimes be less efficient at such filtering of incoming stimuli, their ability to focus attention might be somewhat diffuse and might also be expected to generate anxiety.

Hyperactivity and Impulsivity

The inability to exert control over one's level of activity in developmentally appropriate ways is a frequent, but not essential, symptom of ADHD. This is what is commonly referred to as hyperactivity. Hyperactivity, at least as is typically associated with ADHD, usually involves presentation of highly excessive and inappropriate locomotor activity, such as running about, fidgeting, talkativeness, or repeatedly tapping hands or feet.

Difficulty with self-regulation is a hallmark symptom of ADHD that frequently appears in individuals who present with the inability to inhibit behaviors in developmentally appropriate ways. This is generally referred to as impulsivity. Impulsivity, at least as customarily associated with ADHD, refers to impetuous behaviors that seem to spontaneously erupt without forethought. They can sometimes have a high likelihood of causing harm to either the individual or to others. These impulsive behaviors may come from either an inability to delay gratification or from a wish to get more immediate rewards and associated gratification. Impulsivity seems to be biologically associated with expression of Delta-FosB transcription factor, which is found primarily in the nucleus accumbens, a brain region that is related not only to expression of impulsive behaviors but also to evaluation of potential rewards. Demonstrations of impulsivity are often characterized by obvious tendencies toward hasty and heedless actions.

Hyperactivity and impulsivity symptoms are combined together under the same diagnostic subtype in DSM-5. Examples of hyperactive and impulsive diagnostic symptoms include frequently being unable to quietly play or participate in leisure activities, often excessively talking, and often intruding on or otherwise interrupting the activities of others. Individuals with higher levels of impulsivity seem to be at greater risk of developing many associated problems, such as criminal activities, eating disorders, and substance use.

AGE-RELATED DIFFERENCES

Toddlers with ADHD tend to present differently than older individuals. A common saying is that these are the children who are constantly moving. They seem to be more fidgety and squirmy than others, talk excessively, and are unable to sit still for activities. These features are routinely reported for those who are hyperactive; unfortunately, those who are more inattentive are not usually identified until they are in school.

Adolescence can be a particularly challenging and difficult period for many individuals in the United States and in other Western societies, but sometimes more so for someone with ADHD. Interestingly, many cross-cultural studies, beginning with Margaret Mead's 1928 pioneering "Coming of Age in Samoa," suggest that adolescence isn't necessarily a stressful developmental stage. Adolescence, at least in contemporary Western societies, is among the riskiest periods for adjusting to serious life challenges, including things such as delinquency, sexuality, substance use, social media, and automobile accidents.

The hormonal changes that typically accompany puberty can present additional challenges for those struggling with ADHD. For instance, elevated levels of the sex hormones estrogen and progesterone in adolescent females are recognized to be associated with dramatic mood changes. Testosterone, another sex-related hormone, typically surges in adolescent males and may consequently result in increased engagement in highly risky behaviors. Fluctuating hormone levels in adolescents can also substantially alter efficacy of respective ADHD medicines that they may be taking.

The functional impairments of ADHD can persist well into adulthood, particularly for those individuals whose ADHD was untreated or undertreated. Persistence of these neurodevelopmental issues can manifest with manifold behavioral difficulties. Accordingly, the symptom profile for an adult with ADHD is typically somewhat different from that of younger individuals. Vocational impacts, for instance, are commonly observed in many adults with ADHD, often including problems with workplace productivity and the causally related problem of maintaining regular full-time employment. Adults with ADHD also commonly experience difficulty establishing and maintaining meaningful interpersonal relationships. Misunderstandings of social situations, routinely experienced by many with ADHD, can place considerable strains on relationships with significant others, family, friends, and colleagues. These issues will be further discussed in chapter 7. Substantial financial problems are also frequently reported by many with ADHD, their families, and social health care systems. The impacts of these and other associated attributes of ADHD typically result in poorer quality of life for adults with ADHD and can seriously complicate the diagnostic process. The variable degrees of psychosocial adversity that potentially impair adults with ADHD, as well as a high prevalence of comorbidity of psychiatric and other disorders, result in extremely diverse life histories for those with ADHD.

Persistence of ADHD-related symptoms well into adulthood could reasonably be expected to be more intense and severe for those with untreated or undertreated ADHD. Similarly, individual differences in degree of behavioral adaptation to ADHD are extremely likely to be differentially reflected across the life span of those individuals. For example, while most of the characteristic ADHD symptoms are likely to persist into adulthood, substantial differences are also likely to be successfully mediated by maturation. The way the respective characteristic symptoms of ADHD manifest, particularly those related to hyperactivity, are highly likely to present differently simply due to myriad age-related changes. Basically, many older individuals have learned, at least to some extent, how to effectively manage and control impulsivity and associated urges. Nevertheless, the inner restlessness that is typical of ADHD is usually still present and is routinely reported by adults with ADHD. Many alternative and complementary health techniques, such as those discussed in later chapters (chapters 5 and 8), including meditation, biofeedback, and other relaxation strategies, can help calm much of this internal restlessness that is so common in ADHD.

EXECUTIVE FUNCTION ISSUES

Many of the problems that are frequently associated with ADHD can be attributed to deficits in executive functioning. Executive functioning impacts nearly all of our goal-directed behaviors. It refers broadly to the cognitive or mental abilities that individuals use to actively pursue their goals. Issues with executive functioning can manifest as difficulties in areas such as balancing multiple tasks, staying focused, handling frustration, following multiple directions, and starting and completing tasks. These are all issues that are commonly experienced by many with ADHD. In fact, most individuals with ADHD exhibit developmental delays in mastery of respective executive functions compared to their neurotypical peers. While most individuals without ADHD tend to develop full mastery of executive functions by about the age of thirty, many adults with ADHD continue to struggle with deficits in executive functioning for several additional decades—sometimes throughout the rest of adulthood.

Executive functioning is primarily mediated by the prefrontal cortex of the human brain. Most individuals with ADHD tend to have different patterns of functional brain connectivity, which allows different brain parts to efficiently exchange information. There are, of course, many different neural pathways involved in different respective executive functions. For example, working memory typically involves neural activity going from the frontal lobe, particularly on outer surfaces of the brain's cortex, and progressing to the basal ganglia, especially to the striatum. This specific brain neural circuit is particularly important in making plans, reaching objectives, and preparing for the future. On the other hand, the neural pathway that typically allows us to sequence behaviors and coordinate the timing of necessary actions usually involves activity moving from the prefrontal cortex back to the cerebellum. Another neural pathway, also originating in the prefrontal cortex, allows control of emotions; this brain circuit runs from the prefrontal cortex, through the anterior cingulate, to the amygdala, and finally to the limbic system. The extent to which neural pathways are more or less impaired would help explain the considerable range of variation seen among individuals with ADHD with respect to problematic issues with executive functioning.

Executive function issues associated with ADHD often manifest as behavioral problems. These include things like difficulty following direction or engaging in quiet activities, discipline issues, or disrespectful attitudes. These sorts of behavioral issues are frequently early signs of ADHD.

It is of paramount importance that we appreciate how critical inclusion of the notion of executive functioning is to our current redefinition of ADHD. Euphemistic, even derogatory, references were formerly made to attributes we now recognize as executive function issues. Fortunately, viewing these through the lens of executive dysfunction permits a more nuanced and balanced understanding of this neurodevelopmental disorder. In fact, such approaches have become integral in recent formulations as to the nature of ADHD.

EXAGGERATED EMOTIONS

A rather common difficulty reported among individuals with ADHD is in the processing and controlling of emotions. This can manifest in various ways, such as a low tolerance for frustration, having a quick temper, being easily excitable, or impatience. Similarly, some with ADHD can appear insensitive or relatively unaware of the needs and emotions of others. Challenges with regulating emotions, as with so much of ADHD, originate in the brain. Deficits in working memory, so typical of ADHD, can make simple emotional responses overpowering, and these may erupt as intense emotional outbursts.

It seems that the brain connectivity networks of individuals with ADHD are considerably less effective at carrying information about emotions than those of neurotypicals. The gating mechanism of the brain that usually allows us to distinguish between minor problems and serious threats doesn't appear to function adequately. What might otherwise be a momentary emotion for most appears to flood the brain and block out the other information that helps most individuals modulate their anger and appropriately regulate behavior. It is the hyperfocused nature of an ADHD brain that makes it rapidly concentrate on single potent emotions and makes it extremely difficult to shift focus to other aspects of the situation. Once the individual has effectively become stuck in experiencing that intense emotion, it can foster heightened sensitivity to social disapproval, thereby triggering extreme self-defensive responses, which can, in turn, prevent otherwise reasonable consideration of alternative views and actions. If the feelings aren't released but are rather internalized, they can lead to depressed emotions and loss of self-esteem. If, on the other hand, they are externalized, they can be expressed as rage, usually with inappropriate verbal outbursts. By being unable to rationally screen out insignificant thoughts or perceptions, panic modes may develop, leading to the over-the-top emotional eruption of unwarranted responses.

A tendency to pursue instant gratification is a basic characteristic of some with ADHD. The dopamine reward system of the brains of some with ADHD seems to be deficient. Less dopamine is released, and thereby fewer neuronal receptors for reward recognizing circuits are activated, in the brains of these individuals with ADHD compared to neurotypicals. These individuals are less able to either anticipate pleasure or gain sufficient satisfaction from behaviors that generally yield delayed gratifications. Tasks that require sustained efforts to obtain rewards over a long term are less palatable. This preference relegates their actions more toward activities with more immediate payoffs. It can also manifest by tendencies to procrastinate engagement in tasks that typically have delayed rewards. This appears to culminate in immature behavioral repertoires.

Another rather common result of this emotional conundrum is what seems to be insufficient sensitivity by some with ADHD to recognize the emotional importance of certain activities to others. This can evolve into states of social anxiety, a chronic problem for more than one-third of adolescents and adults with ADHD. These individuals frequently experience persistent fear of being regarded by others as incompetent, undesirable, or simply weird.

STIMULATION CRAVING

The brain serves to regulate responses to stimuli and needs to be fully engaged in order to work well. Arousal allows the brain to be receptive, remain alert, and be ready to optimally attend to tasks and learn. Appropriate functioning of executive skills permits more effective response selection. ADHD brains are driven by the need to maintain optimal stimulation, while neurotypical brains can be adequately aroused by the normal changes that tend to occur with the internal and external stimulation of activities of everyday life. Sustained focus and appropriate regulation over behavior is only possible by means of dependable coordination and regulation of neurotransmitters. The ADHD brain, which is typically dopamine deficient, normally finds internal motivations intrinsically more potent than external demands, as more dopamine is typically available via these channels. This neurotransmitter flooding tends to fuel desires to pursue activities that garner more pleasurable reinforcement over externally driven concerns regarding issues such as time or potential consequences of behaviors. Further, after the dopamine flood is removed, the ADHD brain returns to its prearousal baseline level of being dopamine deprived, and, consequently, there are immediate declines in motivation. This, in turn, leads to broadly scattered searches for possible sources of adequate stimulation, involving rapidly shifting focus, but remaining desperately unsatisfied.

Many individuals with ADHD have relatively low thresholds for outside sensory experiences, since their own monitors are frequently set on high intensity to internal stimuli. ADHD is a neurodevelopmental disorder, not so much of deficit of attention but, rather, of too much attention. The ADHD brain is generally trying to focus on multiple stimuli at once but in so doing, fails to concentrate on the most relevant stimulus at the moment. In order to seek sufficiently pleasurable levels of brain arousal, those with ADHD are usually simultaneously spreading their attention over too many internal and external stimuli. As a consequence, however, they are typically unable to achieve undivided attention to appropriately sustain their focus, and, thus, nothing gets properly attended to or acted upon.

When scanning the environment, an ADHD brain will endeavor to find engaging stimulation, even if such pursuits interfere with attaining more goal-oriented responses. Mundane, irrelevant stimuli, therefore, cannot be easily avoided by these individuals due to their innate drive to try to fulfill the intense craving for stimulation. The incentive-salience model of neurobiology suggests that the dopamine reward system regulates things such as positive reinforcement, motivation, and pleasure fulfillment in all human brains. However, it would also imply that ADHD brains would find any behaviors that increased dopamine levels as inherently far more gratifying than others, even if they were cognitively recognized as not helping them reach their desired objectives.

A direct consequence of the pervasive lack of dopamine available within the synapses of an ADHD brain is the loss of significance attached to task completion. If most stimuli seem equally compelling to a dopamine-deprived brain, then it becomes harder to attend to demands that might be more important and relevant compared to others. This lack of salience produces a state of motivational deficiency. It has been suggested that this problem in the reward pathway of human brains should be referred to as reward-deficiency syndrome to at least partially explain why someone with ADHD requires far stronger incentives than someone with a neurotypical brain. Repeated deficiencies in dopamine would lead to decreased production of dopamine receptors, and this would result in decreased motivation. This explains both why mild rewards and those dependent on long-term gratification lack sufficient salience for someone with ADHD. The ADHD brain constantly craves stimulation that will raise dopamine levels more quickly and intensely.

Many behaviors elevate dopamine production, including food, sex, competition, exercise, and music, as well as certain high-risk activities, such as skydiving or ski jumping, generate more intense rewards, as do gambling; compulsive shopping; risky sex; and misuse of psychoactive substances, including alcohol, caffeine, tobacco, and opioids. This at least partially explains why so many individuals with ADHD gravitate toward certain high-intensity, high-risk careers, such as firefighters and emergency medical technicians.

The inhibition of the release of another critical neurotransmitter substance, serotonin, is also a common feature of ADHD brains, and this deficiency results in decreased ability to inhibit impulsivity. Fidgeting, laughter, noise, or intentional conflict are some of the more common strategies someone with an impulsive ADHD brain resorts to in an attempt to compensate for a low-stimulation, mundane environment. Unfortunately, the pursuit of immediate rewards usually wins out over pursuing those tasks that require delayed gratification.

Even minor sensory motor activities, such as fidgeting of hands or tapping of feet, boost levels of dopamine and norepinephrine, neurotransmitters that are essential to increasing attention and sharpening focus. Accordingly, these sorts of peripheral activities, which could be regarded by some as mere distractions, could help satisfy the constant craving for stimulation and help someone with ADHD to maintain attention to a task that might be seen as less than stimulating in itself. Recent popularity in the use of fidget spinners among elementary- and middle-school children with ADHD might be indicative of this type of behavioral adaptation.

Many individuals with ADHD can become highly addicted to seeking constant states of psychological and physiological arousal. However, there are both good and bad forms of arousal. One of the most costly strategies is to pursue excitement in order to get a stress response, fueled by a nearly instantaneous injection of adrenaline and other stress-related hormones. When we get stressed, our attention becomes more focused, but this response exists largely as a condition of survival, and there is a hefty physiological price to pay for utilizing this approach. Adrenal hormones are released in the flight-or-fight syndrome in order to prepare for physical activity, but, unfortunately they effectively elevate our heart rates, blood pressure, respiration, and blood-sugar levels, and may also cause immune system suppression. The craving for stimulation feature of typical ADHD brains can actually sometimes result in states of overarousal. Unable to modulate responses, it isn't uncommon for those in pursuit of stimulation to exceed their capacity to handle the onslaught and to reach a state of psychological and physiological overload, thereby becoming depleted and likely feeling irritable, aggressive, restless, and even tearful. Too much stimulation could actually accrue to the point of becoming overwhelmed and needing to make a sudden and total withdrawal from the source of arousal in order to regroup. This consequence of stimulation craving often results in a seemingly paradoxical lack of motivation and apparent inactivity, yet the internal gyrations continue.

OTHER SIGNS

There are numerous other signs that can be indicative of individuals who may have the neurodevelopmental disorder of ADHD. Individuals with ADHD might have problems with issues with disorganization, time management, and sleep.

There are diverse conditions identified as having relatively high levels of comorbidity with ADHD, such that evaluation for ADHD should be considered for anyone with one of these respective conditions. Greater awareness of and monitoring of these possible signs can be helpful in identifying individuals who might reasonably be considered for diagnostic evaluation for ADHD, and, thereby, they will be more likely to receive proper management and treatment.

Disorganization

Clutter is a commonly observed sign of individuals who might have ADHD. To some individuals without ADHD, cluttered desks or workplaces might appear chaotic and dysfunctional, but to an individual whose brain functions better with extra stimulation, this may be an effective coping strategy. A messy room might cause more stress to parents or partners of those with ADHD, but it might actually be an attempted solution for an individual with the disorder. Hoarding, on the other hand, is a condition generally associated with anxiety and obsessive compulsive behaviors and seems to affect between 2 and 5 percent of the general population, but it isn't ADHD. Individuals with ADHD can learn organizational strategies and modify their tendency to accumulate clutter.

Poor Time Management

Many with ADHD have a distorted sense of time and, accordingly, tend to be out of sync with the demands of daily living. This desynchronization can sometimes result in considerable deficits in performing required tasks and routines.

Procrastination is a phenomenon commonly experienced by someone with ADHD. The sense of underachievement typically experienced by many with ADHD frequently contributes to procrastination. Guilt over not having met objectives in the past can contribute to paralysis when starting new activities. A helpful tactic can sometimes be to imbue completion of these apparently less glamorous but necessary activities with the sense of pride of accomplishment. Posing them as challenges also frequently helps to keep one on task. Many individuals with ADHD inherently enjoy the pursuit of challenges. Listing and prioritizing a few tasks, such as creating to-do lists, can also help them identify and visualize the core sets of activities to tackle.

One of the most difficult time-management problems for many with ADHD is being able to postpone unnecessary activities until after more-important, required tasks are completed. Many with ADHD find unexpected opportunities more appealing; it is simply part of the disorder. Distracting activities have inherent attraction to ADHD brains. Focusing attention on the often less-interesting tasks or routines requires intentional discipline. Many individuals with ADHD report that customary engagement in multiple tasks simultaneously helps them be more productive and find it more difficult to work on only one thing at a time.

Sleep Problems

Sleep problems, such as insomnia, are common complaints from individuals with ADHD. Untreated individuals often turn to self-medication, such as with alcohol or sedative medications. Sleep problems are also common if the individual is receiving treatment for ADHD, particularly when taking psychostimulants. Physicians who are treating individuals with ADHD who also have insomnia tend to prescribe an antipsychotic medication, such as quetiapine (Seroquel) off-label at low doses for help with sleeping.

Many infants with ADHD tend to be restless or sleepless, and some appear to refuse affection. All infants cry, but many of those with ADHD seem to be constantly crying. The American Academy of Pediatrics recommends that babies sleep on their backs, without soft bedding or toys, and in their own cribs, even if restless or crying; parents can share a room with a baby, but not the same bed.

Comorbidities

Comorbidity with other conditions is another common sign of ADHD—this is, in fact, more often the rule than the exception. Comorbidity is so extremely common among individuals with ADHD that some have suggested it occurs over 90 percent of the time. Comorbidity doesn't simply mean that individuals have only one other disorder along with ADHD—they can actually have several. It is assumed that more than half of all individuals with ADHD have four or more other disorders. At the very least, several disorders are relatively more likely to be comorbid with ADHD than others. It is assumed that around one-third of all individuals with ADHD also have specific learning disabilities, and about half also have ODD.

Many diverse conditions are identified as having high degrees of comorbidity with ADHD. It is well established, for example, that many children with fetal alcohol spectrum disorders (FASD) also have comorbid ADHD. It is similarly recognized that somewhere between 20 and 50 percent of adults with ADHD also meet full diagnostic criteria for having alcohol or other substance use disorder, and it is conservatively estimated that about one-quarter of adults in substance-use-disorder treatment programs could also meet diagnostic criteria for comorbid ADHD.

The rate of comorbid conditions varies with respect to the age of the population being considered. For instance, while CD and ODD appear to be the most prevalent comorbid psychiatric conditions among younger children, antisocial personality disorder, depression, bipolar conditions, and substance use disorders are more prevalent, comorbid psychiatric conditions among older children, adolescents, and young adults. Gender differences have been observed with respect to conditions comorbid with ADHD as well. While males with ADHD are more likely to be diagnosed with comorbid conditions such as CD and ODD, females with ADHD are far more likely to receive a diagnosis for separation anxiety disorder. Other variables identified by researchers as having high comorbidity with ADHD include things such as anxiety, binge eating, mood disorders, premature fatality, tobacco use, and suicidality.

Many studies have helped us better understand the nature of various conditions that have high likelihoods of being comorbid with ADHD. For example, the Project to Learn about ADHD in Youth (PLAY) is a ten-year-long, population-based research project funded by CDC and conducted by the University of South Carolina and University of Oklahoma Health Sciences Center to better understand the public health impacts of ADHD. From the findings of PLAY and related studies, we now know that children with ADHD are more than twice as likely as neurotypical individuals to have another psychiatric disorder in addition to ADHD. More than half (60 percent) of children with ADHD have another comorbid psychiatric disorder, and about one-quarter have two or more. Children with ADHD and either CD or ODD are more likely to have difficulties with school and friendships and to get into trouble with the police. PLAY also collected and analyzed data on trends in ADHD medicines and related treatments.

5

Diagnosis, Treatment, and Management

There are varied approaches to diagnose, treat, and manage ADHD. It is important to know how diagnoses are made, including the instruments used, related conditions, and metabolic testing. Varied approaches to address ADHD must be recognized, particularly medications, along with behavioral and other approaches.

DIAGNOSING ADHD

ADHD is hard to diagnose, as whether someone does or doesn't have it isn't always apparent. No single questionnaire, brain scan, or blood test determines if someone has or doesn't have ADHD. It's a subjective diagnosis made by professionals who gather information from others, such as family members, teachers, or friends. The number of diagnoses has dramatically increased; there were over nine hundred thousand U.S. cases diagnosed in 1990, but more than two million by 1995. The CDC reported that ADHD diagnoses for children rose 42 percent from 2003 to 2011. In the past eight years, there was again another 42 percent increase.

For ADHD to be diagnosed, symptoms must be observed before the age of twelve—they typically appear between the ages of three and six—and must occur within two or more settings, such as home, school, or work. Symptoms must interfere with, or at least reduce, academic, social, or vocational functioning.

The average age of diagnosis is seven in the United States. Children who exhibit severe symptoms tend to be diagnosed younger—eight is the average age of diagnosis for U.S. children with mild ADHD, seven for moderate, and five for severe. Of the 6.4 million U.S. children with ADHD, around 2 million were diagnosed between the ages of two and five.

Medical tests can help diagnose ADHD, even though they are not necessary, or even sufficient in and of themselves. Diagnosis can be supported by functional magnetic-imaging abnormalities commonly found in respective brain regions. Some prefer positron-emission-tomography (PET) scans to assess brain activity, blood flow, and glucose metabolism, while others utilize single-photon emission-computed tomography (SPECT) imaging, employing less radiation to evaluate brain activity and blood flow. The Neuropsychiatric EEG-Based Assessment Aid (NEBA) system has FDA approval for those six- to seventeen-years olds as part of medical and psychological examinations. NEBA measures beta and theta brain waves; the theta/beta ratio is higher among children and adolescents with ADHD.

Diagnosis of ADHD is made through clinical assessment within recognized medical classification systems, usually DSM-5 or ICD-10. ICD-10 characterizes hyperkinetic disorder by features of inattention and overactivity.

Diagnosis often involves multiple clinicians, including psychologists, educators, and physicians. Diagnosing from behavioral perspectives includes assessment instruments, such as rating scales completed by parents, teachers, and others; educational perspectives, including the evaluation of symptoms based on academic performance, often using classroom observations; medical perspectives include assessing inattention, impulsivity, or hyperactivity, and excluding or diagnosing comorbidities.

Assessment Instruments

Assessment instruments have been used for over fifty years to screen, evaluate, and monitor ADHD in children and adults. Behavioral scales, particularly those completed by parents and teachers, are available, such as various Conners Rating Scales; Behavior Assessment System for Children (BASC); Swanson, Nolan, and Pelham-IV Questionnaire (SNAP-IV); Cognition and Motivation in Everyday Life (CAMEL) scale; and Vanderbilt Assessment Scale (VAS). Conners Parent Rating Scales are completed by parents and ask about the child's symptoms. Conners Teacher Rating Scales are completed by teachers to assess symptoms in classrooms. BASC is for four- to eighteen-year-olds. SNAP-IV is a ninety-item instrument for six- to eighteen-year-olds that evaluates emotional behaviors and physical symptoms at home and school. CAMEL consists of sixty items to provide parental assessment of neuropsychological impairment. VAS is for six- to twelve-year-olds and has parent and teacher forms.

The Developmental and Well-Being Assessment (DAWBA) assesses mental health problems, including ADHD, in five- to fifteen-year-olds, consisting of interviews, questionnaires, and rating techniques, which can be rapidly scored. DAWBA can be administered by computer or individuals and includes interviews with parents, teachers, and the child. Parent interviews take about fifty minutes, and child interviews thirty minutes. DAWBA is most widely used in the United Kingdom.

Concomitant Difficulties Scale (ADHD-CDS) evaluates the presence of the more commonly found problems associated with ADHD, such as disruptive behavior, emotional management, fine-motor coordination, impaired academic achievement, time management, sleep patterns, and quality of life. The thirteen-item ADHD-CDS is completed by parents or guardians. It demonstrates good sensitivity with high convergent validity.

Many self-reported scales are available, including Adult ADHD Self-Report Scale (ASRS) Symptom Checklist, Conners Abbreviated Symptom Questionnaire (ASQ), Conners-Wells' Adolescent Self-Report Scale (CWASR), and Weiss Functional Impairment Rating Scale Self-Report (WFIRS-S). ASQ provides a brief self-report, with good sensitivity and specificity, and high diagnostic accuracy. CWASR is intended for self-reporting by teenagers. WFIRS-S is a fifty-seven-item self-report instrument assessing how one functions that has high internal consistency and excellent sensitivity to symptom change and improvement.

Other instruments are completed by clinicians, like Barkley's Quick-Check for Adult ADHD Diagnosis and Brief Semi-Structured Interview for ADHD in Adults. Barkley's Quick-Check for Adult ADHD Diagnosis is an eighteen-item instrument for current or retrospective reporting producing six scores. The first three are summations for inattention, hyperactive-impulsive, and a total ADHD score for retrospective responses, plus another three scores for current responses. Brief Semi-Structured Interview for ADHD in Adults is a thirty-three-item instrument developed by the National Association for Continuing Education. The Brown Attention-Deficit Disorder Symptom Assessment Scale for Adults is similar.

A screening instrument is generally administered initially. For those whose scores suggest they may have ADHD, a more-sophisticated instrument is usually administered, and, if warranted, in-depth evaluations are conducted. For instance, Structured Adult ADHD Self-Test is a twenty-two-item self-administered instrument for screening adults to distinguish between inattention and hyperactivity-impulsivity. Similarly, Adult ADHD Self-Report Scale (ASRS) is a highly validated six-item symptoms checklist, developed in conjunction with WHO, for screening adult ADHD. ASRS can be completed in about one minute, so it is acceptable for general practitioner and similar settings, with high sensitivity and moderate specificity. Those screening positively on ASRS would then be administered a more specific instrument, like the Conners Adult ADHD Rating Scale Self Report—Short Version (CAARS-S:S), a twenty-six-item instrument. Those scoring positively on CAARS-S:S usually get a more-thorough, personalized medical examination, including a detailed history looking for signs and symptoms, and evaluation for comorbidities.

Comprehensive assessment should include multiple strategies, including self-reporting; rating by others; tasks of attention and impulsivity; clinical interview, with detailed patient histories; and complete medical examination, excluding conditions that present with lack of attention, such as central nervous system infections, hypothyroidism, cerebral-vascular disease, or Reye's syndrome. Many instruments are available as tests of attention or impulsivity, such as Continuous Performance Tests, Matching Familiar Figures Test, and Wisconsin Card Sort. Children or adolescents who are being evaluated for ADHD are frequently tested for intelligence, typically using Kaufman Assessment Battery for Children, Stanford-Binet Intelligence Scales, or Wechsler Intelligence Scale for Children.

Many health care professionals, such as psychiatrists, psychologists, and some general practitioners, are trained to administer instruments to diagnose ADHD. The instruments discussed are helpful for both assessment and monitoring.

Related Conditions

Many symptoms listed for diagnosing ADHD might apply to anyone at certain times. Many of us are sometimes distracted or have difficulty getting organized—features that are associated with many conditions. To consider symptoms as indicative of ADHD, impairment and distress must be caused by ADHD and not by other disorders. It is important to thoroughly assess individuals to exclude the possibility that symptoms reflect another disorder.

Many factors present with symptoms easily mistaken for ADHD. Young children are often very active and have developmentally appropriate short attention spans. Changes appearing at puberty can create hyperactivity in teenagers. Other conditions can present with hyperactivity, such as children experiencing problems at home, including sexual abuse, or emotional conflicts, including major life changes, such as the death of family members, parental divorce, or recent moves. Hyperactivity may be exhibited by those bored at school, some of whom may actually be gifted and talented, while some may have specific learning disabilities or other issues. Certain food colorings and preservatives have been identified as increasing hyperactivity. Individuals with thyroid disease have similar symptoms; overactive thyroid may cause hyperactivity or inattentiveness, underactive thyroid may cause lethargy and lack of focus. Someone with chronic sleep problems can appear inattentive. Certain substances, such as cocaine, can cause distractibility or hyperactivity that can sometimes be mistaken for ADHD. Many conditions, such as hearing, vision, and psychiatric problems and seizures cause symptoms similar to ADHD and these must be excluded before diagnosing.

Many factors besides genetics have been implicated as potential causes. Head injury is one, particularly to frontal regions. Similarly, if the brain is oxygen-deprived for too long or exposed to toxins, then ADHD is more likely. Low oxygen levels, whether from umbilical cord obstruction, premature birth with underdeveloped lungs, or choking or drowning, can decrease brain activity and cause permanent damage. Fetal exposure to substances like alcohol, tobacco, or other drugs also raises risk. Exposure to toxins, like lead from paint or plumbing, food additives, colorings, preservatives, mercury, molds, and pesticides are risks. Brain infections, such as encephalitis or meningitis, can cause inflammations that damage brain tissues. When other psychiatric problems occur along with ADHD, it is impossible to say which came first. We know there is comorbidity for conditions like ODD and antisocial personality disorder, but it is hard to establish if one did or didn't cause the other.

Metabolic Testing

Tests are available to evaluate the metabolic irregularities that are implicated in ADHD. Electrodermal testing evaluates food allergies or sensitivities. Fasting blood tests assess levels of blood sugar and essential fatty acids. Amino-acid levels can be evaluated through fasting blood tests or urinalysis, which evaluates intestinal permeability. Hair samples, as well as urine, can be analyzed for toxins. Stool analysis identifies candida and flora imbalances. These are a few tests to assess metabolic deficiencies that may underlie or contribute to ADHD.

ADHD MANAGEMENT APPROACHES

Management of ADHD should consist of multimodal, individualized treatments, typically including medications, behavioral therapy, psychoeducation and, often, more holistic approaches, such as lifestyle and dietary modifications.

Different forms of cognitive and behavioral therapies are used to treat ADHD. Structured practical assistance, such as helping children complete schoolwork or organize specific tasks, teaches self-monitoring. Assisting children in learning to think before talking or acting is a goal of many approaches. Establishing clear rules and reasonable expectations and sticking to structured routines are advisable. Counseling and psycho-education help adults learn how ADHD impacts them, how to address it, and how to consistently implement organizational and planning skills into daily routines. Coaching has become a treatment tool—coaches assist in improving coping skills in areas such as goal setting, scheduling, organi-zation, building confidence and self-esteem, and maintaining persistence.

For preschoolers, those aged four to five, nearly one in two receive no behavioral therapy, and about one in four only get medications. Best prac-tice for this age is behavioral therapy before medicating. However, less than one in three six- to seventeen-year-olds currently receive both behav-ioral therapy and medication; best practices suggests they get both. The CDC says that about seven out of ten U.S. children with ADHD between 2011 and 2012 were taking medications.

Behavioral and Cognitive Approaches

Behavioral therapy includes reducing or eliminating self-defeating or problematic behaviors—features that are associated with ADHD. Behav-ioral therapy is based on principles of operant and classical conditioning. Operant conditioning uses techniques to make desired responses more or less likely to occur, depending on consequences, such as using demerits to reduce impulsively blurting out. Classical conditioning transforms neutral stimuli by pairing with others that already elicit the desired responses. This is also referred to as respondent or Pavlovian conditioning.

Behavioral and cognitive therapeutic approaches are considered effect-ive for ADHD. Medications by themselves are often insufficient to meet all needs. These approaches provide appropriate social and psychological sup-ports to address problems. Individual psychotherapy is usually the initial approach. Cognitive Behavioral Therapy (CBT) is one of the best-known and widely used approaches, along with medication, to treat ADHD, par-ticularly with adults. CBT focuses on thoughts and behaviors, assuming those with ADHD have positive and negative beliefs arising from inaccur-ate thought processes. They acquire skills to avoid negative behaviors and thoughts and learn to cope with, if not eliminate, undesired consequences. They learn to avoid high-risk situations and better understand how choices can lead to positive or negative results. Albert Ellis developed a type of CBT known as Rational Emotive Behavioral Therapy; this version of CBT is based on resolving behavioral and emotional problems by reducing the catastrophic thinking that is characterized by negatively distorted perceptions. Online CBT has been demonstrated as efficacious for treating mental health disorders, including anxiety and depression, as well as reducing hallucinations, insomnia, and paranoia. It may be equally effective for ADHD.

Another type of behavioral and cognitive therapy that is often used with children and adolescents with ADHD is contingency management. In this approach, individuals earn points in a voucher system for demonstrating appropriate behaviors. Vouchers could be used to "purchase" privileges, reinforcing healthy lifestyles. Direct contingency management requires intervention by professionals, such as therapists or teachers who monitor the implementation and effects. Point-reward systems can be implemented at home. Motivational incentives serve as positive reinforcement for appropriate, balanced behaviors; the goal is to monitor and control behaviors. Strategies that promote self-control include self-evaluation, self-instruction, and problem-solving. Individuals learn to assess specific situations, contemplate actions and consequences, and respond accordingly.

Dynamic psychotherapy assumes that symptoms arise from deep, underlying unconscious psychological conflicts. It teaches someone that conflicts exist and encourages adaptive coping strategies.

Group psychotherapy can be part of ADHD treatment, as it addresses the social stigma that is often associated with loss of control and inappropriate behaviors. Members of psychotherapeutic groups benefit from hearing others share experiences and feelings. Knowing others feel and experience things comparably helps normalize them and reduces isolation. Group approaches help refine social skills, increase self-esteem, and promote success.

Multimodal family therapy treats individuals and family members of those with ADHD. Multimodal therapy considers seven discrete, but reciprocally interactive personality modalities or dimensions—behavior, affect, sensation, imagery, cognition, interpersonal relationships, and drugs/biology (BASIC ID)—encouraging professionals to improvise and individualize brief therapies. Family therapy works with members to explore and improve family relationships and promote the mental health of individuals and families.

Other therapeutic approaches can also be used. Relaxation exercises, guided imagery, and other complementary techniques can help. Eye movement desensitization and reprocessing (EMDR) therapy is an approach to lessening stress by processing the meanings of events within the context of one's autobiographical memory. It works by eliciting distressing memories and immediately distracting the individual with directed physical stimuli, such as following the tip of the therapist's finger. As the distressing memory is verbalized, the individual is instructed to notice ideas or feelings that arise, while the therapist encourages positive associations that are reinforced with repeated eye movements.

Medication Approaches

Medicating to treat ADHD is common, and though it may not address the underlying reasons on its own, it can help to manage symptoms while other approaches are introduced. Examples of first-line ADHD medications are psychostimulants, such as amphetamines and methylphenidate. Other medications are also used.

Which medicine is used depends on factors including personalized symptom profiles, age, comorbidities, other health issues, side effects, risk of addiction, and personal and familial preferences. Of the approximately 6.4 million U.S. children diagnosed with ADHD, about half are currently on some medication. Prescriptions to U.S. adults with ADHD rose 53.5 percent between 2008 and 2012. The largest increase—86 percent—was among females aged twenty-six to thirty-four.

ADHD medications work by changing the brain chemistry, generally neurotransmitters. Although medications frequently help, they appear only partially effective, particularly with adults. Despite appropriate medication, many adults report residual symptoms. Medications don't typically resolve quality-of-life issues that are routinely experienced by adults, such as unemployment, underachievement, economic difficulties, and relationships. Over half of adults with ADHD report that it interferes with work. Behavioral techniques that promote active problem solving can yield results over and above medications alone.

MEDICATIONS USED TO TREAT ADHD

Assorted medications are used to treat ADHD. Psychostimulants are the most commonly prescribed, but many nonstimulants are also used. Nonstimulants include amantadine, atomoxetine, antihypertensives, some anticonvulsants, and eugeroics, among others.

Psychostimulants are normally prescribed initially and are, for many, efficacious. Amphetamines and methylphenidate are the major psychostimulants used, and there are formulations combining multiple drugs. Psychostimulants are easily abused and many have high addiction potential. Abuse can result in hypertension, hyperactivity, insomnia, irritability, cardiac irregularities, psychosis, and even death from convulsions, overexhaustion, or cardiac arrest.

Nonstimulants are sometimes used. There are different effects, applications, and routes of administration available for varied medications. Awareness of drug effects helps understand how they help individuals calm down, particularly as they stimulate attention and self-regulation. Knowing how medications work in individuals with ADHD helps determine their potential applications.

Effects of Medications

ADHD medications have diverse effects, some minor and others more profound. Pharmacological effects are of concern in the brain and elsewhere in the body. It is essential to understand approved applications of ADHD medications, and particularly the ages that each is approved for.

Psychostimulants stimulate the release of dopamine from the basal ganglia and also stimulate the prefrontal cortex and temporal lobes, increasing dopamine and norepinephrine levels, improving concentration and lessening fatigue. Amphetamines cause catecholamine release, primarily dopamine and norepinephrine, from brain neurons. Amphetamines also inhibit activity of the monoamine oxidase enzyme, helping block neurotransmitter reuptake, and thus increasing neurotransmitter levels to improve cognitive control, generate euphoria, and promote wakefulness. Methamphetamine has profound effects in the brain, but lesser effects than amphetamines elsewhere in the body—it causes fewer increases in heart rate, blood pressure, respiration, and blood-vessel dilation.

Methylphenidate is a nonamphetamine psychostimulant and one of the most commonly prescribed ADHD medications. Its mechanism of action is to block the reuptake of dopamine and norepinephrine, reducing activation in the right inferior frontal gyrus, left anterior cingulate, and bilateral posterior cingulate cortex. Some combined formulations, such as Adderall, both stimulate release and produce reuptake inhibition of norepinephrine and dopamine, thus enhancing cognition and related factors.

Nonstimulant medications also impact brains, but differently than psychostimulants do. Amantadine appears to stimulate the synthesis and release of dopamine and inhibit reuptake, increasing the central dopaminergic tone to help control impulsiveness. Atomoxetine is a slow and longer-acting nonstimulant that selectively inhibits presynaptic norepinephrine reuptake in the prefrontal cortex. It has a high affinity for norepinephrine transporters, but little for neurotransmitter receptors. Increased norepinephrine, resulting from atomoxetine, increases attention span and wakefulness and decreases hyperactivity and impulsiveness. Atomoxetine can be more helpful for those with predominantly inattentive subtypes.

ADHD antihypertensives have profound brain effects. Evidence suggests that these act directly on the prefrontal cortex, improving executive functioning. Immediate-release guanfacine and clonidine help treat ADHD. Both increase norepinephrine production, increasing focus, lessening distractibility, and helping control inappropriate behaviors by promoting impulse-control. Guanfacine increases attentiveness; decreases sedation; and improves executive functioning, including working memory.

Anticonvulsants control seizure activity. Carbamazepine blocks sodium-ion channels and is anticholinergic, stimulating serotonin release.

Valproate inhibits the enzymatic activity of gamma-aminobutyric (GABA) transaminase, increasing brain GABA levels. It may also block sodium-ion channels.

Modafinil is a selective, but weak, atypical dopamine reuptake inhibitor that mainly acts in the nucleus accumbens and, more generally, in the striatum. As modafinil is selective for only the dopamine transporter, it blocks methamphetamine-induced dopamine release. Modafinil and other eugeroics inhibit GABA transmission and activate orexin peptides to produce wakefulness without the need for compensatory sleep. They also promote electronic coupling, enhancing neural communication.

ADHD medications have diverse effects throughout the body. Effects vary depending on the substance, but psychostimulants have roughly similar effects, elevating heart rate and blood pressure, while producing vasoconstriction. For example, lisdexamphetamine increases heart rate, but increases blood pressure less so, and poor circulation in fingers or toes or skin turning blue has been reported. Lisdexamphetamine also alters the digestive system, and appetite loss and even anorexia can result. Methamphetamine effectively decreases appetite and elevates blood pressure. Other amphetamines have similar, but less pronounced, effects. Amphetamines dilate pupils and close bladder sphincters, making urination difficult, and causes lungs to expand, which is why they are used for asthma and related conditions. Methylphenidate causes respiratory stimulation and decreases appetite.

Nonstimulant ADHD medications also have substantial effects throughout the body. Antihypertensives, like clonidine and guanfacine, lower peripheral resistance, heart rate, and blood pressure. Anticonvulsants, like carbamazepine and valproate, are both GABA-receptor agonists. Eugeroics create loss of appetite and weight loss. Nicotine elevates blood pressure and heart rate and constricts pupils.

Approved Applications

ADHD medications are approved for specific applications for use with individuals of certain ages. The variables are different for respective medications, including psychostimulants and nonstimulants.

There are minor differences but considerable similarities in the applications of psychostimulants. Lisdexamphetamine was formulated as a long-lasting ADHD medicine. It is approved for those six and older with ADHD and for those with binge-eating disorder who are eighteen and older. It is not approved for obesity or weight loss and often takes a few weeks to reach therapeutic levels. Individuals with ADHD typically notice improvements in attention and possibly better control of hyperactivity and impulsiveness. Adderall is approved in an immediate-release formulation for those three years of age and older with ADHD, and in extended-release formulations for those six years and older. Formulations of amphetamine, like Dyanavel XR, have been approved for those three years and older with ADHD. Similarly, formulations of dextroamphetamine, like Dexedrine or Dextrostat, are approved for those three years old and older with ADHD. Methylphenidate, like Concerta or Ritalin, is approved for those six years and older with ADHD.

Considerable differences exist for the application of ADHD nonstimulants. Amantadine is approved for those one year old and up. Bupropion, which is available in hydrobromide (Aplenzin) and hydrochloride (Wellbutrin) formulations, is approved for those who are eighteen and older. Atomoxetine is approved for those six years old and up with ADHD. Clonidine and guanfacine are approved either alone or in combination with stimulants for those with ADHD who are six years old and older. ADHD anticonvulsants, like carbamazepine and valproate, are approved for those of any age. Eugeroics, like modafinil, are approved for those who are eighteen years old and up.

Use of most nonstimulants, at least for ADHD, is generally off-label. Many of these same medications have been used off-label for many other conditions. For example, some of these, like amantadine, have been used to treat cocaine dependence.

HOW CAN PSYCHOSTIMULANTS CALM PEOPLE DOWN?

Psychostimulants generally stimulate physiological processes, but they help calm individuals with ADHD. This apparent contradiction is understandable when one recognizes how ADHD works. This is even clearer when we examine the different effects psychostimulants seem to have in those with ADHD.

Different Effects with ADHD

Psychostimulants generally tend to decrease very high responding rates, as mentioned earlier. This happens the same way in all people, whether they have ADHD or not. Psychostimulants don't work differently in those with ADHD, although they were once assumed to. We know that those with ADHD differ from neurotypicals with respect to brain chemistry and functioning. It is thought that there is more activity in the posterior part of the brain with ADHD, but less activity in the front parts than in neurotypicals. It is now believe that the neurotransmitter systems in brains of those with ADHD operate inefficiently—such individuals may produce less, or more, of respective neurotransmitters, changing how they process and respond to stimuli and, thus, how they behave. Individuals with ADHD, who tend to respond at very high rates, would, under psychostimulants, be expected to lower their rates of responding. The brains of these individuals would, under such conditions, behave in more expected ways. Many with ADHD who take psychostimulants experience improved self-control, working memory, hyperactivity, and other improvements. This doesn't mean that ADHD medications work differently in those with ADHD than in neurotypicals, as was thought. There is no pharmacological support for this. ADHD medications work in specific but standardized ways, but there are considerable psychological and physiological differences in those with ADHD.

Stimulating Attention

The ability of psychostimulants and other medications to improve attention is important in treatment planning. Inattention or weakness in focusing or paying attention is common in ADHD. Psychostimulants generally increase blood flow to the parts of frontal cortex involved with attention. Other medications also improve attention.

Psychostimulants paradoxically appear to calm individuals down. Such medications help individuals focus and pay attention, whether they have ADHD or not. If, as many believe, when the brains of those with ADHD are not sufficiently stimulated, they tend to shift attention, move, and seek thrills to remediate boredom, then these medications stimulate their brains, mainly by directly or indirectly changing brain chemistry, so that distracted individuals with ADHD are able to calm down and stay focused.

Stimulating Self-Regulation

The ability of psychostimulants to assist with behavioral inhibition is significant. Self-regulation indicates the extent to which subjective experiences are fundamentally social phenomena. Individuals must have a sense of self and others, including a pervasive sense of self-being. Structuring of functions and regulatory controls is a lifelong developmental task, but individuals with poor inhibitory control, typical of ADHD, find this harder. Fortunately, certain ADHD medications enhance their abilities to inhibit behavior. Antihypertensives increase functional connectivity in the prefrontal cortex, improving self-regulatory behaviors. Amantadine is an ADHD medicine that helps control impulsive behaviors by stimulating dopamine synthesis and release. Atomoxetine, clonidine, and guanfacine also help maintain impulse control.

EFFECTS OF SPECIFIC ADHD MEDICATIONS

The effects of psychostimulants and nonstimulants vary considerably with respect to pharmacological variables, including dosage, duration of action, and pharmacokinetics and elimination.

Dosage

Dosage refers to the rate of application of dose, including the size and frequency administered. The recommended initial dosage of amphetamine for ADHD is 5 mg twice a day, which can be increased by 10 mg per week until the therapeutic effect is achieved. The recommended dosage for dextroamphetamine is up to 40 mg per day; Lisdexamphetamine is 30–70 mg per day; methamphetamine is up to 25 mg per day; and methylphenidate 5–60 mg per day. Since longer-acting ADHD psychostimulants have become available, the need for multiple daily dosing has reduced, thereby reducing barriers such as noncompliance, activity restrictions, and stigma.

Dosages for nonstimulants are more varied than for psychostimulants. Antihypertensives differ markedly in dosages. While clonidine is 100–600 mcg per day, guanfacine is 1–3 mg per day, once a day, typically taken at bedtime. The range for amantadine is 100–200 mg per day for those over age sixty-five.

The dosages for ADHD anticonvulsants differ substantially. Recommended dosages for carbamazepine are, for maintenance, between 800 and 1200 mg per day in divided doses, while dosages for valproate are 10–60 mg per kg per day, and, if the dosage exceeds 250 mg per day, it should be in divided doses. Recommended initial dosage for atomoxetine is 40 mg per day, which may be increased up to 100 mg per day. While the effective dose of atomoxetine ranges from 5 to 100 mg per day, doses less than 40 mg per day might often be appropriate, especially for young children.

Some with ADHD can differ with respect to dosage needs. Some need relatively small doses of psychostimulants, like 2.5–5 mg twice per day, while others need the same ADHD medicine four or even five times every day. However, most with ADHD, particularly if taking an extended-release formulation, typically take ADHD medications once per day. Others may need higher doses of the same psychostimulant, or perhaps even a nonstimulant. Body weight doesn't necessarily correlate with therapeutic dose. Trial and error is often needed to determine the right dosages of the right ADHD medicine.

Duration of Action

Duration of action refers to the time drugs persist with therapeutic effects, and it can be highly variable. For example, the duration of action of both amphetamine and dextroamphetamine is three to seven hours with immediate-release formulations, and twelve hours with extended-release formulations, while duration of action of Lisdexamphetamine is twelve hours, and methamphetamine is between ten and twenty hours. Similarly, methylphenidate has a duration of action of between three and six hours with immediate-release formulations, five to eight hours with extended-release formulations, and twelve hours with long-acting formulations. Duration of action of combination formulations like Adderall is eight to twelve hours. Duration of action is important for treating those with ADHD so that they can perform without symptoms resurfacing. Unfortunately, if a child or adolescent is in school and took ADHD psychostimulants with a three-hour duration before school, symptoms can reemerge, unless another dose is administered. Extended-release formulations were developed to avoid this.

Nonstimulant ADHD medications generally have less variation in duration of action, generally permitting once-a-day dosing. For example, guanfacine's duration is two hours for a single dose, while clonidine's is six to twenty-four hours. Modafinil's is five to fifteen hours, averaging twelve hours, while armodafinil's is fifteen hours. Relatively long durations for ADHD nonstimulants make the need for administration of another dose in the middle of the day generally less of an issue than for psychostimulants.

Pharmacokinetics and Elimination

Pharmacokinetics refers to activities within the body after the administration of a mediation, including many of the previously discussed factors. Half-life is a function of both distribution and elimination, whether by metabolic disposition or excretion. The rate of absorption is impacted by several factors, including route of administration; solubility; and certain body conditions, such as lipodystrophy and liver health. The amount of a substance that is excreted unchanged in urine is usually expressed as a percentage of that administered dose.

ADHD medications are eliminated in various ways. Kidneys are the major organs excreting medications and metabolites as urine. Liver enzymes break down medications into simpler compounds to be excreted. If medications are not absorbed following oral administration, they can be eliminated in feces. Metabolites are excreted as bile via the liver. Some drugs are secreted in breast milk, which can harm nursing infants. Small amounts of some are eliminated by perspiration, and some by exhalation.

Pharmacokinetics of ADHD medications explains why some may not respond to what for others are effective dosages, while some may be sensitive to side effects. Understanding pharmacokinetics medications helps providers select the best medications for an individual and also adjust dosages to optimize outcomes. ADHD medicine selection should be individualized based on pharmacokinetic and pharmacodynamics, and individualized with respect to factors such as previous response patterns, preferences, and comorbidities.

Amantadine is well absorbed orally. Peak concentration is reached in 1.5–8 hours, averaging 3.3 hours. It is excreted mainly in urine. Atomoxetine is rapidly absorbed, with water solubility of 27.8 mg/mL. It is metabolized by hepatic CYPO2D6 and is excreted with urine. Clonidine is almost completely absorbed in the gastrointestinal tract, but it is subject to rapid liver metabolism. Approximately half of guanfacine is eliminated in urine, and about 40 percent is excreted unchanged.

ALTERNATIVE WAYS TO MANAGE

The use of complementary medicine and other alternatives to manage and treat ADHD has increased. It is estimated that 65 percent of the parents of children who are diagnosed with ADHD use complementary medicine and other approaches to relieve symptoms. When these techniques are consistently used, we expect associated prevalence declines. Many of these techniques would enhance health and well-being of the general population, even those that are not at higher risk for ADHD.

Dietary Supplements

What we put into our bodies impacts how our bodies and brains work. Nutritional deficiencies affect many factors, including short- and long-term memory. Low levels of certain amino acids that serve as precursors lead to diminished neurotransmitter levels, while elevated amino-acid levels create excessive levels. Aspartame has been linked to high amino-acid levels that are associated with increased hyperactivity. Many substances have been used to supplement diets, hoping that they would help ADHD. However, there is no conclusive evidence supporting their safety or efficacy. In fact many are toxic, and dosage control is difficult. Another concern is self-diagnosing and self-prescribing, as well as the harm that might come from delaying treatments with known effectiveness.

Herbal Remedies

Herbal remedies have been used for millennia to help calm hyperactivity, including in India as part of Ayurveda and in traditional Chinese healing. More commonly recommended herbal remedies for ADHD include green oats, water hyssop, gotu kola, and Korean red ginseng. Herbal teas composed of herbs and flowers, such as chamomile, lemon grass, and spearmint, are also often recommended. Herbal remedies are broadly regulated by the FDA, but not for safety or efficacy.

Vitamin and Mineral Supplements

The human body, including the brain, requires many substances to function normally. Vitamins are substances that are necessary for normal metabolism and minerals and trace elements are essential to various bodily functions. Deficiencies in some nutrients could cause symptoms similar to ADHD, and some believe supplements could remediate these. However, most Americans get enough nutrients in well-balanced diets. Excessive use of supplements can lead to hypervitaminosis, a toxic condition that results from unnecessary and potentially fatal accumulation of certain vitamins. Excessive intake of certain minerals can also be dangerous.

Acupuncture

Acupuncture originated in ancient China and involves inserting thin needles at specific anatomical points, along what are referred to as the meridian lines of twelve energy channels that purportedly flow beneath the surface of the body. Acupuncture is known to have been practiced as far back as 4,500 years ago in China and neighboring lands. There are at least 365 specific sites identified along meridians, where specialized acupuncture needles can be inserted and twirled by acupuncturists in specific ways for specific periods of time to produce therapeutic results. Chinese medicinal specialists who perform this revered alternative ancient practice are said to help balance life forces, known as yin and yang, that flow throughout the body as chi. Acupuncture needles produce gentle tingling and can make part of the body numb by apparently changing brain signals. It is theorized that acupuncture selectively blocks transmission of nerve impulses.

Acupuncture has long been practiced in the East, used for everything from childbirth to treating psychiatric conditions. It is thought that it works by stimulating the release of endorphins and other neurotransmitters which block signals from being sent to the brain or delivered from there back to the extremities. Whatever the mechanism, acupuncture appears to be a safe and effective nonpharmacological therapeutic modality. Acupuncture can change brain activity, particularly within the dorsomedial prefrontal cortex, the dominant site of hyperactivity. Acupressure techniques, closely related to acupuncture, can be taught to even young children when they feel upset.

Aromatherapy

Aromatherapy is an alternative therapeutic approach that employs the perfumed scents from the essential oils of selected plants. (Essential oils are the fundamental compounds that produce a plant's aroma.) Essential oils, generally used in diluted formulations, can be applied directly to the skin, such as rubbing on the face or as body wraps, inhaled, or bathed with. Essential oils are recommended for the relief of symptoms that are commonly associated with ADHD, such as peppermint for increasing mental alertness, calmness, and decreasing depression. Basil, eucalyptus, hyssop, lemon, and rosemary are similarly used, and cedar-wood oil is also thought to reduce ADHD symptoms. The calming effects of lavender have promoted relaxation for centuries and may help reduce hyperactivity; lavender has been shown to reduce the rate of neuronal firing. Bergamot, frankincense, and patchouli have similar uses. Chamomile is used for reducing anger, irritability, and resentment, and brahmi is said to improve memory and enhance brain functioning. Essential oils appear to relieve many minor and sporadic ailments.

Aromatherapy is another complementary modality used for thousands of years by peoples scattered around the globe, including in ancient China, India, and Persia, to manage and control emotions and actions. It can, at the very least, probably be useful in assisting some with ADHD achieve more calm, tranquil states. The area of the brain where olfactory senses are processed is known to be close to the hypothalamus, which may explain how fragrances elicit specific emotions and memories.

Art Therapy

Art therapy uses modalities such as drawing, painting, and sculpting to help individuals with ADHD explore emotional challenges, manage behaviors, develop interpersonal skills, reduce stress, and increase self-awareness. Art therapy provides accessible, nonverbal ways to build skills. Art therapists elicit verbal processing of produced images to help resolve conflicts and problems and otherwise achieve insight and improve self-esteem. Progressing through directed activities helps improve controlled attention and strengthens working and long-term memory. Art therapy furnishes opportunities for someone with ADHD to practice problem-solving and enhance frustration tolerance.

Occupational Therapy

Occupational therapy utilizes sensory processing and other techniques to create individualized plans to improve performance. Occupational therapy helps improve fine- and gross-motor coordination difficulties and fidgeting, all common with ADHD. It teaches individuals to break down required tasks into manageable units so as not to get overwhelmed and to reduce impulsivity across diverse settings. Occupational therapy also assists with organization, planning, and independence related to activities of daily living.

Chiropractic

Chiropractic is an alternative medical practice utilizing specific techniques that are based on the belief that dislocations in vertebral arrangement causes nerve impingement, resulting in health problems, including some ADHD symptoms, such as restlessness. Realignment by manipulation, known as subluxation, is the primary technique to purportedly adjust or realign the structural integrity of the spinal column.

Chiropractic treatment usually begins with detailed personal health histories, along with extensive physical examinations. Laboratory tests or diagnostic imaging, such as MRIs or X-rays, may be conducted to identify abnormalities—usually those related to musculoskeletal structure. Chiropractic care frequently consists of specific manual adjustments delivered by techniques such as high-velocity, low-amplitude spinal manipulation. Chiropractic practitioners frequently dispense dietary advice, usually advocating specific nutritional supplements, as well as employing other modalities, including hot or cold compresses, infrared or ultraviolet light, ultrasound, or traction. General health benefits claimed for chiropractic care usually include greater joint mobility and less physical discomfort, but such relief is typically temporary and routinely requires long-term treatment. Chiropractic doctors are not legally permitted to perform surgery, prescribe drugs, or practice obstetrics.

Electrotherapy

Therapeutic types of electrotherapy have been developed as alternative approaches to control sensations and reduce excessive locomotor activity that is commonly exhibited with ADHD. Electrotherapeutic approaches use equipment to help control and manage muscular tension and associated physical sensations. Transcutaneous electrical nerve stimulation uses safe, relatively mild electrical signals, released by small, battery-powered electrical devices that can be attached to the skin, while spinal cord stimulation has an electrode surgically implanted near the spinal cord so that neuromodulation can selectively block neurotransmission signals. Peripheral nerve stimulation is an alternative therapeutic technique that utilizes tiny electrodes, inserted through small surgical incisions and placed on a nerve. A less-invasive approach is peripheral nerve-field stimulation, where electrodes are inserted under the skin by needles. Deep brain stimulation is the most invasive, but rarely used technique, as it places electrodes directly into the brain, usually in the sensory thalamus or periacueductal gray regions. Transcranial magnetic stimulation is a noninvasive technique that utilizes rapid cycling of electromagnetic induction to direct electrical stimulation to control extravagant locomotor activity. Low-energy neurofeedback systems utilize weak electromagnetic fields to stimulate generalized brain-wave activity and promote brain flexibility.

Hypnosis

Hypnosis is an alternative therapeutic approach using techniques to improve focus and concentration, inhibit distractions, and increase responsiveness to suggestions that are presented while in an induced trancelike state. Some better respond to hypnotic suggestions than others, and expectations and motivations significantly influence possible efficacy of hypnotherapy. Varied hypnotherapeutic techniques are used to manage ADHD symptoms, such as interpersonal approaches and hypnoanalysis.

Hypnotic regression is another technique considered best for getting someone to identify underlying causes of issues, recognition of which can be sufficient to better accept and gain relief. Autogenic training, pioneered in the early twentieth century by German psychiatrist Johannes Heinrich Schultz, is a desensitization-relaxation technique based on self-hypnosis and shown to induce vasodilation, produce feelings of warmth and heaviness useful in maintaining concentration and enhancing body awareness, and increase alpha brain-wave activity that is associated with calmness. Most hypnotic techniques intend to alter awareness, often enough to sufficiently open one to integrate specific suggestions, like being less distracted.

Massage

Massage therapy is an alternative therapeutic technique that is somewhat similar to chiropractic, as it manipulates muscles, skin, ligaments, and other soft tissues to change muscular, circulatory, lymphatic, and nervous systems. The characteristic chopping, friction, kneading, pummeling, rubbing, squeezing, stroking, and vibration of muscles and other body tissues, as practiced in different massage-therapy techniques, increases metabolism, enhances lymphatic drainage, and effectively releases substances into the circulatory system to achieve physical and mental comfort and relaxation. Assorted liniments, lotions, oils, and other substances are sometimes used.

Studies indicate that massage stimulates the release of endorphins, internally produced neurotransmitters, higher levels of which produce euphoria. Massage therapy promotes moving toward states of relaxation and, apparently by increasing serotonin levels, it seems to provide opportunities for higher levels of concentration and improved daily functioning.

Respective massage approaches have demonstrated clinical efficacy in increasing mental focus and concentration, and these techniques may help manage distractions. Reiki is a traditional Japanese style that is based on balancing chi. There are numerous forms of massage, including Ayurvedic, craniofacial, Feldenkries, manual lymph drainage, myofascial release, postural integration, reflexology, rolfing, shiatsu, stone therapy, Swedish, and Traeger. Hydrotherapy is a closely related modality to promote relaxation and provide relief from sensory bombardment; simple immersion in warm water causes dilation of peripheral blood vessels, which decreases the rates of neuronal firing at motor end plates, reducing muscular tension.

Other Products

Many products have been developed and marketed for treating ADHD, including Listol, Addasil, and Synaptol. Listol is a formulation of natural substances that are used to manage ADHD symptoms in children and adults. Its active ingredients are mainly minerals and amino acids. Addasil is a liquid nutritional supplement containing phospholipids, essential amino acids, and assorted minerals and vitamins. It is marketed as stimulating attention and concentration, as well as promoting focus in children and adults with ADHD. Synaptol is a liquid homeopathic formulation that is marketed as alleviating ADHD symptoms. It consists of herbal extracts and other ingredients that are claimed to improve attention span and enhance mental focus and concentration.

LIFESTYLE CHOICES

Your lifestyle is dynamic and changes throughout your life. Activities integrated into the lifestyles of children differ from those of adolescents and adults. A healthy, balanced lifestyle should be instilled early to reduce the likelihood of problems later. Children or adults with treated or untreated ADHD who adopt healthier lifestyles can reduce, and possibly even eliminate, negative impacts. Someone who exercises regularly, eats properly, and sleeps sufficiently is less likely to experience symptoms than someone who makes poorer choices. Further, if taking ADHD medications, less may be needed. Making lifestyle choices that keep the body and brain healthy aids in the management of ADHD.

Stress Management

An array of stress-management techniques is available to help individuals with ADHD cope with stress. While stress—and specifically distress—is generally considered a problem, it is not always bad. In fact, eustress, the good stress, makes life enjoyable and rewarding. Too much stress creates problems, such as anger, anxiety, depression, headaches, mood changes, and sleep problems. All of these are problems that some with ADHD experience, and too much stress makes them more problematic. However, one can learn to deal with stress. Much has to do with how we interpret the stress we experience and how we react to it.

There are general procedures that can help. Being optimistic and focusing on the potential positive outcomes can turn most stressful conditions into opportunities to grow and improve. The same phenomenon can be perceived as either eustress or distress, depending on how we frame it. Talking things out with trusted family members, friends, a therapist, or other special individuals can help someone sort out feelings, and this helps see different perspectives on possibly stressful situations.

One easy stress-management technique is deep breathing. Get into a comfortable position, and relax your stomach. Next, place one hand over your stomach, just slightly below the ribs. Breathe in slowly through your nose, feeling your stomach rise. Hold the breath briefly, and gently exhale through your mouth, attempting to empty your lungs as completely as possible, while feeling your stomach going down. Repeat a few times, until you feel calm and relaxed.

PMR is another easily implemented stress-management technique. Begin by laying or sitting comfortably. Roll up the fingers on both hands and clench your fists tightly. Next tighten your forearms, then tighten the upper arms, and move to the shoulders, upper back, abdomen, lower back, buttocks, and upper legs, and then the lower legs, both feet, toes, neck, face, and the top of your head. Gradually reverse, from the head on down, progressively releasing tension in each body part until you have relaxed the whole body.

Visualization is another popular stress-management technique. When practicing visualization, sit or lie comfortably. Close your eyes and imagine a pleasing, peaceful place, such as a sandy beach or lush forest, and then imagine yourself in that gentle setting. Focus on that scene. Imagine what the air feels like and any smells, sounds, and so forth. Gradually return to the present and resume your personal activities, hopefully in a more relaxed, peaceful state.

Many basic guidelines can help manage stress. For example, taking regular breaks helps keep you refreshed and relaxed. When those with ADHD take a break, such as when studying or working, it can energize them and help them maintain focus. Laughing also helps relieve tension and brighten anyone's mood. Finding something humorous in situations can help. Laughter changes brain chemistry, altering neurotransmitters, and makes us feel better. Writing things down that make you feel good or that stress you can help identify stressors and things that can help you relax. Maintaining optimistic outlooks helps you work on things you can change. Finally, don't be afraid to ask for help.

Time Management

Time management is the process of planning and intentionally allocating how much time is spent on specific activities to increase effectiveness. This can be challenging for someone with ADHD, but time management helps them become more productive and efficient. With proper execution, many tasks can be performed better in less time, leaving more time for leisure and other activities.

Time is fixed for everyone, but techniques to allocate it more effectively can relieve stress and demands made upon someone with ADHD. Begin by selecting environments that are conducive to effectiveness. For some, this might be a pristine, quiet location; however, for many with ADHD, such settings are too stimulus poor, and they may prefer what might seem by neurotypicals to be cluttered, confused, noisy spaces. Personal preferences are essential in evaluating this stratagem.

Creating action plans can aid in setting goals and prioritizing activities by importance. Breaking tasks down into smaller, more manageable units and setting time limits for each step helps keep one moving toward task completion. Use of daily and weekly planners can help.

Creative problem solving can assist with time management—and, fortunately this is a skill many with ADHD are proficient in. Looking at a problem in different ways is an acknowledged benefit of ADHD. Making novel combinations can be appealing to someone with ADHD, and this can help, as long as it isn't allowed to spiral on excessively. Thinking metaphorically and utilizing diagrams and imagery can be useful in problem solving.

Many time-management systems incorporate time-management tools. A clock, timer, or hourglass could actually be a simple, helpful tool. Many software applications are available, such as web-based ones that are available for download onto a cellular telephone. Any way to help monitor the use of time and provide clear feedback can be beneficial in time management. Automation of such processes as part of some time-management systems simply exploits this principle. There are a plethora of well-known time-management systems available, like Getting Things Done, Pareto Analysis, and Pomodoro Technique. Whatever approach is taken, it is essential for individuals to take ownership over managing their time.

Time management should be incorporated into ADHD management and treatment, which are more likely to be successful when tasks are defined and measured in terms of real-life contexts and implemented with appropriate timing details. Treatment efficacy for ADHD medications is known to vary with different administration protocols, thus when and how often respective medications should be taken must be considered. Chronotherapy, or timing administration of medications according to individual circadian rhythms, or internal clocks, could lead to more optimal therapeutic results for ADHD medications and also to fewer adverse side effects.

6

Long-Term Prognosis and Potential Complications

ADHD is a highly treatable disorder and responds well to varied treatments. Unfortunately, there are complications associated with ADHD, but they are different, depending on whether ADHD is treated or untreated. Most of the complications associated with treated ADHD are related to the side effects of the medications that are used to treat it. These include abuse and addiction concerns, particularly to psychostimulants. On the other hand, the long-term prognosis for those whose ADHD is properly treated and managed is very positive and includes many success stories.

UNTREATED VERSUS TREATED ADHD

Untreated ADHD can exact considerable problems on individuals and on those around them. The toll of not treating the disorder includes higher levels of academic failures, automobile accidents, juvenile delinquency, substance use, unwanted pregnancies, and venereal diseases. Costs attributed to a lack of appropriately treating ADHD are estimated to be in the hundreds of billions of dollars annually. The effects of untreated ADHD are most obvious in school, psychosocial, and work arenas.

Educational Impacts

Educators acknowledge that between 10 and 20 percent of school-age children will have difficulties with their academics. In any elementary or secondary classroom, there are likely at least two students seriously affected by ADHD to the extent that it causes problems. Reasons for such difficulties are many. Due to ADHD, some will have trouble maintaining attention, sitting still, and thinking through answers before responding. Many students with hyperactivity have difficulty sitting still for common academic activities, such as having books read to them or quiet writing exercises. Inattentive students are more likely to be overlooked and allowed to drift. Distractions are inherently more rewarding to someone with an ADHD brain, and they will naturally attend more activities than typically acceptable in most educational settings, where reading and other language-based activities are common. Similarly, homework assignments are usually more challenging with untreated ADHD, and they routinely generate conflict and result in frustration for both parents and children.

ADHD can make school more challenging for those afflicted than for neurotypicals. Academic failure, including higher rates of grade-level retention and dropping out, are predictable consequences. In fact, around one-third of those with ADHD never finish high school, compared to the national average of 8.7 percent.

Psychosocial Impacts

The psychosocial complications of untreated ADHD are manifold and commonly results in serious consequences. Complications include aggression, interpersonal problems, and comorbid mental health issues. Not surprisingly, untreated ADHD is more associated with lower self-esteem and poorer social acceptance.

Aggressive outbursts are common with untreated ADHD. Abusive, destructive, or even intentionally disruptive behaviors are typically punished severely, and this, not infrequently, results in escalating, counter-challenging reactions. Most social environments are structured to punish rather than to gently curb and redirect impulsivity, which may work for neurotypicals but often causes those with ADHD to be stigmatized as "bad" and poorly behaved. Unfortunately, children generally mimic what they see. As we expect many untreated children with ADHD to have untreated parents, they are less likely to observe how to remain calm and composed when stressed and are more likely to learn to respond in kind and even to escalate a situation. Rather than learning to relax, breathe, and collect thoughts, they are more likely to lash out and suffer adverse consequences. As individuals mature, these behaviors frequently result in delinquency and criminal infractions.

Interpersonal troubles seem to be more challenging to those with undiagnosed and untreated ADHD. Minor annoyances are likely to result in frustration and overreacting as individuals are more easily overwhelmed. Between 50 and 60 percent of children with ADHD are thought to have difficulties with peer relationships. Difficulties managing emotions are more likely if ADHD is not properly treated. Emotions seem to erupt more often and with greater intensity. Further, those with untreated ADHD usually have trouble calming down when they are angry or annoyed. They also appear to be more sensitive, have harder times accepting constructive criticism, and are more likely to be avoided or rejected by social peers. The impulsivity, emotionality, and aggression in those untreated make it more difficult to make friends and socialize, which impairs their social lives and often manifests in social avoidance. Further, after the initial infatuation fades, dopamine levels plummet. This makes interpersonal relationships more difficult for those untreated. Additionally, the rejection sensitivity that is commonly developed leads to loss of control, with tendencies to lash out at those around them. A common sign of ADHD is an inability to recognize the needs and desires of others. Misunderstandings and miscommunication with parents, siblings, friends, teachers, coworkers, and partners/spouses are more frequent when untreated. These factors make interpersonal relationships all-the-more difficult.

Negative psychosocial impacts that begin in childhood often erupt in adulthood for those untreated. Approximately three-quarters of adults with ADHD also have other comorbid mental health disorders. The most common mental health comorbidities include various anxiety, mood, and personality disorders. Suicidal ideation can be a severe and potentially fatal complication. Eating disorders are more common among adolescent and young adult females with untreated ADHD.

It must be recognized, on the other hand, that the overall prognosis for individuals with properly treated ADHD is good. Most individuals with treated ADHD have higher quality of life. Similarly, most mental health disorders that are commonly comorbid with ADHD are highly treatable.

Employment Impacts

The vocational consequences of untreated ADHD include higher rates of adverse employment indices, such as changing jobs, a lack of promotions, and unemployment. WHO estimates that untreated adults with ADHD annually lose, on average, twenty-two days of work productivity.

Employers consistently report that employees with ADHD have lower work performance, impaired task completion, a lack of independent skills, and poor relations with coworkers and supervisors. These and related issues generally lead to a lower socioeconomic status of adults with ADHD.

An economic impact study estimated that up to 83 percent of overall incremental costs of ADHD (estimated at $143–$266 billion annually) are incurred by adults—so between $105 and $194 billion per year. Workplace issues, primarily productivity and income losses, represent the largest share of costs of adult ADHD to the U.S. economy, accounting for $87–$138 billion each year. Workers with ADHD are more likely to have at least one sick day per month than neurotypicals are. Adults with ADHD are eighteen times more likely to be disciplined at work for perceived behavior problems and are 60 percent more likely to lose their jobs than are colleagues without ADHD. Adults with ADHD, on average, earn from $5,000–$10,000 less per year. These factors contribute to ADHD societal costs, estimated to total $12,005–$17,454 annually per individual in the United States.

SIDE EFFECTS OF PSYCHOSTIMULANTS

There are concerns over risks associated with use of ADHD psychostimulants, including side effects. Some concerns are unwarranted once one understands what is actually known. Concern is understandable, since these are the most commonly prescribed substances for individuals with ADHD.

Preliminary studies suggested that psychostimulants might stunt children's growth. However, little well-designed research supports this. Recently, better-designed studies found that this is untrue. Although there might be minimal suppression of growth in some children who are administered high doses of psychostimulants, this is remediated as dosage is adjusted. Research demonstrates that children who took ADHD medications attain normal adult heights. Stopping the use of psychostimulants once children reached adolescence was formerly routine, due to thinking that not doing so would lead to permanent height loss. It is now more common to slightly decrease doses, but such adjustments aren't generally necessary.

Side effects are occasionally experienced by psychostimulant users. Some are due to pharmacological stimulation of the autonomic nervous system, producing physiological responses like increased heart rates or tachycardia, blood pressure, and respiration. Other side effects include dry mouth, pupillary dilation, and anorexia. Blood glucose and blood coagulation rates can also increase. Increases in skeletal muscular tension but relaxation of bronchi and intestines is common. Urination sometimes becomes difficult. Acute toxicity to large doses can cause profound psychological changes, such as intense paranoia and psychoses, including a condition known as amphetamine psychosis, which consists of states of extreme panic, delusions, hallucinations, mania, and schizophrenic-like behavior.

There are somewhat different side-effect profiles associated with the use of respective ADHD psychostimulants. Dextroamphetamine side effects include constipation, diarrhea, appetite loss, dry mouth or xerostomia, headaches, diminished sex drive, sleep difficulties, uncontrollable shaking, unpleasant taste, and weight loss. Serious, but rarer, side effects include aggressive or hostile behaviors, abnormal movements, blurred vision, chest pain, believing untrue things, excessive tiredness, frenzied mood, hallucinations, paranoia, seizures, tachycardia, verbal tics, and weakness in legs or arms. Methylphenidate side effects include decreased appetite, dry mouth, headache, insomnia, nausea, tachycardia, and vomiting. Rarer side effects include anxiety, excessive sweating, irritability, and tics.

Route of administration alters the likelihood of which side effects are experienced. Snorting or intranasal use is more likely associated with congestion, hoarseness, loss of smell, nose-bleed, and sinusitis, as well atrophy of nasal septum, necrosis or perforation of septum, and problems swallowing. Smoking, in addition to pulmonary complications, can produce throat ailments, productive coughs with black sputum, and increased addiction susceptibility. Injection drug use is associated with risks of unsterile equipment, which can result in abscesses, bacterial or viral endocarditis, cellulitis, hepatitis, HIV infection, lung infections including pneumonia, renal infarction, thrombosis, and tuberculosis. Extended oral administration is associated with ischemic colitis and pulmonary edema.

SIDE EFFECTS OF NONSTIMULANTS

Side effects experienced using nonstimulant ADHD medications are numerous and vary by substance. Amantadine side effects, for instance, include blurred vision, dizziness, faintness, light headedness, and sleeping problems. Rarer, but potentially serious, side effects include difficulty urinating, shortness of breath, and swelling of extremities.

Side effects associated with ADHD antihypertensives relate mainly to blood pressure. Clonidine side effects include hypotension, bradycardia, constipation, diminished libido, dizziness, drowsiness, dry eyes, dry mouth, dry nasal mucosa, fainting, irritability, nausea, and stomach pain. Use of clonidine patches can result in skin reactions and possible burns when having an MRI. Chronic clonidine use can cause edema and fluid retention. Guanfacine side effects include constipation, dizziness, drowsiness, dry mouth, headache, tiredness, and weakness. Serious, but rarer, side effects include severe allergic reactions, fainting, and slow or irregular heart rate.

Side effects for ADHD anticonvulsant carbamazepine include anxiety, back pain, constipation, diarrhea, dizziness, drowsiness, dry mouth, headaches, heartburn, memory problems, nausea, unsteadiness, and vomiting. Carbamazepine can cause life-threatening allergic reactions, such as Stevens-Johnson syndrome or toxic epidermal necrolysis. These allergic reactions can cause severe damage to skin and internal organs. Carbamazepine may also decrease red blood-cell production. Valproate side effects include abdominal pain, alopecia or hair loss, anorexia, congenital abnormalities, diarrhea, dizziness, drowsiness, infection, low red blood-cell production, nausea, tremor, vomiting, and weakness.

Side effects for ADHD eugeroics are benign and typically only cause temporary discomfort. Dizziness, headaches, and nausea are most common. Diarrhea is often reported for modafinil; thus, hydration is important. If modafinil is taken late at night, insomnia is likely. Since armodafinil has similar therapeutic effectiveness but fewer side effects than modafinil, it is more often recommended.

MANAGING SIDE EFFECTS

Side effects of ADHD medications typically dissipate after a few weeks. There are easy-to-follow recommendations to help prevent or reduce most side effects. Recommendations include being well informed and following simple precautions. Learning as much as possible about particular ADHD medications adults, or their children, are taking is a good beginning. Reading package inserts provides valuable information. Monitoring effects helps determine if dosage or medicine should be changed.

Precautions to manage side effect are essentially common sense. Most should be taken with food to minimize the likelihood of stomachaches. Start with small recommended doses, and progressively work up to larger ones if needed. If the dose is effective and no serious adverse reactions occur, then increasing dosage is unwarranted. Psychostimulants should usually be taken early in the day to minimize sleep difficulties. If extended-release formulations cause insomnia, switching to shorter-acting formulations is indicated. If one wishes to discontinue ADHD medication, and after discussing with health care providers, it is usually advisable to taper off slowly. Stopping abruptly can cause irritability, fatigue, or depression. Proper health checkups are critical, particularly checking blood pressure if dizziness experienced. Problems with hypertension might mean the dosage needs adjustment, or a longer-acting formulation or different medicine might be prescribed. It is important to drink plenty of fluids while taking ADHD medications, as this can minimize dizziness. Mood changes should be noted and discussed with health care providers, as this can indicate that effectiveness is wearing off, and either different formulation or even a different medicine should be tried.

ADHD MEDICATION INTERACTIONS

A medication interaction refers to when some substance or condition adversely impacts how an ADHD medicine works. Interactions result not only from mixing different medications but can also result from mixing medications with various beverages, foods, nutritional supplements, and other substances.

Avoiding Interactions

Easy-to-follow suggestions can help avoid interactions of ADHD medications with other substances. Suggestions include being well informed and following simple precautions. With respect to being well informed, it is recommended that one carefully reads drug labels and package inserts, and researching and learning about particular medications that one, or one's child, is taking, paying attention to what each is for, possible side effects, and special warnings.

Recommended precautions to avoid drug interactions are essentially common sense. Medications should be kept in original containers and clearly marked. Mixing medications in containers is dangerous. One should always talk to health care providers as to what beverages, foods, and medications—including over-the-counter products—to avoid when taking respective ADHD medications . Psychostimulants and other medications should not be taken with citrus juices, as they decrease the effects. It is helpful to maintain lists of all medications, over-the-counter medications, and supplements taken and sharing them with health care providers. It is advisable to only fill prescriptions at one pharmacy, which could alert consumers to dangerous drug interactions.

ABUSE POTENTIAL OF ADHD MEDICATIONS

The abuse potential of ADHD medications, particularly psychostimulants, is underscored by common diversion to illicit venues and propensities for nonmedical use. More compelling evidence of abuse potential is the dramatic differences in addiction among those with untreated ADHD.

ADHD medications are misused by many for what are often similar reasons. ADHD medications are typically misused by those wanting to stay awake, study, and improve school or work performance. Another reason for misusing ADHD medications is to suppress appetite. Some misuse for recreational purposes, primarily for the euphoric "highs" that are experienced. Psychostimulant, eugeroics, and cholinergics are the most likely misused ADHD drugs, but others can be also.

Diversion of Psychostimulants

Psychostimulants that are legitimately manufactured for medical purposes, including ADHD, can be diverted for illegal uses. Drug diversion consists of use of prescribed and nonprescribed medications, particularly among adolescents and young adults. Drug diversion and misuse are done by those with and without ADHD.

.Studies report the nonprescription use of psychostimulants within the past year was 5–9 percent among eighth to twelfth graders, and 5–35 percent among college students. Lifetime diversion rates by students with psychostimulant prescriptions asked to give, sell, or trade medications is 16–29 percent. Greatest at risk for misusing and diverting psychostimulants are Caucasian fraternity or sorority members with lower grade point averages (GPAs) who use immediate-release, not extended-release, formulations. Misuse is mostly by taking more pills than prescribed or taking them more frequently than prescribed. About half of those engaged in diversion say they deliberately missed doses to save them for diversion. About one-third of those prescribed psychostimulants reported that they gave medications to others, and about one-quarter reported that they sold some, usually to friends or relatives. This is despite the substantial legal penalties that can be imposed. Evidence suggests that those diverting their ADHD psychostimulants are themselves more likely to be frequently victimized. Reasons reported for misuse of prescribed psychostimulants include improving alertness, staying awake, improving concentration, getting high, or curiosity.

There are criminal justice initiatives to reduce the diversion of psychostimulants and other ADHD medications. The DEA estimates that thirteen thousand physicians or pharmacists knowingly provide opportunities for illicit diversion of dangerous and controlled substances, including psychostimulants and precursors. Criminal diversion activities can easily be covered up, such as by falsifying reports of bogus burglaries and robberies, starting suspicious fires, or similar acts. During Barack Obama's two administrations, initiatives were made to enhance efforts against drug diversion, such as the Organized Crime Drug Enforcement Task Force, a partnership of federal and local law enforcement agencies that was created to identify and disrupt criminally organized drug trafficking. Other international, federal, and state initiatives are intended to interdict domestic and international drug trafficking, including diversion of legally manufactured psychostimulants from other countries. These include the Caribbean Basin Security Initiative, Drug Low Attack Strategy, Merida Initiative, and Plan Colombia.

Risk of Addiction in Those Medicated for ADHD

Studies suggest that children with ADHD are more likely than neurotypicals to have serious substance-abuse problems when they become adolescents and adults. Research indicates that children who appropriately took ADHD medications, such as methylphenidate and combination psychostimulants like Adderall, are not at greater risk for substance-abuse problems later. Evidence shows those with ADHD who don't take prescribed ADHD medications are at greater risk. Increased risk to developing substance problems is observed among those with untreated ADHD. It is estimated that up to 25 percent of those with a lifetime history of addiction also have ADHD. It is recognized that ADHD is often comorbid with other psychiatric conditions, many of which are associated with greater abuse risk, such as depression or schizophrenia. Those with ADHD who become adults but do not receive pharmacological treatment are more likely to experience substance-abuse problems. As there are over twenty-four million Americans who abuse amphetamines annually, it may be assumed that many of these do so as a result of untreated ADHD.

SIGNS OF PSYCHOSTIMULANT ABUSE AND ADDICTION

Individuals who abuse or are addicted to psychostimulants exhibit individualized constellations of symptoms. One prominent sign of psychostimulant abuse and addiction is the intense cravings for the drug of choice. Other subtle, but diffuse effects include anxiety, excessive fatigue, extreme depression, and increased hunger. Abuse symptoms include dry mouth and blurred vision.

Physical symptoms reflect the specific physiological effects of psychostimulants, such as dilated pupils, increased respiration, hypertension, elevated body temperature, muscular tension, and cardiovascular system abnormalities. Other physical symptoms include angina pectoris, arrhythmias, headaches, malnutrition, nausea, seizures, and skin disorders.

Behavioral signs of psychostimulant abuse and addiction include some that are considered positive but are nevertheless indicative of abuse. Purported positive signs include improved academic or occupational performance, enhanced athletic prowess, improved memory and recall, staying focused and awake for extended times, less sleep needed, and increases in energy. Other behavioral signs include altered sexual behaviors, talkativeness, and decreased appetite, and fewer behaviors are exhibited that are normal, socially expected behaviors. Dangerous behavioral signs include setting unrealistic goals, unrealistic beliefs in personal abilities and power, and engaging in risk-taking, all of which are associated with mania. Pronounced mood changes, such as pronounced mood swings, being overly euphoric, or appearing unusually anxious or depressed have been observed.

Psychological signs that are indicative of psychostimulant abuse and addiction include being overly aggressive or hostile. Other psychological manifestations include feelings of paranoia, delusions, hallucinations, and psychotic symptoms.

Adverse social consequences to psychostimulant abuse and addiction that are shared with ADHD include strained interpersonal relationships. Divorce is common. Many experience financial ruin, and job loss is common, as are criminal justice problems.

The physical ravages of chronic psychostimulant abuse and addiction include dehydration, malnutrition, and vitamin deficiencies. Emaciation is frequently observed. Sometimes there is an apparent lack of physical coordination, periods of incoherence, and even total physical collapse. Potentially fatal signs include respiratory depression and seizures. Other severe medical conditions include stimulant-induced psychosis and toxic psychosis. Unsuccessful attempts to cut down or stop; continued use despite awareness of associated problems; and development of tolerance, manifested by progressively larger doses, taken for longer periods, are hallmarks of abuse and addiction. Another prominent feature is when the psychostimulant and its pursuit become central to one's life, to the point that concern with other important areas, such as personal safety, family, friends, and work, is diminished, if not ignored.

OVERDOSE ON ADHD MEDICATIONS

When excessively large doses of ADHD medicine are consumed, effects vary, depending on variables such as the particular substance, the amount consumed, the individual's personal history with that and closely related substances, and whether other substances were taken in combination. In considering overdoses, we must recognize that ADHD medications come in different dosages.

Toxicity for ADHD psychostimulants is related to excessive extracellular levels of dopamine, norepinephrine, and serotonin. The clinical syndrome associated with overdose primarily involves cardiovascular and neurological effects, but secondary complications can include gastrointestinal, muscular, pulmonary, and renal effects. Someone overdosing might present with symptoms such as agitation, anxiety, combativeness, confusion, delirium, excessive sweating, hallucinations, hyper-reflexes, movement disorders, paranoia, and seizures. Seizures can be fatal or can produce lifelong disabilities, including brain damage, as can arrhythmias, heart attacks, or heart failure. The rapid pulse associated with psychostimulant overdose can damage blood vessels or heart valves or cause stroke or bleeding in the brain. Difficulties with breathing can cause low blood oxygen, resulting in blue lips or fingernails. Elevated body temperature associated with psychostimulants can lead to hyperthermia, which can cause dehydration, malfunctioning of vital organs and body systems, or paradoxical hypothermia. Management of psychostimulant overdose is primarily supportive, although benzodiazepines may be used judiciously. If the patient is unresponsive to benzodiazepines, second-line approaches include antipsychotics, such as haloperidol (Haldol) or ziprasidone, or alpha agonists, such as dexmedetomidine or propofol.

Individuals experiencing methamphetamine overdose typically present with altered mental status, including confusion, delusions, hallucinations, paranoia, or suicidal ideations. As methamphetamine tolerance is developed rapidly, there is less likelihood of cardiovascular complications. Route of administration also alters risk. For instance, oral administration of methamphetamine is less likely to cause cardiotoxicity, and, as oral administration takes longer to reach peak-blood concentration, it is associated with less susceptibility to addiction, certainly relative to smoking, while intravenous and other injection methods are more associated with toxicity.

Numerous signs are associated with overdose of respective nonstimulant ADHD medications. These are naturally variable, as are the pharmacological properties of different ADHD medications. For example, someone experiencing amantadine overdose may present with agitation, aggression, breathing difficulties, confusion, convulsions, diminished or ceased urinary output, fainting, fever, hallucinations, severe headaches, personality changes, problems with balance or walking, tachycardia, and tremor.

Clonidine overdoses mostly involve cardiovascular and neurological effects, mainly bradycardia, depressed senses, and hypotension; however, early in some overdoses, paradoxical hypertension occurs. Guanfacine overdoses can include diaphoresis, drowsiness, dry mouth, and lethargy. Clinical management of clonidine or guanfacine overdoses is largely supportive but includes blood pressure support.

Overdose of the ADHD anticonvulsant carbamazepine can involve coma, sleepiness, and epileptic seizures and, in fatal cases, may include respiratory depression or arrest. Valproate overdose includes symptoms such as arrhythmia, coma, and sleepiness. Managing anticonvulsant overdoses is mainly supportive but may include enhancing elimination and decontamination.

Modafinil overdose typically produces excessive extracellular dopamine, norepinephrine, and serotonin levels in the brain. Neurological effects of modafinil overdose include agitation, anxiety, dizziness, dystonia, headache, insomnia, and tremors. Managing modafinil overdoses is largely supportive, including concern with blood pressure and sedation. Armodafinil overdose typically produces symptoms similar to modafinil overdose and may include chest pain, diarrhea, nausea, and unusual bleeding or bruising.

Avoiding Overdose

Commonsense steps can be taken to decrease the likelihood of overdosing on ADHD medications, particularly for different ages. Preschooler precautions include containers with child-resistant caps and storing containers up high, ideally locked, out of sight and reach. If more than one adult administers ADHD medicine to a child, procedures to prevent double dosing should be established. Labels should be carefully read and fully understood. Children should be taught that medications aren't candy and should only be taken when given by caregivers. For elementary-aged children, ADHD medications should be securely stored between administrations, and only caregivers should administer them. For high school and college students and other young adults, they should not be allowed to take their own medications unless it is certain that they understand how to do so safely. For the elderly, ADHD medications should be kept in original containers and not mixed with other medications, unless someone else is sorting daily medications for them and putting them in pill minders. As about 40 percent of those aged sixty-five and older take five or more prescription medications, the chance of dangerous interactions is high. It is important for the elderly, or their caregivers, to communicate effectively with physicians, pharmacists, and other health care providers to ensure that there is no conflict, including paying attention to dietary supplements and consideration of interactions from food and beverages.

SUCCESSFUL MANAGEMENT OF ADHD

Two major approaches used to manage ADHD are pharmacological and behavioral. Psychostimulants are the most commonly prescribed, but 10–30 percent of those with ADHD don't respond well or cannot tolerate their side effects. There are many forms of behavioral psychotherapy. Most have been shown to be most effective when used along with ADHD medications, but they can be effective on their own. Behavioral approaches can help reduce unrealistic expectations and assist with skill acquisition.

When schools work along with parents, using behavioral therapeutic or modification strategies such as behavioral classroom management and parent training techniques, to create supportive, mutually reinforcing environments with consistent expectations, chances are increased that those with ADHD will behave appropriately. Unfortunately, cognitive behavioral therapy and similar approaches can be frustrating to some who may not have the patience or organizational skills to master the techniques. Alternative strategies, such as lifestyle choices, can be incorporated. Whatever approaches are used, they should be personalized to address individualized needs.

SUCCESS FOR PEOPLE WITH ADHD

Many with ADHD can be highly successful. Individual success is more likely for those who receive accommodations and services, particularly related to education and employment.

Adults with ADHD often develop coping skills that enable workplace success. Someone with the hyperactive ADHD subtype might appear to be overworking or have atypical competitive drive. Adult workers with ADHD often learn coping mechanisms that permit them to function on the job and discover ways to adjust work environments to their needs, such as relying on coworkers for assistance and selecting careers and work environments that accommodate their needs.

Successful Individuals with ADHD

Many with ADHD, whether treated or not, have been successful in diverse areas. Numerous individuals with ADHD have contributed to making the world better in disparate fields, including explorers, entertainers, artists, musicians, business leaders, entrepreneurs, political leaders, scientists, inventors, authors, and athletes. It is difficult to state with certainty that a particular individual in the past, before ADHD was recognized, actually had ADHD or not. Nevertheless, reviewing biographical or autobiographical details about specific historical figures permits reasonable assessment of whether they exhibited characteristics that are indicative of ADHD.

Some noted explorers had qualities that are consistent with ADHD, and the condition may have benefited them in developing and maintaining their visionary pursuits of the undiscovered. Some better-known explorers who probably had ADHD include Christopher Columbus, Sir Walter Raleigh, Meriwether Lewis, and William Clark.

Many entertainers, such as actors and comedians, probably had or have ADHD. Contemporary comedians who have publicly stated that they have ADHD, which might help them with spontaneity and creativity, include Howie Mandel, Jim Carrey, and Patrick McKenna. Some celebrity chefs and restauranteurs who have declared that they have ADHD include Jamie Oliver and Alexis Hernandez. Karina Smirnoff, a professional dancer on *Dancing with the Stars*, acknowledges being diagnosed with ADHD as an adult and says she channels her high energy into her work.

Famous artists are included among well-known individuals who probably had ADHD. Some with ADHD seem to demonstrate higher creative thought levels than neurotypicals. Artists who probably had ADHD include da Vinci, Van Gogh, Picasso, and Dali.

Several noted musicians probably also had or have ADHD and might have benefited from the creativity that often accompanies it. Classical musicians such as Mozart and Beethoven may have had ADHD. Other musicians who probably had ADHD include Elvis Presley and Kurt Cobain. Among contemporary musicians who have publicly admitted having ADHD are Justin Timberlake, Solange Knowles, and Phillip Manuel. Justin Bieber, the popular Canadian singer and songwriter, admits being prescribed Adderall.

U.S. business leaders and entrepreneurs who probably had ADHD include Andrew Carnegie, Frank Woolworth, Henry Ford, Walt Disney, Howard Hughes, and Malcolm Forbes. Contemporary entrepreneurs who publicly stated that they have ADHD include Richard Branson, David Neeleman, and Paul Orfalea. Some of their success may be partially attributed to the fact that some with ADHD demonstrate increased spontaneous idea generation than most neurotypicals.

Many past political leaders exhibited behaviors consistent with ADHD. Several U.S. presidents probably had ADHD, including Abraham Lincoln, Theodore Roosevelt, Woodrow Wilson, Dwight Eisenhower, and John Fitzgerald Kennedy. In addition to Eisenhower, other military generals who likely had ADHD include Napoleon Bonaparte, George Patton, and Norman Schwarzkopf. Political figures who have publicly stated that they have ADHD include former U.S. Representative Kendrick Meek, James Carville, and Glen Beck.

Many scientists and inventors, who tend to be highly inquisitive and approach subjects from novel perspectives, probably also had ADHD. This could include Einstein, Newton, and Galileo. Among well-known U.S. inventors who probably had ADHD are Benjamin Franklin, Orville and Wilbur Wright, Alexander Graham Bell, and Thomas Edison. English mathematician and writer Charles Dodgson, better known as Lewis Carroll, also exhibited signs that are indicative of ADHD.

Authors, including playwrights and poets, are represented among successful individuals who probably had ADHD. Playwrights who probably had ADHD include Oscar Wilde, George Bernard Shaw, and Tennessee Williams. Famous poets who probably had ADHD include Samuel Taylor Coleridge, Lord Byron, Emily Dickinson, Robert Frost, and Anne Sexton. Other well-known writers who probably had ADHD include Hans Christian Anderson, Charlotte Bronte, Ralph Waldo Emerson, Henry David Thoreau, Jules Verne, and Mark Twain. Among contemporary writers who publicly announced that they have ADHD are Jenny Lawson and Katherine Ellison.

Numerous athletes from diverse sports are known to have ADHD. This may be, in part, because some with ADHD are able to hyperfocus better than neurotypicals. Michael Phelps has publicly stated that he has ADHD and takes ADHD medications. Simone Biles also acknowledges that she takes ADHD medicine, as have Olympic athletes Cammi Granato, Adam Kreek, and Louis Smith. Other athletes who have also publicly acknowledged that they have ADHD include Greg LeMond and Terry Bradshaw. Professional golfers with ADHD include Bubba Watson and Payne Stewart. Current professional football athletes who have publicly stated that they take ADHD medications include Josh Freeman, Virgil Green, and Andre Brown.

7

Effects on Family and Friends

ADHD is a disorder that impacts not only individuals who are identified with the condition, but it can also have profound effects on their family and friends. Family concerns can present serious issues in relationships with parents, children, siblings and other extended family members. In a similar vein, there are commonly difficulties for individuals with ADHD in finding and maintaining friendships. Despite the numerous difficulties of living with someone with ADHD, there are many gifts. Accordingly, these must be recognized as well.

FAMILY CONCERNS

ADHD can potentially affect all aspects of an individual's life throughout his or her entire life. It impacts not only individuals with ADHD but can also severely impact all those around them. Having a family member with ADHD can be very stressful for the entire family. While ADHD can strain relations between parents and children, it can also stress relationships with siblings and other extended family members.

Negative effects of ADHD on individuals and their families and peers can change across the life span, with different aspects being more or less prominent and problematic at various times. Further, due to the highly heritable nature of ADHD, there is, more often than not, more than one individual with the disorder in a family and across generations. This common reality can often create even more complex family dynamics issues.

Parenting Issues

ADHD can affect families in many different ways, particularly depending on the age of the individual with ADHD. As a general rule, family conflicts are more likely the older the child with ADHD is. This is not to say that parenting younger children with the neurodevelopmental disorder of ADHD will not be challenging. Parents will probably be somewhat stressed if they have a preschooler who doesn't follow their advice or respond appropriately to their requests. However, this isn't entirely unexpected, particularly due to the delayed development that is so typical of many children with ADHD. These younger children will often exhibit oppositional behaviors and may also have poorly developed social skills, but these issues are not as dramatically age inappropriate as they would be for older children. However, such challenging behaviors are typically more pronounced in children with ADHD than in their same-aged neurotypical peers. It is generally true that preschoolers with ADHD may typically require considerably more supervision than same-age neurotypicals without ADHD, but if parents of children with the disorder are consistently vigilant and regularly monitor behaviors of their children, they can often successfully modify such behavioral repertoires for more desired outcomes, particularly if they consistently model appropriate behaviors themselves. If, on the other hand, parents don't agree on the best ways to address particular situations, then this division may be manipulated by the children and can result in greater parental strains. The additional time and expense that is sometimes involved in caring for a young child with ADHD can also create additional stress for parents and other family members.

Children with ADHD, like all children, typically model behaviors after the individuals around them, particularly including their parents and other caregivers. Individuals regarded as having power are considerably more likely to be modeled than those who are perceived to be without such power. Fathers, in most traditional Western societies at least, are expected to possess instrumentality, such that they demonstrate desire for achievement, orientation toward task completion, and effective coping with demands of everyday life. Perception of paternal power is naturally enhanced if they exude greater levels of expertise, more physical prowess, and associated prestige. Maternal power is traditionally, at least in most Western societies, demonstrated by giving comfort, as well as by typical talents at being more adept at establishing good human relations, aided by their stereotypical proficiency at expressing emotions. These stereotypical, traditional parental modeling roles are less likely to be available if one or both of the parents has ADHD as well, which, due to the highly heritable nature of ADHD, is more likely than not.

Due to often reported difficulties adults with ADHD have in maintaining meaningful relationships, it is somewhat more likely that parents with ADHD may be absent from day-to-day parenting responsibilities. Studies have repeatedly found that paternal absence, in particular, can adversely affect a son's masculine self-concept and has also consistently been associated with greater probability of various psychopathologies developing later. Further, research indicates that the younger the child is when the father leaves the household, and the longer he is absent, then the more severe such psychopathologies are likely to eventually be.

Disorders such as ADHD can often have devastating impacts on family dynamics. These dynamic processes can sometimes take over the lives of individuals with ADHD and those of family members, as well as challenging their emotional and physical health, sense of hope, and peace of mind. Manifestations of these maladaptive behaviors are expressed by myriad psychosexual problems that are regularly found in association with ADHD. These challenges of the disorder interact dynamically with the qualities of families affected, such as the family's life cycle stage and the roles of various family members, leadership resources available in the family, degrees of isolation felt by family members and the understanding and beliefs about the nature of the disorder and how best to address it.

Parents of school-age children with ADHD often experience some common difficulties. For instance, they typically have little time for themselves and must expend considerable time and resources on monitoring the unpredictable behaviors of their children. However, they often get some relief from contact with various educational and medical professionals, who are at least aware of and somewhat familiar with ADHD, and from the process of seeking and ultimately obtaining thorough professional evaluations. This enlightenment routinely provides the beginnings of explanation to parents of the myriad problems they have been experiencing. Such parents are mostly without prior understanding or awareness of the nature of the disorder and of commonly associated challenges. They simply tend to be overwhelmed with the daunting challenges. Once an ADHD diagnosis is made though, new parental responsibilities often emerge, such as overseeing the child's medication schedule and additional appointments with therapists and other professionals. These additional demands, initially at least, can exacerbate and further stress already wearied parents. From the point of view of considering a family as basically a homeostatic system, tendencies of ADHD symptomatic behaviors to sometimes serve as equilibrium-maintaining factors must be recognized. As families often form and develop around the disorder, they learned how to live with it, even if somewhat irrationally. Changing such a cybernetic system would naturally be disruptive to all family members involved. Resistance is, of course, a rather typical response to such phenomena and must sometimes be worked through with professional assistance.

Friction between parents and their adolescent children with ADHD is not uncommon. Some reasons behind these difficulties may be inherent physiological and psychological differences between members of respective age groups. Adolescents, as a class, tend to be physically more active, energetic, and vigorous than their parents. Adolescents also usually experience an intensification of sexual interests, augmented by changes occurring at puberty. There is also typically an increasing preference for companionship of age-mates, which can foster feelings of loss in some parents—this is actually rather common among parents of children with ADHD. Friction that commonly erupts between parents and adolescent offspring is, unfortunately, often more severe in family systems that are already strained by failing to adequately address that additional challenges that are routinely associated with ADHD.

Parenting styles are highly variable and, of course, significantly affect parent-child relations in all families. Styles of parenting can be classified as varying from autocratic and authoritarian, through democratic, equalitarian, and permissive, to somewhat laissez-faire, or even characterized as generally ignoring. Respective parenting styles are highly correlated to a child's levels of confidence, independence, and self-esteem. More autocratic and authoritarian parents of children with ADHD tend to be more likely to raise offspring who will resist and rebel and exhibit low self-esteem. Less rigid parental control and allowing children with ADHD to participate in decision-making when possible is more likely to permit these children to become more confident and independent. Similarly, degrees of appreciation, dominance, and protectiveness that are regularly expressed by parents will substantially influence their children's psychosocial development. Under-appreciated children, for instance, are far more prone to be overbearing and unrealistic with respect to interpersonal relationships, which is already more likely in those living with ADHD. Over-dominated children, on the other hand, are far more likely to be both emotionally and physically withdrawn or timid or overly pushy and assertive. Further, many families with ADHD can be characterized as having poor communication and serious problem-solving deficits, which is only more likely to produce problematic family dynamics.

Many parents of a child with ADHD feel guilty over the disorder. These parents need to clearly understand that ADHD isn't caused by bad parenting. Nevertheless, parents will often begin to doubt themselves and their parenting skills and knowledge. These negative thoughts can only further impair their already strained abilities to provide solid, nurturing care and they often require professional assistance.

Parents with ADHD can experience additional parenting challenges, particularly if they are untreated. They may be easily frustrated with their children and with themselves. If they exhibit characteristic disorganized and impulsive behaviors, it can make it more difficult for their children to learn appropriate, consistent behavioral responses to situations. Sometimes a responsible child will take on some parental roles and duties, which can hinder their own normal emotional growth and development. Fortunately, once family members openly recognize and discuss family issues associated with ADHD, unhappy relationships typically improve, including unhappy marital relationships, unhappy parent-child relationships, and unhappy sibling relationships.

Parent Training

The American Academy of Pediatrics clinical practice guidelines recommend prescribing behavioral therapy as the initial line of treatment for very young family members with ADHD—those who are four to five years old. Further, these children should only be given ADHD medicines if behavioral therapy approaches were first attempted and found unsuccessful. Parent-training approaches have been found to be most effective for this particular age group. Parent-training behavioral therapy is referred to by many different terms, including Parent Training, Behavioral Parent Training, Behavioral Management Training for Parents, Parent Behavioral Therapy, and Parent Management Training. Parent-training behavioral therapy usually involves teaching parents to utilize behavioral therapeutic principles through approaches such as role playing, modeling, and home practice, to learn how to more effectively interact with their children. These therapeutic approaches seem to have been most successful in working with parents of younger, preadolescent children.

Some specific programs of parent-training behavioral therapy that have been found to be fairly effective in reducing hallmark ADHD symptoms are the Incredible Years Parenting Program, Helping the Non-Compliant Child, New Forest Parenting Programme, Parent-Child Interaction Therapy, and Positive Parenting Program (Triple P). These particular types of parent-training programs are designed to teach parents skills they need to be able to encourage and reward positive behaviors in their children. This usually includes the utilization of systems of rewards and consequences that can effectively help change undesired behaviors, particularly with immediate and positive feedback to create situations that help support desired behaviors. For example, Incredible Years Basic Parenting Program is designed for parents of children at high risk for ADHD and related behavioral problems. It is focused on helping parents strengthen relationships with their children and includes training on setting limits, establishing ground rules, providing praise and incentives, and addressing misbehaviors. It operates as a twelve- to fourteen-session training program that has demonstrated effectiveness at providing long-term benefits to preschool children at risk for ADHD.

Relatively simple behavioral techniques, such as keeping to routines, making lists of tasks and activities, using reminder notes, assigning special places to routinely place important items, and breaking down large tasks into more manageable smaller units, can be helpful for both children and adults with ADHD. Behavioral therapy not only gives parents strategies and skills to help their children, it has also been shown to be as effective as ADHD medicines for treating symptoms of ADHD in preschool children. Further, preschool children typically experience more side effects from ADHD medicines than older individuals, and, in addition, long-term effects of most ADHD medicines haven't been well studied in younger individuals. In addition, being involved in parent-training programs typically helps to reverse the helplessness and demoralization parents of those with ADHD often feel when they are unable to successfully deal with the undesired behaviors of their children with ADHD.

Sibling and Other Family Member Issues

Stresses in dealing with someone with ADHD can easily spill over to adversely impact siblings and other members of the extended family. These demands can impair family dynamics, create havoc with family routines, and generally disturb the fragile balance of interpersonal relationships by putting everyone in the family on edge. Normal family roles can become distorted and exaggerated when ADHD is added to complex cauldron.

Family relations are often adversely impacted by ADHD. Siblings of those with ADHD commonly report being victimized by aggressive acts, ranging from manipulation to verbal aggression, and even including repeated acts of physical violence from other siblings with ADHD. Parents frequently expect siblings without ADHD to help with caretaking to compensate for the emotional and social immaturity that is characteristic of those with ADHD. Siblings of individuals with ADHD often complain of feelings anxious, sad, or worried.

Sibling conflicts can intensify the stress that is typically present when a family member has the neurodevelopmental disorder of ADHD. Younger children often emulate the behaviors of older siblings; thus, if an adolescent with ADHD acts inappropriately and gets attention for it, then younger siblings might be more inclined to imitate those behaviors, endeavoring to obtain similar parental attention. Negative parental attention can even be considered to be desirable by younger children, who may often feel somewhat overlooked by parents or caregivers who are likely trying to deal with the typically very challenging behaviors of the older sibling with ADHD. This sense of feeling ignored by parents can manifest with feelings of jealousy and depression, including suicidal ideation and attempted suicide. Such parenting actions of apparent neglect are also highly likely to result in lowered self-esteem and can sometimes even fuel intense feelings of anger and result in aggressive outbursts in the family members without the disorder. How parents or caregivers handle the child with the identified disorder of ADHD is extremely likely to impact how they deal with any neurotypical siblings.

Siblings of individuals with ADHD, particularly if they don't have ADHD themselves (which, of course, is highly unlikely), can easily come to resent the amount of extra time and attention the affected sibling seems to get. They may not only be jealous but can sometimes become sad or even angry at their sibling or at their parents for disturbing the family. In general, families of individuals with ADHD tend to have fewer contact with others, including with other members of their extended families, such as grandparents, aunts and uncles, or cousins. This lack of meaningful interaction can lead to social isolation and result in more stressful responses. In fact, parents of children with ADHD are more at risk of becoming separated or divorcing.

Due to the highly heritable nature of the neurodevelopmental disorder of ADHD, other extended family members of individuals with ADHD are also likely to have the condition. This can add additional layers of complexity to the family dynamics that are often observed in association with ADHD. Grandparents with commonly undiagnosed and untreated ADHD can sometimes be more challenging than helpful, as can other extended family members. The adverse impacts of untreated ADHD, such as frequent arrests, divorce, unemployment, comorbid disorders, and so forth, often only serve to further complicate and confuse the dynamics around the family situation. Role modeling that is sometimes furnished by extended family members, as well as the scapegoating often resorted to by other family members, frequently harms, rather than helps, an already difficult scenario.

FAMILY STRATEGIES

Many different strategies are available that have been found to be helpful for some families who are dealing with a family member or members with ADHD. These strategies include things such as early intervention, practicing emotional control, organizational techniques, establishing structure, and soliciting support.

Finally, we should try to maintain a sense of humor and remain persistent. Persistence can help overcome many issues that, at first glance, can seem nearly insurmountable. It often helps to remember the many positive aspects of living with someone with ADHD. These typically include things such as high levels of energy, a profound sense of intuition, and the intense creativity that is often exhibited by individuals with ADHD, as well as their general tendency to be both good-hearted and compassionate.

Early Intervention

Early intervention is widely recognized as being crucial for young children with ADHD for greater improvements, not only in the short-term but also in the long-term. Preschool-age children with ADHD carry added risks for being suspended or even expelled from varied child-care settings, where many staff members may be unfamiliar with and are often untrained in dealing with ADHD. Accordingly, there is an all too common tendency for some child-care staff at such settings to unprofessionally assert that a child challenging them must have ADHD. This is further complicated by cultural differences in accepted ranges of what is considered normal behavior. There are also elevated risks for individuals with ADHD of sustaining physical injuries.

Reducing excessive disruptive behaviors in young children has been found to be strongly associated with decreases in mental health problems, substance use, criminality, and even premature mortality in adulthood. For instance, disruptive behavior in young children, as commonly associated with ADHD, is strongly linked to smoking at early ages and to greater likelihood of adolescent intoxication, as well as to poorer life-management skills and excess weight gain. Early intervention efforts must, of course, begin with a thorough evaluation, since professional diagnosis is essential before appropriate strategies can be developed.

Practicing Emotional Control

Parents can be highly effective in changing behaviors of their children with ADHD. This basically comes down to teaching the children how to maintain emotional control and how to formulate plans of action with the support of assorted coping strategies. Prevention of problems is, of course, generally the best strategy. Thus, taking proactive measures to avoid emotionally challenging situations is a good initial step, such as not pairing up with partner who is known to be difficult to get along with.

However, sooner or later, the individual with ADHD will have to learn how to handle these sorts of demanding scenarios. Helping the child to formulate plans for handling potentially difficult situations, such as asking for assistance to start working on a specific task, can be helpful. Taking steps to help someone prevent the likelihood of feeling overwhelmed can aid not only in avoiding the sense of frustration but also reducing the chances of an emotional outburst occurring as a consequence. Some parents engage in role-playing activities with their children as practice for how to possibly respond to potentially challenging situations.

By offering a stable, supportive home environment, the child is better able to handle future challenges in other settings, such as at school or play. Accordingly, it is important for parents of those with ADHD to keep to daily routines and to assure that the children get enough sleep; fatigue can make it more likely that emotional outbursts might surface.

Teaching someone to recognize the feelings that usually accompany emotional outbursts, such as an accelerated heart rate, muscle tension, and shallower breathing, can be useful. When such skills are learned, it is much easier to employ stress-management techniques that can assist with maintaining emotional control.

Organizational Techniques

Being organized is one of the most important skills for being successful, but unfortunately, it is something that individuals with ADHD often struggle with. Poor organizational skills are often inferred from the tendency to create cluttered environments, which is typical of many with ADHD. Organizational techniques can apply to demands at home, school, and work.

Mastery of organizational techniques enhances many aspects of one's life. Staying focused on tasks is helpful in remedying the disorganized habits that are so typical of individuals with ADHD. Thinking about the end results can help these individuals remain on track and develop better organized efforts.

Organizing events and assignments can immensely help one become more productive. Making a list of responsibilities and ordering them by due dates or other priorities can help one more regularly complete and accomplish their demands. Such organizational lists continually need to be revised as new tasks arise and need to be incorporated.

Breaking tasks down into smaller, more manageable units can help ease burdens and make them seem less overwhelming. Tackling small, achievable objectives helps maintain motivation and lets one integrate these into meeting larger goals.

Establishing Structure

Deficits with respect to maintaining structure are common in individuals with ADHD. Structure comes more naturally to many neurotypicals, whose brains help them perform in accordance with internally generated structures. Most individuals with ADHD must work harder to learn how to incorporate more structure into their daily lives.

Children with ADHD are intrinsically overactive and energetic and need structure to help them achieve reasonable control. Parents, teachers, and supervisors must learn to be more patient and tolerant and help create outlets for the release of excess energy. Further, moderate amounts of realistic praise help enhance their self-esteem and reinforce the likelihood that positive behaviors will garner attention, rather than the negative behaviors that are much more likely to be noticed and mentioned by parents, teachers, supervisors, and others.

Establishing structure in home, school, and work environments greatly assists those living with ADHD. Structured routines help individuals with ADHD accept order. Keeping times, such as those for meals, breaks, and bedtimes, consistent increases predictability for all concerned. Formulating clear, reasonable rules and consistently adhering to them minimizes disciplinary conflicts. Maintaining feelings of acceptance is necessary for survival of self-esteem and self-confidence.

Weaknesses in planning ahead and in determining and setting priorities are common issues among those with ADHD. Consequently, acquiring planning skills with the guidance of parents, teachers, or other "coaches" is essential to helping individuals with ADHD learn the requisite skills to successfully establish more structure in their daily lives.

Soliciting Support

Family members of individuals with ADHD need to remember to cultivate as many supports as possible. These supports, hopefully, include professionals who are familiar with and knowledgeable about ADHD, such as family physicians and therapists, as well as teachers and other educational specialists. Friends and other family members are, of course, important sources of support for most of us. There are specialized support groups for parents of individuals with ADHD. Participation in these sorts of support groups helps one keep things in proper perspective and can also be useful in generating solutions to solve myriad problems, many of which other group members have likely already struggled with.

Affiliation with local and national organizations related to ADHD can help supply additional sources of support and access to invaluable resources. Attending state, regional, or national conventions can potentially expand the pool of relevant resources available.

FRIENDSHIP DIFFICULTIES

It is widely acknowledged that those with ADHD have difficulties in making and keeping friends. Many of these problems are related to the very nature of the characteristic symptoms of ADHD. Children with ADHD can tend to be emotionally reactive, domineering, aggressive, intensive, and otherwise difficult and demanding, and thus seem undesirable to befriend.

Individuals with ADHD are known to have difficulties in recognizing and understanding the cues given by others as to their desires and needs. ADHD often makes them pay more attention to interesting things over other people. Friends require being regularly acknowledged and appreciated, something that is often not given great priority by those with ADHD. When someone with ADHD begins to feel overwhelmed or frustrated, paying attention to the needs of friends fades.

Impulsivity, so characteristic of ADHD, can easily make some with the disorder seem insensitive. However, many individuals with ADHD are actually very emotionally sensitive—in fact, they are commonly oversensitive. Since they may have more difficulties in learning from past experiences, they can be readily labeled as troublesome and can experience social rejection by peers. This can evolve into isolation as a coping strategy.

It is hard for someone with ADHD to remain a consistent friend. Boredom rapidly sets in, and other things easily divert attention from friends. The erratic, sometimes capricious nature of ADHD makes it even harder for those with the disorder to make friends. Neurotypical children are less likely to befriend a child who seems to consistently interrupt, fails to wait to take turns, and so forth, as is typical of many individuals with the disorder. Memory deficits that are so common in ADHD make it harder to recall the small, personal details that are so helpful in maintaining friendships, like the names of siblings and parents and important dates, such as birthdays and anniversaries. Friends like to feel valued, which is hard when the other person cannot remember important things about them.

It is natural for someone with ADHD to get easily distracted and change topics. Friends don't appreciate those who regularly bounce off on unrelated tangents, so characteristic of ADHD. It can make them and their personal needs seem unvalued.

Parents become concerned when their children has persistent problems in playing with others. Social exclusion and rejection can become more prominent and acutely personal as school-age friendships develop. It is difficult for parents of those with ADHD to see their children struggling to make and keep friends. It is sad for a child to not be asked for play dates or sleepovers and not get invited to birthday parties and other social activities.

BENEFITS OF FRIENDSHIP

Meaningful relations with friends greatly enrich our lives. The enthusiasm, creativity, and energy that often accompany ADHD can contribute to solid friendships, if they are channeled appropriately. Working on keeping friends helps keep someone with ADHD on track. Remembering what is important to friends—their likes and dislikes, interests, special values, birthdays and other special dates, and such—enhances memory skills and nurtures friendships.

Friendships provide opportunities for dealing with the emotions of interpersonal relationships, sometimes including the painful feelings of rejection. Relations with parents, other caregivers, siblings, and others serve as a basis for learning how to communicate, interact, and deal effectively with others. Friendships with peers allow opportunities to build relationships on a more-equal basis. Unfortunately, this is an area many with ADHD have considerable difficulties with.

Early interpersonal relationships that lead to feelings of affiliation have been shown to play a substantial role in assisting in the maturation of a range of neurophysiological processes, particularly those in the frontal cortex. They are also linked to the development of alliance formation, attachment, and friendships, as well as inhibiting expression of certain genetic predispositions, such as that for ADHD. Affiliative social relationships are recognized to be calming, improve immune functioning, and raise pain thresholds. Affiliation has also been demonstrated to help regulate threat processes by means of generating feelings of social safeness. Psychopathologies, such as ADHD, are understood to be less likely when individuals feel safer and more connected by means of greater affiliations to their social environment.

Working at keeping friends helps foster empathy, a frequently cited deficit of those with ADHD. It takes concerted effort for someone with ADHD to let others know how much they are appreciated. This purposeful effort will generally be recognized and reap friendship rewards. Keeping long-term friends helps reinforce one's sense of self-esteem, often identified as being weak in those with the disorder.

Developmentally appropriate peer relations help us learn how to more meaningfully connect to others. Social skills that are usually acquired through friendships help us learn things such as cooperation, reciprocity, negotiation, and conflict resolution, which those individuals with ADHD generally have to work harder to master than most neurotypical individuals do.

8

Prevention

Preventing ADHD is important because the more severe symptoms are, and the earlier they appear, the greater the chances long-term negative impacts will be experienced. ADHD professionals are interested in which risk factors are modifiable and how actions or behaviors can reduce negative effects and, perhaps, even prevent the disorder from developing in the first place. Although prevention and lifestyle choices represent our "best guess," there are no guarantees. Recommendations for preventing ADHD can be considered common sense guidance and may prevent many conditions. At the very least, these sorts of approaches could also help reduce the severity of ADHD symptoms should they appear, as well as reduce the likelihood they ever do.

PREVENTION

Prevention is intended to stop ADHD before it appears and also reduce its impacts. Public health recognizes three levels of prevention: primary, secondary, and tertiary. Primary prevention is mainly intended to block the appearance of ADHD, including educational efforts such as media campaigns encouraging abstinence from alcohol, tobacco, and other drugs during pregnancy, as well as those eliminating exposure to lead or pesticides during early childhood. Secondary prevention is directed more at early detection of conditions and also at reduction of symptoms before

ADHD or related disorders have fully developed. Secondary prevention efforts are mainly intended to avoid, or at least reduce, associated problems. Tertiary prevention is intended to halt the progression of problems that have occurred and is more treatment oriented.

Many prevention efforts cut across these somewhat arbitrary levels and, not surprisingly, can vary considerably by target population, such as attempting to identify individuals at higher risks for ADHD or focusing on the general population. Both approaches are valuable and would contribute to overall prevention objectives. Some who may not have attributes that are recognized as putting them at higher risk can still experience the disorder. On the other hand, not everyone who has even multiple risk factors will necessarily ever get ADHD. It is hoped that implementation of the techniques and practices discussed here will contribute to lowered incidence of this neurodevelopmental disorder.

Prevention professionals distinguish between risk and protective factors. Effective broad-based prevention campaigns endeavor to reduce the impacts of risk factors while augmenting the impacts of protective factors. Earlier, we discussed the risk factors for ADHD, and here we focus on techniques that can reduce the likelihood someone ever develops ADHD, even with identifiable risk-factors, and to substantially reduce and maybe eliminate negative impacts. Health-promoting techniques have the potential to serve as primary, secondary, or tertiary prevention activities, depending largely on the intended target population. Identifying and intervening with any modifiable risk factors is desirable, and ways to prevent ADHD and healthy lifestyle choices contribute to both these goals.

While diagnosis and treatment have improved for ADHD, prevention offers the best protection, as it does for most diseases and disorders. Research indicates that preventative strategies reduce and sometimes eliminate the occurrence of ADHD. Individuals play major roles in maintaining their health, and this applies to ADHD, as it does to other conditions. Individuals must maintain healthy lifestyles that not only reduce the likelihood that they will experience ADHD but lessen its impact if they do.

ADHD Awareness

Recognition and awareness of ADHD is necessary before any effective prevention campaigns, strategies, tactics, techniques, procedures, and programs can be designed and implemented. Awareness is generally part of what public health professionals consider to be primary prevention, and usually includes not only awareness but also education, empowerment, advocacy, and other prevention goals. It is believed that ADHD awareness is one of the best ways to continue the progress made in ADHD education and advocacy. One of the simplest and most effective things people can do is promote greater awareness of ADHD among those around them, beginning in their own homes, schools, and communities. Small efforts can reap huge dividends in increasing awareness of ADHD and related concerns. Awareness efforts can range from activities like posting fact sheets on bulletin boards to large-scale public events. As to the former, fact sheets about the challenges that individuals with ADHD experience in school, at work, and in social relationships can be helpful. Writing elected officials to inform them about ADHD issues, such as letting them know about ADHD Awareness Month, can be effective.

Each October around the world is set aside to observe and celebrate ADHD Awareness Month. ADHD Awareness Month started in 2004 as National Attention Deficit Day, established with a resolution from the U.S. Senate. The ADHD Awareness Month Coalition consists of leading organizations that are devoted to providing information, advocacy, and support for individuals, families, and professionals affected by ADHD. The purpose of ADHD Awareness Month is to educate people about ADHD by disseminating information that is based on scientific findings, particularly including peer-reviewed research. During each ADHD Awareness Month since 2009, an online virtual event known as the ADHD Awareness Expo has been held, where people can get tips and strategies from experts in the field, engage in twenty-four hour per day chat rooms, and access a showcase of products and services. During ADHD Awareness Month, wearing an orange awareness ribbon is encouraged to signify support for those with the disorder.

In 2010, Janssen-Cilag, a subsidiary of Johnson & Johnson, launched a social-media campaign to raise awareness of people living with ADHD. It is a strategic and targeted awareness campaign aimed at those either living with or treating ADHD. The Janssen-Cilag awareness campaign includes an animated film, *Living with ADHD*, created by Story Worldwide and shot through the eyes of a child with ADHD to help dispel many of the misconceptions about the disorder.

GENETIC SCREENING

Genetic screening, also more commonly referred to as DNA testing, is a technique to identify and diagnosis individuals with vulnerabilities to inherited conditions, including ADHD. Genetic screening involves biochemical, molecular, and other analyses, including family history questionnaires, to predict who may be at risk for having or transmitting certain conditions. Genetic tests on blood, saliva, and other tissues can be used to find out if individuals carry genes for specific diseases and if they might pass risks on. Results could be used for family planning and to test for disorders before they arise by identifying those at risk who should receive focused prevention and early intervention options.

Availability of genetic screening services and genomic technologies is constantly evolving. Unfortunately, risks, benefits, and costs of these approaches raise many complex moral issues, and, thus, our collective societal values need considerable public and professional debate before consensus is reached. Potential for discrimination, denial of insurance coverage, and psychological effects are some of the major concerns.

As ADHD appears to be a disorder of complex, multifactorial inheritance, caused by interplay of genetic, behavioral, and environmental factors, it is unclear how useful genetic screening will be. Genetic screening is recognized as a secondary prevention strategy, as it identifies the risks for conditions before they develop. The DNA of many individuals with ADHD appears to have multiple copy-number variants—these are missing or duplicated chunks of DNA, particularly in areas of chromosomes that are implicated in related neurodevelopmental disorders such as autism or schizophrenia. Genetic screening for ADHD has a high degree of uncertainty, particularly as the disorder has many nongenetic factors. Individuals are faced with complex decisions related to screening; how to interpret the results; and what actions, if any, to take based on what are often somewhat indeterminate results.

WAYS TO HELP PREVENT ADHD

There are many ways to help prevent ADHD. Prevention, including delay in the onset, of ADHD is important, as earlier onset is a leading determinant of adverse long-term clinical and functional outcomes. It is highly desirable to be proactive and identify and intervene with modifiable risk factors before ADHD or related conditions manifest. Ways to prevent ADHD, including healthy lifestyle choices such as developing proper habits for sleep, diet, and hydration, can contribute substantially to achieving these goals. Effective mobilization of resources before problems actually surface can be one of the most effective approaches to preventing ADHD and related conditions.

It is understood that stress isn't always bad in our lives. In fact, Hans Selye, a pioneer of stress research, reminded us that the only time we are without stress is when we are dead. However, it is also true that too much stress can create problems, including anger, anxiety, depression, headaches, mood changes, and sleep problems. All of these are often experienced by many people with ADHD, and too much stress only makes them more problematic. Further, one can learn to deal productively with stress, as it is, fundamentally, a nonspecific response of the body to any demands made upon it. Much of how it affects us has to do with how we filter stressors and how we react to them. Being optimistic and focusing on positive outcomes turn most stressors into opportunities to grow and improve.

Nutrition

Nutritional therapy can be highly effective in preventing and managing ADHD, and many parents of children with ADHD have willingly tried it. Maintaining body weight through proper nutrition and regular physical activity helps prevent certain comorbid conditions recognized as having a high association with ADHD, such as obesity and diabetes. Vegetarian diets have been suggested to help prevent or minimize ADHD symptoms. The Feingold diet, which focuses on the elimination of food additives and other nutritional components that are suspected of promoting, or at least increasing, the likelihood of ADHD, has been widely promoted. However, research is far from conclusive as to efficacy of such regimens for both the prevention and management of ADHD symptoms.

Taking nutritional supplements like melatonin may help improve sleep problems for those who are taking ADHD psychostimulants. Vitamin D is essential for the nervous system to transmit messages from the brain to the rest of the body. B-complex vitamins are essential for supporting the brain and nervous system and improving focus and may also reduce aggression and antisocial behaviors. Vitamin B3, or niacin, helps nerves function appropriately; vitamin B6 is believed to increase dopamine in the brain to improve alertness; and vitamin B12 helps improve energy levels and cellular function. B vitamins also help with processing and metabolizing carbohydrates and other critical functions. Inositol, part of the vitamin-B complex, has been shown to have calming properties for ADHD brains. Picamilon is a nutritional supplement that is a combination formulation of the B vitamin niacin and GABA and appears to enhance blood flow to the brain and also has stimulant effects.

Mineral supplements can help prevent and manage ADHD symptoms. Low iron levels are associated with cognitive deficits and with severe ADHD symptomology, which makes sense, since adequate levels of iron are essential for the production of dopamine. Magnesium seems to have a calming effect on the brain, while zinc aids in the synthesis of dopamine and further assists with reducing impulsivity.

Spices also help prevent and manage ADHD symptoms. Parsley, sage, rosemary, and thyme, for instance, help with memory, and cinnamon is said to boost attention. Preliminary research suggests that saffron may be as effective as methylphenidate for treating ADHD.

Herbs are sometimes suggested. Passionflower is recommended to calm children with ADHD. *Rhodiola rosea* is said to improve accuracy, alertness, and attention, while valerian and lemon balm can help individuals with ADHD relax. St. John's wort helps with depression. Pycnogenol, which is rich in antioxidant polyphenols that protect our brains from free radicals, is an extract made from French maritime pine bark that is thought to lessen hyperactivity and improve attention, concentration, and visual-motor coordination. Herbal remedies, omega-3 fish oils, and other nutritional approaches, such as gluten-free diets, have been suggested, but additional evidence-based research is necessary before legitimate recommendations can be made.

The consumption of balanced diets with appropriate caloric intake is critical, as the human brain utilizes about one-fifth of the total energy consumed by the body. Well-balanced diets can decrease, if not even completely eliminate, the amount of ADHD medicines required to achieve therapeutic results. High-protein diets, such as those that include lean meat, fish, beans, eggs, cheese, soy, and nuts, particularly in the morning and for afternoon snacks, may improve concentration and help some medications have longer duration of action. Amino acids in proteins provide building blocks for our neurotransmitter substances, the imbalances in which are so critical to the emergence of ADHD. High-protein and -fiber diets also help prevent spiking and plummeting in blood-sugar levels, which can manifest in the hyperactive behaviors that are so characteristic of ADHD.

Exercise

Regular physical activity promotes blood flow, strengthens muscles, improves flexibility, restores muscle tone and balance, enhances immune-system effectiveness, stimulates metabolic functioning, and promotes overall health. The benefits associated with exercise assist in preventing and managing ADHD. Research indicates that the brains of those who regularly exercise have more gray matter, which is important, as it equates to greater processing power. Exercise has been conclusively demonstrated to activate the reward center in the prefrontal cortex, thereby providing motivation to focus. It has been suggested that engaging in physical activity triggers the release of the brain-derived neurotropic factor that helps maintain healthy neurons and promotes maintenance of cognitive factors, such as attention, memory, and processing time and have been shown to directly correlate with rates of learning. Regular exercise, accordingly, improves concentration, focus, and even stimulates genesis of new neurons. Exercise improves functioning in the hippocampus, the center of memory storage. Regular physical activity also enhances functioning of the locus coeruleus, making us less irritable as a consequence.

Regular physical activity not only reduces the risks of neurodegenerative diseases but can also prevent or at least slow down the course of certain disorders, including ADHD. Exercise helps improve many factors associated with the prevention of ADHD, including energy level, sleep, sense of well-being, and brain health. Regular exercise reduces the risks for developing depression, anxiety, and many other disorders, including, of course, the neurodevelopmental disorder of ADHD.

Many physical activities grant health benefits. Tai chi, a traditional Chinese practice consisting of gentle, slow, controlled movements, for example, increases flexibility and concentration. Likewise, diverse schools of yoga that are practiced in India have been used to achieve mind-body balance and promote more pervasive relaxation and concentration. Walking is a simple and yet effective exercise; individuals who walk at least one mile each day have more gray matter than those who don't. Dancing has been shown to increase hippocampal volumes, associated with learning and memory, and serves as a promising prevention strategy that enhances mental functioning. There are many other physical therapeutic techniques and corrective exercises that could enhance physical and emotional health, while improving focus and concentration. The important point to recognize is that any form of physical activity that is engaged in on a regular basis will engender these same sorts of positive changes that have been identified as helping prevent ADHD.

One of the highly desirable consequences of engaging in physical exercise is in becoming calmer and more focused. Other benefits are derived from regular physical exercise that could help prevent, as well as manage, ADHD symptoms and promote overall health. Regular use of cardiovascular, strength, and flexibility exercises improves physical and psychological health and reduces, if not entirely eliminates, the need for medications. However, the wrong types of activity, such as those requiring hyperflexion of the knees, or any form of exercise that is performed improperly, can lead to injury. Professional guidance is always recommended.

The commonly used punishment of denying participation in recess is contraindicated for students with ADHD, as such restriction may exacerbate ADHD symptoms. Any teacher who has had students with ADHD will readily tell you that they were much calmer and more focused after recess. Our understanding of the evidence at this point further indicates that if individuals engage in regular physical activity at any age, but particularly at younger ages, this may even help reduce the incidence of the neurodevelopmental disorder of ADHD.

Biofeedback

Biofeedback is a therapeutic approach using specialized equipment that amplifies body signals to teach gaining better conscious control over involuntary physiological functions such as heart rate, blood pressure, blood and saliva serum levels, muscular tension, respiration, sweating, and surface skin temperature. Clinical biofeedback is based on individuals using their minds to consciously control what is happening inside their bodies to better control themselves, their emotions, and their overall states of health, all of which could contribute to preventing ADHD.

Electromyographic biofeedback uses equipment to monitor muscle tension to selectively and effectively relax areas of intense muscular tension, such as the forehead, jaw, neck, or back, which can lessen stress, including that associated with anxiety disorders, depression, and headaches. Similarly, electrocardiogram biofeedback measures the electrical activity of the heart, particularly with respect to frequency and amplitude of heartbeats. Electroencephalographic biofeedback, known as neurofeedback, utilizes monitoring equipment to measure brain-wave activity and can help prevent and manage conditions such as ADHD, seizure disorders, or epilepsy.

The goal is to help someone with ADHD learn to increase levels of alpha and theta waves, which cycle, respectively, at 7–14 waves per second and 0.5–4 per second, and lower beta wave activity, which is associated with stress and cycles at more than 15 waves per second. Similarly, galvanic skin response, known as electrodermal activity, is a biofeedback technique used to monitor sweating, a physiological response that is associated with stress-related conditions such as anxiety. Biofeedback devices typically provide auditory or visual feedback to help someone learn to voluntarily gain control over basic autonomic physiological processes. Unfortunately, respective biofeedback techniques take time and practice to master, and require equipment that can be expensive and challenging to interpret and maintain.

There are other closely related approaches similar to biofeedback techniques that have been advocated for preventing and helping with ADHD. Use of an interactive metronome has been recommended to improve planning and sequencing, which are common deficiencies in ADHD. A related technique is integrative sensory training, which is intended to stimulate neuronal connections to help the brain better organize itself to cope with overwhelming incoming sensory stimuli, which is common with ADHD. Accordingly, the thinking is that if these sorts of techniques were introduced and mastered prior to the initial appearance of ADHD, they could help prevent it from occurring. More generally, they could be helpful in reducing the severity of symptoms and helping individuals learn to better manage ADHD.

Relaxation

Relaxation approaches, such as guided imagery, meditation, and progressive muscle relaxation (PMR), are designed to reduce stress. These not only help individuals learn to consciously relax specific groups of muscles to attain calmer, more restful mental states, but also reduce stress hormones, like cortisol, epinephrine, and norepinephrine. PMR, as pioneered by Herbert Benson, is a systematic, progressive technique of tensing and relaxing respective muscle groups, usually beginning in the lower extremities and working up to the head, to achieve neuromuscular homeostasis for relaxation and rejuvenation.

Meditation produces heightened mind-body inner focus and peaceful, concentrated levels of awareness to maintain attention and focus by increasing frontal lobe activity. Relaxation approaches include yoga, autogenic training, rhythmic breathing practices, transcendental meditation, mindfulness meditation, and visualization exercises. Since most of these help one achieve deeper contemplation states, they lower blood pressure, slow metabolism, and lessen anxiety, all of which are helpful with ADHD to make one less distractible and better able to sustain focus and attention. Relaxation techniques help someone systematically reach balanced homeostatic physiological states that are essentially opposite to the generalized stress response. Several approaches to relaxation therapy have been demonstrated to reduce anxiety. Meditating, for example, appears to increase the ability to maintain focus and concentration. This, in turn, leads to decreased frequencies and severities of respective ADHD symptoms, which may not only help prevent ADHD but also assist in reducing, if not eliminating, the need for ADHD medicines in those who actually develop it.

LIFESTYLE CHOICES

Lifestyle choices help determine the extent to which we all will live with health or disease. For prevention of ADHD and general optimal health, it is ideal to strive for coherent and comprehensive lifestyles. A lifestyle is, fundamentally, a compilation of choices made throughout one's life. Individuals who acquire habits that can be characterized as making healthier lifestyle choices are far less likely to experience the negative behaviors that ultimately lead to an ADHD diagnosis.

Lifestyle choices an individual's parents, siblings, grandparents, and earlier ancestors made all contribute to the chances an individual will or will not have ADHD. It is important to recognize that genes work differently in different environments. A fetus whose mother was persistently stressed during gestation could be exposed to higher cortisol and other stress-related hormone levels, and epigenetic changes altering the amygdala could make him or her more hyperactive when growing up. Even the individuals one or both of your parents associated with, if they were adventurous and risk takers and perhaps more likely to have a genetic predisposition for ADHD, could have altered your risk for ADHD as they were, by association, more likely to be selected as partners.

Healthy prenatal and infancy care are important in preventing ADHD. This care, of course, includes healthy nutritional choices. Omega-3 fatty acid levels in pregnant women and breastfeeding women are related to better brain development in offspring, thereby helping to prevent ADHD. Reducing infant exposure to foods with heavy pesticide levels and to foods with artificial colorings and other artificial ingredients is important. Reducing the unnecessary use of antibiotics during childhood contributes to preventing ADHD, as intestinal flora produce more neurotransmitters than our brains do. Excessive antibiotics during childhood, resulting in impaired intestinal health, is a recognized risk factor for ADHD.

The intense emotional feelings many with ADHD routinely experience can be effectively prevented with a few simple strategies. Often the crises come from overcommitting, since novel things seem more appealing to an ADHD brain. Making fewer commitments in the first place and not being afraid to back out when begin to feel overwhelmed can minimize the pressures. Getting enough sleep permits all of us to remain positive and be less reactive. Engaging in regular physical activity has been shown to increase neurotransmitter levels to help us maintain equilibrium. Untreated comorbid conditions make it more difficult to establish emotional control. For example, about 30 percent of individuals with ADHD have had a depressive episode. Planning ahead for how to cope with situations we know will be emotionally difficult makes them less evocative. When feelings begin to bubble up, it is helpful to step back and take a quick break to regroup. It can be reassuring to remember that however bad something feels in the moment, it will dissipate with time. By proactively learning and internalizing these sorts of practices into their daily lives, individuals will be less likely to experience many of the characteristic negative symptoms and traumatic incidents that typically lead to pursuing an ADHD diagnostic evaluation.

Sleep

Restful sleep, the physiological state of relative unconsciousness and relative inaction of voluntary muscles, is essential for optimal health, yet it is a common problem for many with ADHD. The reticular activating system of the brain stem, partially responsible for regulating sleep-wake cycles, tends to be less effective in ADHD brains. Circadian rhythms in those with ADHD skew toward higher activity levels in the evenings, pushing back the time they go to bed and making it more difficult to wake in the mornings. Our attention and ability to concentrate and focus lessen as we sleep less. Mental function is less effective in those who regularly don't have normal, restful sleep. Maintaining regular sleep routines, such as going to bed and waking up at the same times each day, helps our brains work best at any age.

Sleep disorders are relatively common, with 8–18 percent of the general population being dissatisfied with sleep, and 6–10 percent diagnosed with insomnia disorder. The National Sleep Foundation says that up to 80 percent of adolescents don't get sufficient sleep. Having a sleep disorder is predictive of psychiatric symptoms, including those associated with ADHD. In fact, the DSM-III actually included moving about excessively while sleeping as one of the diagnostic symptoms for ADHD.

Many individuals with ADHD tend to sleep poorly and get less sleep than neurotypicals. Drinking caffeinated beverages, including soda, or alcoholic beverages before going to bed can disrupt sleep patterns. Insufficient sleep or sleep disorders exacerbate ADHD and can also lead to other negative health consequences, such as cancer, diabetes, heart disease, hypertension, obesity, and mood disorders. Poor sleep adversely effects mood and alertness. In some cases, treating sleep problems may be enough to resolve hyperactivity and attention difficulties. Inadequate sleep can cause not only inattention but can also lead to more procrastination, forgetfulness, and other symptoms that are easily mistaken for ADHD.

Following a few simple strategies can make it less likely that one will become sleep-deprived. Establishing and sticking to a specific, realistic bedtime increases the likelihood of feeling well-rested. Having a regular pre-bed routine can also help prime one for a more restful night of sleep. Making sure the bedroom is dark—not only turning off the lights but also shutting curtains or blinds and blocking the light and noise from all electronic devices, such as phones, clocks, and computers—removes potentially disruptive stimuli. Keeping the bedroom temperature a bit cooler encourages snuggling under the blankets. A tidy, uncluttered sleeping environment also helps promote more restful conditions.

Regularly getting deep, rejuvenating sleep reduces the chances that the characteristic ADHD symptoms appear in the first place, thus effectively preventing the disorder from occurring. The amount of deep, delta sleep has been highly correlated to performance on memory tests in both children and senior citizens.

It should be acknowledged that there is individual variation with respect to chronotypes—that is, differences among individuals with sleep timing. Morning types, for instance, tend to sleep less on the weekends, while evening types tend to exhibit longer sleep latencies. Further, "morning-ness" seems associated with agreeableness, conscientiousness, and extra-version, while "eveningness" is more associated with neuroticism and openness to experience. Relationships between personality factors and sleep behavior should be considered when working with individuals who might develop ADHD or are trying to manage ADHD symptoms.

Diet

Proper diet is important to all, including those who have ADHD or are at risk for developing it. Although the research is not entirely conclusive, many studies have examined the role of nutritional factors, such as relative levels of sugar, dietary fiber, and food additives, as well as pesticides in the foods and beverages that are consumed in contributing to the cause or continuation of selected ADHD symptoms. Sugars include disaccharides and monosaccharides that have been added to foods and beverages and natural sugars, such as those in fruit, milk, honey, and syrups. Low glyce-mic foods help to furnish steady sugar flows, making it easier for someone with ADHD to control behaviors and improve performance. Conversely, peaks and steep drops in blood-sugar levels only increase the likelihood that an individual will be hyperactive and, consequently, develop ADHD, or at least be evaluated for it.

Nutritional supplements, as discussed earlier, can be helpful in prevent-ing this. For instance, omega-3 fatty acids reduce inflammation and improve mood, which would be clearly helpful in ADHD. They also appear to help cognitive skills, such as focus and concentration. Omega-3s also help regulate triglyceride levels and slow the progression of atherosclero-sis. There are three main omega-3 fatty acids: alpha-linolenic acid (ALA), eicosapentaenoic acid (EPA), and docosahexaenoic acid (DHA). It is rec-ommended that individuals with ADHD eat diets that are rich in omega-3s or take supplements with at least two to three times more EPA than DHA, as these ratios seem more effective in ameliorating ADHD symptoms, par-ticularly aggression and mood swings. Omega-3s taken in phospholipid formulations and those that attach phosphatidylserine to omega-3s (PS-Omega-3s) seem to foster greater decrease of symptoms relative to those in triglyceride formulations. It is understood that low omega-3 levels increase risk for ADHD, and it is thought that omega-3 fatty acids are degraded faster by those with ADHD. Certain foods are better sources of certain omega-3s—for example, flaxseeds and broccoli are particularly good sources of ALA, while seaweed is a good source of both EPA and DHA. Mackerel, tuna, and salmon are good general sources, as are lignans, which also reduce free radicals, which helps keep neurons healthy.

Other nutritional supplements can be helpful, such as magnesium to aid with relaxation and sleep, and zinc to reduce impulsivity and hyperactivity.

Maintaining healthy human biomes is essential to benefit from well-balanced diets. The activity of the hundred trillion microorganisms inhabiting our gastrointestinal tracts impacts the health of our brains. Human biota, and particularly dietary supportive bacteria, such as Lactobacilli and Bifidobacterium, aid in digestion and nutrient absorption and produce many neurotransmitters that are essential for brains. High-fiber diets help maintain healthy microbiomes. Reducing refined starches and sugars is also beneficial. The absorption of vitamins A, C, K, certain B-complex vitamins, and other essential nutrients is enhanced by the activity of probiotic bacteria.

Hydration

Dehydration affects the ability to concentrate and impairs memory. It is correlated with fatigue and mood swings. As little as 1 percent dehydration adversely affects your attention, memory, mood, and motor coordination. Approximately 55–65 percent of the human body, 83 percent of blood, and 70–80 percent of the brain consists of water. The average human needs to replace eighty-one fluid ounces (2.4 liters) of water each day. When someone gets thirsty, the blood becomes concentrated, and kidneys send less water to the bladder, making urine darker. Dehydration raises body temperature, since we sweat less and heart rate increases to maintain oxygen to the brain and other tissues. Keeping properly hydrated and well-nourished is essential to achieving optimal brain functioning and proper health, including preventing or lessening the effects of ADHD.

9

Issues and Controversies

Many issues and controversies surround ADHD, including overdiagnosis, concern over medicines, the choice to medicate even though other treatments work, medicine misuse, and clinical trials. Criminal justice involvement is controversial, as are policies such as drug scheduling and social stigma.

OVERDIAGNOSIS

ADHD exists along a severity continuum. Thorough evaluation is necessary for diagnosis. Unfortunately, cursory assessments can result in labeling and stigmatizing someone who is not fully manifesting the disorder. Further, it could lead to unnecessary treatment.

There are children and adults diagnosed with ADHD who may not actually have it, and such misdiagnosing could cause overdiagnosis. Conditions with symptoms similar ADHD, if not excluded, could lead to overdiagnosis. For example, iron-deficiency anemia produces impaired cognition, irritability, difficulty concentrating, and short attention spans. These could be mistaken for ADHD. Hypoglycemia and other nutritional deficiencies produce symptoms such as hyperactivity, aggression, difficulty sitting still, or impaired concentration. Children with intellectual disabilities or autism can have limited social skills, appear immature, and have academic difficulties, all of which are ADHD characteristics. Children with autism or sensory disorders can become hyperactive if they are overstimulated. Children with sensory disorders or hearing impairments can seem inattentive and take risks, unaware of the dangers, and be accident prone. After mild absence seizures, children can be disoriented or confused, which can easily be mistaken for ADHD. Hypothyroidism, as well as lead poisoning, can present with impaired memory, diminished concentration, decreased cognitive skills, and poor academic performance. Many factors can cause inattention, even transitory events such as arguing with significant others. These and other phenomena contribute to overdiagnosis.

Another factor contributing to overdiagnosis is immaturity. A study of kindergarteners found that 10 percent of those born in August were diagnosed with ADHD, while only 4.5 percent of those born in September were. Furthermore, those born in August were twice as likely as those in September to get psychostimulants. A study from Iceland found that the youngest third of students in classes was 50 percent more likely to be diagnosed and prescribed psychostimulants.

Many professionals believe that ADHD is actually underdiagnosed. Although ADHD may sometimes be overdiagnosed in children, it is underdiagnosed in adults, and particularly in older adults. An estimated 20–30 percent of psychiatric patients diagnosed with anxiety, depression, or substance use probably also have ADHD. Many adults with psychiatric disorders also have ADHD. Comorbid ADHD is often unrecognized, or at least undertreated. It is difficult to make a differential diagnoses of adult ADHD, since symptoms overlap with other conditions. Additionally, current DSM-5 criteria make it difficult to conduct appropriate diagnoses, as symptoms might be accounted for by various disorders. Further, many adults are unable to provide evidence of childhood symptoms.

ADHD is often comorbid with conditions like anxiety, impulse control, mood, and substance disorders. ADHD can impact the expression of comorbidities, making it difficult to comply with treatment. Unrecognized ADHD can be mistaken for a poor treatment response, typical of several comorbidities. This underscores the importance of managing ADHD appropriately, typically by prescribing ADHD medicines. This generally helps stabilize daily functioning and leads to recovery.

CONTROVERSIAL USE OF ADHD MEDICATIONS

Concerns have been raised about many people, particularly children, taking medicines for ADHD before they are fully diagnosed. Medicines have been administered to treat what we now call ADHD since 1937, when Bradley used Benzedrine for children with behavioral problems.

Methylphenidate, first synthesized in 1944 and better known as Ritalin, was approved in 1955 for hyperkinetic behaviors, as ADHD was then called. By the mid-1950s, it was prescribed for depression, lethargy, and narcolepsy. Since the mid-1960s, it has been used for ADHD. Methylphenidate increases the abilities of those with ADHD to focus attention and reduce disruptions and impulsivity. From 1985 to 1995, methylphenidate production increased almost eightfold in the United States, reaching over ten tons annually. By 1995, around 6 million prescriptions were written annually for methylphenidate, and 2.5 million U.S. children were taking it. The United States then accounted for over 90 percent of the production and consumption of methylphenidate. From 1990 to 2005, the U.S. production of Ritalin increased sixfold. In 2004, 29 million U.S. psychostimulant prescriptions were written. Of these, 14.5 million were for methylphenidate.

The United Nations (UN) issued a warning in 1996 about the widespread use of methylphenidate for treating what was then called ADD. They noted a special interest group of parents received substantial contributions from the main U.S. Ritalin manufacturer. Since then, other groups of parents and physicians campaigned against Ritalin and related medicines, citing dangers such as abuse, dependence, and other long-term problems. Questions have been raised about the long-term efficacy. Studies of Adderall failed to find reliable improvements on cognitive ability, even though subjects reported feeling that their academic performance was enhanced. Many parents, physicians, and others contend that medicines have been used safely, with many benefits and improved quality of life. For instance, 70–80 percent of children diagnosed with ADHD demonstrate improved attention span, improved on-task behavior, and reduced impulsivity while taking psychostimulants.

In the 1990s, around 1–3 percent of U.S. school-aged children were taking psychostimulants for ADHD. Over eleven million psychostimulant prescriptions were written in the United States annually. The global use of ADHD medicines rose threefold from 1993 to 2003. Taking inflation into account, spending on ADHD medicines increased ninefold, reaching $2.4 billion by 2003. Although use of ADHD medicines and spending on them rose in developing and developed countries, the United States, Canada, and Australia had greater than predicted increases in use and spending, due mainly to more expensive, longer-acting formulations.

There have been dramatic increases in prescriptions for ADHD medicines. Of the approximately 6.4 million U.S. children diagnosed with ADHD, about half take medication. There were 49.1 million U.S. prescriptions for ADHD medicines in 2015—a 21 percent increase over 2008. In 2010, 46 percent of prescriptions for ADHD medicines were for those aged twenty and older, 42 percent more than in 2008. Prescriptions for adults with ADHD increased 53.5 percent from 2008 to 2012. The largest increases were in females aged twenty-six to thirty-four, which increased 86 percent. There was a 32 percent increase in 2015 over 2008 for ADHD prescriptions for men aged twenty to fifty-nine. Over the same period, there was a 38 percent rise in prescriptions for same-aged women. In 2015, 8.2 million prescriptions were for men, and 11.4 million were for women aged twenty to fifty-nine.

The more ADHD medicines that are available, the more likely it is that they will be abused. Associations between availability and abuse have been demonstrated for many drugs, including alcohol, nicotine, and opioids. Further, over one-third of those legally who are receiving ADHD medicines have been asked to trade or sell them to those without prescriptions. Over 4.2 million individuals are currently prescribed ADHD psychostimulants. While over 19 million legal U.S. prescriptions for amphetamines were filled in 2000, increases in nonprescription psychostimulants was a greater problem.

WHY MEDICATE IF OTHER TREATMENTS WORK?

ADHD medicines don't work for some people, but they work for most individuals most of the time. However, their initial use isn't always successful. A particular medicine or its dose may be the problem, both of which can be adjusted through trial and error, with proper monitoring. Expectations may be unrealistic, both by patients and, more often, their parents. Psychoeducation usually handles this.

There is reluctance to prescribe and use ADHD medicines, particularly psychostimulants, despite studies that show their safety and efficacy. Not everyone with ADHD will necessarily experience the same results taking the same medication, nor should everyone necessarily need medication. Treatment approaches are different and varied. Discussing treatment options with health care providers is important.

Medicine to treat ADHD is generally recommended, but it may not fully address underlying reasons on its own. Its use generally keeps symptoms under control while other treatments are introduced. Medicines that can be part of ADHD treatment include psychostimulants, such as amphetamines, methamphetamine, and methylphenidate. Other medicines that are used to reduce and manage ADHD symptoms include antihypertensives, anticonvulsants, eugeroics, and cholinergics. All the psychostimulants mentioned above have FDA approval for ADHD. Several nonstimulants were FDA approved in 2003 for ADHD, including atomoxetine, clonidine, and guanfacine. Most other medicines are used off-label.

If ADHD medicines are working properly, most people will experience sustained focus, improved mood, less impulsivity, better memory, better attention to details, and even better sleep. However, if individuals don't feel these improvements, or if they experience side effects, such as headaches, nausea, or loss of appetite, they should talk with their health care providers.

Although ADHD medicines are recommended as first-line treatments in the United States for children above preschool age, this is not the case in other countries. Practice guidelines in the European Union and other places state that ADHD medicines should be used only if behavioral therapies are first tried and found insufficient. The American Academy of Pediatrics and American Psychological Association recommend behavioral therapy as a front-line treatment for young children aged two to five before medication. This, unfortunately, isn't always done, and younger children are routinely prescribed off-label use of myriad medicines, including atypical antipsychotics and other potent medicines, before behavioral therapies are attempted.

ADHD Medications Don't Work for Everybody

Unfortunately, ADHD medicines don't work for everyone, as individuals respond differently. A medicine that effectively resolves symptoms in one person may not help another. Physiological and medical differences change how medicines work in one person and vary in others.

There sometimes are differences between brand-name and generic formulations of ADHD medicines. These may be only minimal, but, as everyone is somewhat different, one version may not digest or work the same as another for some people. Finding the right medication that works optimally, if at all, is key to the appropriate treatment of ADHD.

MISUSE OF ADHD MEDICATIONS

ADHD medicines are misused by many people for often similar reasons. ADHD medicines are most commonly misused by those wanting to stay awake, study, and improve school or work performance. Another frequent reason is appetite suppression to lose weight. Some misuse them to get "high." Psychostimulants, eugeroics, and cholinergics are the most likely to be misused, but others also can be.

The Drug Abuse Warning Network (DAWN) monitors drug-related hospital emergency visits. DAWN reported emergency visits for ADHD psychostimulants increased 234 percent from 13,379 in 2005 to 31,244 in 2010. While emergency visits for psychostimulants among males nearly doubled from 9,059 in 2005 to 17,174 in 2010, they rose even more among females, going up 326 percent from 4,315 in 2005 to 14,068 in 2010.

DAWN reported that the most significant increase in emergency-room visits for psychostimulants was in adults eighteen and older. Although visits for psychostimulants among children under eighteen years of age didn't significantly increase from 2005 to 2010, there were modest increases. For five- to eleven-year-olds, emergency-room visits rose from 3,322 in 2005 to 3,791 visits in 2010, and, for twelve- to seventeen-year-olds, they rose from 2,702 in 2005 to 3,461 in 2010.

Between 2005 and 2010, increases in emergency-room visits for ADHD psychostimulants among adults, as noted, were statistically significant. For those eighteen to twenty-five, visits rose from 2,131 in 2005 to 8,148 in 2010; for twenty-six- to thirty-four-year-olds, they rose from 1,754 in 2005 to 6,094 in 2010; and for those thirty-five and older, they increased from 2,519 in 2005 to 7,957 in 2010. Emergency-room visits for psychostimulants involving nonmedical misuse significantly increased from 5,212 in 2005 to 15,585 in 2010. This nonmedical misuse accounted for half of all U.S. emergency-room visits for ADHD psychostimulants. Additionally, nearly one-third (29 percent) involved adverse reactions.

Of 31,244 visits for psychostimulants in 2010, one-quarter involved the use of one other drug, and nearly two-fifths (38 percent) involved two or more. Drug combinations also involved many nonstimulant ADHD medicines. In 2010, 8,083 (26 percent) visits involved the misuse of psychostimulants plus an anti-anxiety or insomnia medicine, such as eugeroics. There were also 3,199 (10 percent) visits involving misuse of psychostimulants and antidepressants; 2,050 (7 percent) visits involving psychostimulants and antipsychotics, and 1,150 (4 percent) visits involving psychostimulants and anticonvulsants.

About one of every five U.S. college students between the ages of eighteen and twenty-five misuses ADHD psychostimulants. Male college students with slightly lower grade point averages than non-misusers are the most likely to misuse an ADHD medicine, and are likely juggling academics, work, and their social lives, suggesting that they are coping with multiple tasks and responsibilities. Similarly, one of every seven nonstudents the same age also misuses ADHD psychostimulants. The most commonly misused psychostimulants by this group are those prescribed for ADHD, mostly combination amphetamine formulations (Adderall), methylphenidate (Ritalin), and lisdextroamphetamine (Vyvanse). Nearly 50 percent of U.S. college students reported misuse of ADHD psychostimulants to improve academic performance. Around 33 percent of young adults believed these would help them get better grades or be more competitive in school, athletics, or work. Around 40 percent of U.S. young adults said they misused psychostimulants to stay awake, while 25 percent reported misuse to improve work performance. There are numerous anecdotal reports of high school and college students using psychostimulants at times of academic deadlines, such as during midterms and finals. Sporadic misuse, particularly at times of high stress, results not only in sleep deprivation, but in susceptibility to paranoia and hallucinations.

Many adverse consequences are associated with ADHD medicine misuse. In addition to physiological side effects, those who misuse these medications experience other consequences. They may not normally develop coping skills, such as time-management and study skills, which are essential to having a fulfilling, healthy, and happy life. Someone who uses medicines without prescriptions or sells or shares Schedule-II drugs may be committing a felony. Some colleges and universities consider ADHD medicine misuse cheating, resulting in probation, suspension, or dismissal. There are indications that nonmedical use of ADHD medicines may not result in higher grades. College students with B or lower grade point averages are nearly twice as likely to report nonmedical use of ADHD psychostimulants than those with B+ or higher grade point averages.

ADHD MEDICATIONS USED AS STUDY AIDS

It isn't surprising that using ADHD psychostimulants is slightly higher among college students than same age noncollege peers, as they are commonly used to stay alert and awake, complete assignments, and study. Full-time college students are nearly twice as likely as non-full-time students to use amphetamines. These substances are frequently used for euphoric and energizing effects. College students who used amphetamines are nearly three times as likely to use marijuana, five times as likely to use painkillers, and eight times as likely to use tranquilizers.

Sharing and Misuse in High School and College

"Monitoring the Future" is a federally sponsored, annual survey of U.S. secondary-school students, college students, and young adults, examining behaviors, attitudes, and values related to alcohol, tobacco, and other drugs, including ADHD medicines. Over fifty thousand questionnaires are completed annually by students and young adults, comprising representative samples of same-age Americans.

In 2012, U.S. high school and college students and noncollege young adults all reported similar annual prevalence rates of illicit drugs, about 18 percent. However, by 2014, college student illicit drug use exceeded that of twelfth graders, largely attributable to college students' greater use of nonprescribed amphetamines. Nonprescribed amphetamine use rose among college students, increasing from 5.8 percent in 2008 to 11.1 percent in 2012, but it hasn't risen since, reported at 9.7 percent in 2015.

In 1999, the first time the survey asked about methamphetamine use separately from other psychostimulants, 4.7 percent of high school seniors reported use within the previous year. By 2009, that declined to 1.2 percent, and to 0.6 percent by 2015.

Amphetamine use is higher among U.S. college students than same-age noncollege adults. In 2015, annual prevalence rates of amphetamines among college students was 9.7 percent, but it was 8.1 percent for noncollege adults. Annual use of nonprescription Adderall was higher, at 10.7 percent, for college compared to noncollege respondents, at 7.1 percent, and this has been consistent for over five years. In 2016, past year non-medical Adderall use remained stable at 6.2 percent for U.S. twelfth graders—the same rate reported in 2015—but it decreased to 5.5 percent in 2017. Ritalin use was the same, at 2.0 percent for both college and noncollege respondents, and this decreased to 1.3 percent in 2017. In 2015, nonprescribed Adderall use was reported by more than five times as many U.S. college students as Ritalin was. It seems likely that this increased use is to improve academic performance.

Perceived harmfulness questions for Adderall were added to young-adult surveys in 2012. Results indicated that the perceived risk of using Adderall once or twice was 30 percent. The perceived risk of occasional Adderall use reached 35.9 percent among twenty-five- to thirty-year-olds by 2014, while perceived harmfulness of taking Adderall occasionally remained at 44–45 percent among twenty-seven- to thirty-year-olds from 2012 to 2015. In 2016, when eighth graders were asked if occasional non-medical Adderall use is harmful, meaning there is a "great risk" associated with it, 35.8 percent said "yes," increasing from 32 percent in 2015.

CLINICAL TRIALS OF MEDICATIONS

Clinical trials are how new drugs, including ADHD medicines, are evaluated. This system has four major phases that new pharmaceuticals must pass through to become available. Clinical trials assure confidence in safety and efficacy.

Clinical trials evaluate if medical techniques are effective. They have protocols that describe how testing will be conducted and justify each step. Trials furnish information about which pharmaceuticals or other interventions should be investigated further, with more rigorous studies. Approximately eighty thousand industry- and federal-sponsored trials are conducted annually in the United States, using five to six thousand different protocols, conducted at over ten thousand locations.

Trials evaluate the safety and effectiveness of new treatments and medicines, compared to existing ones or to current standards of care. Studies typically involve human subjects testing safety and effectiveness. However, not all trials necessarily assess safety and efficacy. Some are fundamentally diagnostic, determining better ways to diagnose, which could include symptoms like hyperactivity in children with autism who may or may not have comorbid ADHD. Screening trials look for the best ways to detect conditions, and preventative trials examine ways to prevent conditions, such as ADHD after maternal alcohol drinking during pregnancy. Other trials are to improve quality of life for those with conditions, including ADHD. Trials with different purposes have different research designs.

Trials are intended to examine an intervention or set of interventions and can be considered interventional studies. Interventions could be new medicines or devices or involve different dosages or ways to use these, such as ADHD medicine that is administered through a transdermal patch rather than in pill form, or they could involve lifestyle changes, such as diet, exercise, or caffeine use. Observational studies are another type of trial.

Trials are prospective, not retrospective, in design—that is, they propose intended effects; establish testing; and assess results to determine if they support the hypothesis positively, negatively, or unclearly. The dependent variable is the study outcome, such as the effects of medicines on ADHD. When selecting samples of individuals with ADHD for clinical trials, it must be remembered that they aren't homogenous, so procedures should be used to select representative samples. Certain subgroups might need to be reduced or expanded to increase representativeness.

It takes up to twenty years and $800 million to bring drugs from discovery to marketing. It takes about ten years of testing in test tubes and with animal subjects before drugs are ready for human testing. Only about one of every fifty drugs that are undergoing preclinical testing will be considered safe and effective for human testing.

Critiques of Clinical Trials

Numerous criticisms are directed at clinical trials. These include concerns with the influence pharmaceutical and other companies have, particularly with issues such as sample selection, publication, and dissemination.

Critics suggest that many trials are flawed and that the system is not working. Reforms have been called for. Unfortunately, pharmaceutical or related industries control and influence much of the process. They might, for example, use flawed research designs, comparing their drug against a placebo, when there are already perfectly good medicines available. Under such conditions, many medicines would demonstrate higher efficacy than the placebo, which, by definition, should have no therapeutic effect. Anything is likely to have more effect than nothing, which is what a trial against a placebo tests. Another flawed approach is the administration of unusually high or low doses, making it more likely to find side effects or insufficient efficacy.

Another criticism is with concerns over samples. Many trials have limited numbers of subjects, a practice that is generally rationalized by claiming the excessive costs of larger samples. The selected participants may not be representative of the target populations. Relatively young, healthy subjects are commonly selected, even though, if approved, the drug would be used with different individuals.

It isn't surprising that industry-sponsored trials yield positive results. What might be less apparent is the extent to which industries excessively control or influence the eventual publication and dissemination of the studies. They often withhold negative results and can otherwise manipulate factors that are assumed to be neutral.

Selective publication that indicates only positive findings is common. Companies aren't obligated to publish all the results from all trials. Missing results might suggest that the new approach is actually no better, or even worse, than approaches that are already used. This can result in biased research with misleading, and even false-positive, results. Critics report that findings with negative results or even those that are somewhat unflattering are less likely to be disseminated. Unfortunately, the techniques and strategies used by pharmaceutical and related industries to extol their products often go far beyond this.

Some publications are designed and paid for by pharmaceutical companies but appear to be independent academic research journals. These publications are widely disseminated and are often mailed directly to physicians, who may read them, believing they are legitimate scholarly, research journals, when they are merely vehicles marketing pharmaceutical or related products. Articles printed in these publications often claim to report on objective data, but the materials therein naturally promote the pharmaceutical company's products.

Recent Initiatives

The FDA's Center for Drug Evaluation and Research attempted to streamline the review of new approaches. The FDA approved more new medicines in 2014 than in any of the previous twenty years, including approval of 34 percent more drugs in 2014 than in 2013. More than 75 percent of the medicines were approved in their first review cycle, without calls for additional information, as had previously been common. Nearly two-thirds of new pharmaceuticals were approved under the accelerated FDA-approval programs before being approved in other countries.

The FDA has, since the late 1990s, been increasingly requiring pharmaceutical companies to gather safety and efficacy data on drugs that might have pediatric applications. The Safety and Innovations Act was enacted in 2012, requiring the FDA to expand consideration of medicines for use with those aged seventeen and under. The European Medicines Agency, on behalf of the European Commission, developed the Pediatric Regulation, which went into effect on January 26, 2007, and which, like the Safety and Innovations Act, established a system of obligations and incentives, ensuring that medicines would be researched, developed, and authorized for children. Such measures force pharmaceutical companies to consider pediatric applications of the medicines they develop and improve the availability of high-quality medicines for children, including potential ADHD medicines.

RESTRICTIONS ON PSYCHOSTIMULANTS IN THE UNITED STATES

In the United States, restrictions have been established on access to psychostimulants. Initially, individual states, and then the federal government, passed restrictive laws to regulate drug importation and sales. Amphetamines have only been legally available in the United States by prescription since 1956. Many laws were passed as amendments to CSA, placing psychostimulants and other drugs into schedules. Adderall is, for example, listed as a Schedule-II substance.

RESTRICTIONS IN OTHER COUNTRIES

Other countries have passed laws that are similar to CSA and regulate the manufacture and distribution of medicines and control illegal use. The United Kingdom passed the Misuse of Drugs Act in 1971, and Canada passed the Controlled Drugs and Substances Act in 1996, both analogous to CSA. These and similar laws elsewhere were enacted to comply with treaty commitments under agreements like the Single Convention on Narcotic Drugs and the UN Convention Against Illicit Traffic in Narcotic Drugs and Psychotropic Substances.

Many countries passed more narrowly focused laws, addressing issues of use and addiction of psychostimulants. For example, Norway restricts prescribing psychostimulants to those with substance-use disorders and to those in opioid-maintenance programs. The number of amphetamine-like psychostimulants under regulatory control internationally increased fivefold from 1971 to 1995.

CRIMINAL JUSTICE INVOLVEMENT

Individuals with untreated ADHD are more likely to experience criminal justice involvement than those who are properly treated or than neurotypicals. This involvement is escalated for both juveniles and adults including violent and nonviolent crime.

Misuse of psychostimulants, particularly methamphetamine, is related to crime in many ways. The long-term use of methamphetamine at higher dosages than for therapeutic uses, such as for treating ADHD, can result in amphetamine psychosis, which impairs judgment and ability to control anger and frustration, often resulting in violent outbursts that are disproportionate to the context. In Australia, association is commonly made between methamphetamines and severe psychological psychosis. For instance, whenever an illicit purchase for methamphetamine is considered to go wrong, violence and even murder are thought to result. Similarly, whenever a clandestine methamphetamine lab is raided, firearms, explosives, and other weaponry are frequently found.

Methamphetamines are a major illicit drug problem in the United States and globally. Around twelve million Americans have used methamphetamine at least once. Some get methamphetamine by prescription, usually for ADHD, but others do so illicitly. Methamphetamine was supplied for decades in the United States by localized clandestine trafficking and manufacturing operations, initially by Mexican organized criminal groups and motorcycle gangs. Recently, transnational criminal organizations have gained control over the methamphetamine supply.

The National Survey on Drug Use and Health estimates that, annually, about 353,000 Americans aged twelve or older abuse methamphetamine. The DEA estimates the lifetime prevalence of illicit methamphetamine is 4 percent of Americans, but this number varies substantially by ethnicity. Ethnic group reporting the highest levels of methamphetamine use is Native Hawaiians/Pacific Islanders at 2.2 percent, second is multiracial at 1.9 percent, and third Native Americans at 1.7 percent, while rates are lower among others, with Caucasians at 0.7 percent, Asians at 0.2 percent, and blacks at 0.1 percent.

From 1996 to 2008, there was panic about crystal methamphetamine in the United States, which by 2005–2008 shifted to a secondary moral panic over crystal methamphetamine in the gay community and its relationship to HIV/AIDS and the emergence of super-lethal strains. It has been reported that one out of every ten gay men in San Francisco has tried methamphetamine, and gay men in the United States continue to have among the highest HIV rates. There have been similar indications in other countries, such as Australia, where bisexual and gay men report high levels of methamphetamine use, both in powder and crystal forms.

Methamphetamine arrest rates have risen and fallen. In 1996–1997, the rate was reported at 5 percent. It peaked in 2000 and 2001, when it reached 11 percent and has been declining since. Nevertheless, about 9 percent of U.S. teenagers (about 1.9 million) report that they have misused or abused Ritalin or Adderall in the past year.

Around 80 percent of methamphetamine in the United States is made and trafficked by Mexican cartels, with transnational connections. There was a 75 percent increase from 2002 to 2004 in seizures of methamphetamine at ports of entry between Mexico and the United States. Seizures of methamphetamine along the Mexican-U.S. border increased 87 percent in 2007–2009. The Sinaloa Mexican cartel began trafficking methamphetamine to reduce reliance on Columbian cocaine. Methamphetamine from Mexico is currently up to 90 percent purity and less than half the price of competitors.

The psychostimulant drug trade is especially lucrative within prisons. For example, while one-half ounce (14.2 grams) of crystal methamphetamine sells for up to $1,700 on U.S. streets, in prisons the same half-ounce sells for up to $10,000. Prison drug trading is estimated to be worth $300 million per year.

POLICY ISSUES

Numerous policy issues have been explored around ADHD. These include education of those with ADHD, insurance coverage, comorbidities, military service, and regulation of ADHD medicines.

In October 2017, Education Department Secretary Betsy DeVos, in accord with President Trump's Executive Order 13777, rescinded seventy-two policies that helped students with disabilities, including ADHD. Sixty-three of these originated in the Office of Special Education Programs, and the rest dealt with the Rehabilitation Services Administration. Some of these offered clarification of regulations under the Individuals with Disabilities Act (IDEA) to provide public education in the least-restrictive environment. Professionals worry that these changes will make it more difficult for schools to appropriately serve students and for parents to advocate for children's needs.

Some state governments and insurance companies have policies that impact diagnosis and treatment of ADHD. For instance, prior-authorization policies impact treatments, particularly ADHD medicines. In this regard, twenty-seven states currently have policies that manage access to ADHD medications for children. Reimbursement policies impact access to care, but they may or may not guide professionals toward best practices. However, the Mental Health Parity and Addiction Equity Act requires insurance companies to have the same dollar and treatment limits for mental health conditions that they apply to physical conditions.

Policies on diagnosing and treating comorbidities can change. Prior to DSM-5, clinicians were not supposed to simultaneously diagnosis ADHD and autism. Fortunately that has been corrected. While we recognize that about 20 percent of individuals with ADHD will have some form of bipolar spectrum disorder, doctors refrained from prescribing psychostimulants due to fears that they could induce or exacerbate mania. We now recognize that a mood stabilizer should be introduced to minimize the chances of ADHD in mania.

Armed services policies can restrict individuals with ADHD from enlisting in military services—it can bar someone, on a case-by-case basis, from certain military positions or duties. Prior to 2004, a history of ADHD diagnosis or treatment necessitated a special waiver for enlistment. Currently, ADHD is a disqualifying condition if individuals have been treated with ADHD medicines in past year, or if they display significant symptoms such as impulsivity or distractibility. Any ADHD treatment within the previous three years must be documented prior to military medical examinations.

The making and use of patent medicines for hyperactivity and myriad other conditions eventually lead to passage of the Pure Food and Drug Act in 1906. Later concerns, mainly around production and distribution of both legal and illegal drugs, led to drug-related UN conventions. Production and regulation of ADHD medicines and other controlled substances in the United States is conducted, as discussed, mainly through the CSA.

UPDATING THE CONTROLLED SUBSTANCES ACT

The CSA acknowledges that there may be a need for addition, deletion, or transfer of substances from one schedule to another and has procedures for doing so. Any new drug or concerns over existing drugs can be considered on scientific and medical grounds. The DEA considers any substance for inclusion into schedules based on information from FDA and the National Institute on Drug Abuse, as well as from criminal justice agencies, pharmaceutical companies, or others. A review determines whether a substance should or should not be controlled under schedules or removed from them.

The CSA significantly altered how pharmaceutical companies develop, manufacture, and distribute drugs, including their import and export. Under the CSA, the U.S. attorney general annually establishes production quotas for substances in Schedules I-II, limiting their production. CSA also requires that the pharmaceutical industry keep selected drugs physically secure, such as establishing strict standards for inventories and records. Provisions exist to regulate those whose scope of service involves dissemination or use of controlled substances. For example, prescriptions for ADHD and other medicines must list the physician's DEA license number. DEA registration allows pharmaceutical manufacturers, researchers, and health care professionals to access controlled substances on Schedules I-V.

SOCIAL STIGMA

There is a tendency to stigmatize individuals with ADHD and other disabilities. Social stigma, also known as negative stereotyping, discredits and damages the reputations, or even the identities of, individuals viewed as different, often rejecting and isolating them from mainstream society. A consequence of stigmatization is the devaluation of individuals regarded as "others." Since time immemorial, society has disliked or distrusted those who are disabled or otherwise different. Individuals with a disability were considered cursed, possessed, or otherwise "invalid." Martin Luther asserted that mentally handicapped children were changelings who were possessed by the devil due to the sins of their parents.

Members of dominant groups have perceived individuals with disabilities as less-powerful "others" to be shunned or ignored. This resulted in discrimination in finding employment; getting married; and receiving programs and services, including educational and social services. Stigmatizing individuals with disabilities isn't conducive to education or therapy and could result in academic and therapeutic failure. Stigmatized individuals, such as those with ADHD, internalizes the perspectives of others regarding them as contemptible and unworthy. Internalization produces fear of being labeled "disabled" and obstructs efforts to obtain help and services.

Educational programs and services to counter perceived limitations of individuals with a disability such as ADHD can help to ease stigma. Efforts emphasizing treatability and successes achieved by individuals with a disability could be helpful, but not as much as emphasizing the commonalities rather than the differences.

Psychostimulant users are stigmatized by society, reinforcing beliefs that they are different from nonusers. Crystal methamphetamine users, for example, often pull back and withdraw from situations and associations and are characterized by personal and social isolation. Their behaviors —including that they appear "wired," don't sleep or eat, steal, are paranoid, or are hostile and even collect and use firearms and other weapons—identify them as "others." Injection psychostimulant users bear more blatant signs of use, such as needle scars. These signifiers only enhance the likelihood of stigmatization.

Individuals with hidden disabilities, such as ADHD, can experience trauma associated with stigma. Such individuals often choose to not disclose their disability for fear of discrimination. They may not tell family members or friends, and some even hide their diagnosis from spouses. The stigma associated with disability can be devastating, particularly if individuals don't have adequate coping resources. This emotional health assault can lead to problems, including anxiety, depression, substance use, and related conditions.

Labeling children with ADHD results in lowered expectations. Lower academic expectations lead to delayed skill acquisition. These issues become more problematic by the fourth grade, when reading becomes a larger academic factor.

Understanding the stigma for ADHD may improve understanding of the disorder and help guide therapists. There may be subtypes of stigma that could be categorized to better address aspects of ADHD. Reducing the stigma associated with ADHD will enhance human potential and foster economic productivity.

10

Current Research and Future Directions

These are exciting times for research into ADHD and its future. To find better ways to prevent and manage ADHD, it is crucial to more fully understand what ADHD actually is. Many scientific technologies help us understand the brain and learn more about its functioning in ADHD. Researchers are considering novel areas that may add to ways for addressing ADHD. These developments may help not only better understand ADHD, but also better treat and even effectively prevent it.

Research gives exciting glimpses into what the future might hold for ADHD, including new treatments. Approaches to simplify and improve treatment regimens, including those utilizing multiple medicines are being examined. Potent, well-tolerated multiple drug combinations have potential for coformulation as single tablet regimens. Investigational substances are under development. Some fit within existing drug classes of ADHD medicines, and some don't. Other investigators are developing new drug-administration systems, such as transdermal delivery. Nonpharmacological approaches offer myriad possibilities. Hopefully future efforts will yield new, more effective options for preventing and managing ADHD.

It is assumed that better understanding the past, especially concerning the evolution of understanding of ADHD, will allow the crafting of new solutions and generate additional resources to more fully understand this disorder. Similarly, comprehending the diverse issues surrounding the current situations related to ADHD should help us formulate more effective ways to address them. Awareness provides and informed basis for generating choices and making informed decisions to address areas such as prevention and policy.

LEARNING MORE ABOUT ADHD

An initial step in helping someone with ADHD is understanding the background and nature of the disorder, including the causes, signs, and factors related to treatment success. Promising scientific technologies and sophisticated research designs can be drawn upon. The results should direct successful developments within the many fields for prevention and treatment.

Technological and Other Advances

Myriad areas of scientific research offer valuable insights to improve how we assess and address ADHD. There are new and emerging areas offering opportunities to better understand ADHD and its varied treatments, including medicines and nonpharmacological approaches.

Pharmacogenetics

Pharmacogenetics, defined as identification of genetic variations to predict, positively or negatively, responses an individual will likely have to particular medicines, is a new and rapidly emerging field. It has been suggested that ADHD has a 0.8 degree of inheritability and that up to 80 percent of phenotypic variation is attributable to genes. As noted, concordance of ADHD among monozygotic twins is significantly higher than among dizygotic twins, suggesting significant contributions from genes in the development of ADHD. Several different genes are likely involved in phenotypic expression, some of which have been identified, and more are certain to follow. Clearly ADHD is one of the most heritable psychiatric conditions. Pharmacological responses to specific ADHD medicines are also highly influenced by genetic variations.

Several genes have already been reported as being associated with specific responses to ADHD medicines. These include the alpha-2A-adrenergic receptor gene (ADRA2A), catechol-O-methyltransferase (COMT), dopamine-receptor D4 (DRD4), SNAP-25, and serotonin-transporter genes. Similarly, individuals who carry variants of the CHRNA4 gene, identified as associated with the nicotinic acetylcholine receptor system, who were also exposed to certain environmental risks, such as prenatal alcohol or tobacco consumption, or psychosocial adversity, may respond differently to respective ADHD medicines. However, a few studies failed to find associations between methylphenidate treatment in adults with ADHD and the DAT1 or ADRA2A genes. At any rate, administration of methylphenidate appears to be positively correlated with functioning of the hypothalamic-pituitary-adrenal axis in individuals with ADHD, at least as measured by salivary cortisol, which is significantly and positively associated with measures of neuropsychological performance.

Related research suggests that precision medicines may be developed to reduce the effects of genetic risk factors for ADHD. Genetic risk factors for brain development that might lead to ADHD sometimes appear to converge in particular regulatory pathways.

This convergence seems to be primarily related to the enhancer and promoter activity of genetic factors involved in developing brains. If we more precisely determine how this occurs, we might identify the specific biological processes that are impacted and target them with specifically designed interventions.

Neuroimaging and Related Technologies

Several neuroimaging modalities are available to examine brain structure and function in ADHD. Neuroimaging and related approaches are useful research tools, but they are not yet sufficiently developed to either confirm or deny an ADHD diagnosis for particular individuals. They only provide snapshots of brain functioning at moments in time and cannot examine ranges of the functional variability that is characteristic of ADHD.

Magnetic Resonance Imaging

Magnetic resonance imaging (MRI) and other structural brain-imaging techniques help evaluate phenomenon such as brain size, composition, volume, or organization, while functional brain-imaging techniques can explain brain activity while performing specific tasks. An MRI uses large cylindrical magnets, computers, and instruments to transmit and receive radio waves. These are used to form two- or three-dimensional images of the brain and other body parts. The magnetic field created by MRI devices causes nuclei in the body to line up. Radio waves are directed at nuclei, and, if the frequency is identical, a resonance is formed, permitting nuclei to absorb radio waves. The strength and length of these signals are translated by computers into images. The MRI was developed from an earlier approach, known as nuclear magnetic resonance (NMR) spectroscopy, which provides information about molecular structure. The MRI has the advantage of not using radiation or radioactive tracers.

Numerous studies suggest that individuals with reduced volume in specific brain regions, such as the frontal lobes, amygdala, basal ganglia, cerebellum, caudate nucleus, hippocampus, nucleus accumbens, and putamen, are more likely to have ADHD. However, as there are ranges of individual variability in brain region volumes, we aren't able to exclusively use MRIs for conclusive ADHD diagnosis. Other studies suggest that there are subtle structural differences in select brain regions in ADHD, such as less white matter in the right frontal lobe and a smaller right anterior prefrontal cortex. These structural differences could lead to problems with sustained attention and focus. Structural asymmetries in the caudate nucleus appear to lead to problems with self-control, as it is responsible for integrating information from different brain regions and supporting cognitive functioning, including memory. Similarly, children with ADHD are more prone to be developmentally delayed with respect to variables such as brain volume, cortical thickness, and structure.

Diffusion tensor imaging (DTI) is a relatively new technique that assesses brain structure in individuals with ADHD. A particular benefit of DTI is in examining white-matter integrity across different brain regions that are associated with impulsivity and attention.

Computed Axial Tomography

Computed axial tomography (CAT), also known as computed tomography (CT), is another structural neuroimaging technique. It uses a series of X-rays to generate brain images. CAT/CT scans are mostly used for evaluating brain injuries. As ADHD is not primarily the result of structural brain problems but of more functional, neurochemical issues, CAT/CT scans and other structural techniques, such as MRI and DTI, have limited applicability, except perhaps in ruling out confounding conditions.

Functional Neuroimaging

Functional neuroimaging techniques, as opposed to structural approaches, measure brain physiological functioning. Functional neuroimaging provides detailed information about the activity within specific brain areas, typically comparing activity before and during performance of a specific task. Functional MRIs show degrees of oxygen uptake, associated with high neuronal activity. Functional MRI studies indicate disrupted brain functioning in areas known to be related to neuropsychological processes that are associated with ADHD. Increased activation in the medial-frontal and parietal regions and reduced fronto-striatal activation is related to motor inhibition, which is common in ADHD, although the former may actually be caused by psychostimulant use. Underactivation of the inferior prefrontal cortex and anterior cingulate are associated with interference inhibition, another characteristic of some with ADHD. Underactivation of the dorsolateral and left inferior prefrontal cortex is associated with attention vigilance, another common ADHD characteristic. Likewise, underactivation of the inferior ventrolateral, parietal, prefrontal, tempro-occipital, and cerebellar brain regions appears to be associated with deficits of working memory, another feature that is often experienced with ADHD.

Diffuse Optical Tomography

Diffuse optical tomography (DOT), also called diffuse optical imaging (DOI), is a neuroimaging technique that uses near-infrared light waves to form images of the brain or other body parts. This functional approach is based on optical absorption of hemoglobin, which generally varies in relation to the oxygenation status of brain regions, reflecting where greater activity occurs based on greater blood flow. DOT/DOI is comparable in application to functional MRIs.

Positron Emission Tomography

Positron emission tomography (PET) imaging techniques examine metabolic processes in the brain. PET scans are typically done while individuals perform specific tasks, such as reading, thinking, or listening. PET scans use low-dose, radioactive, metabolically active isotopes bound to glucose, which is injected into the blood and accumulates differentially in respective brain regions to measure neurotransmitter activity. After entering the brain, radioactive-labeled glucose emits positrons, which collide with electrons in the brain tissues and emit gamma rays. These gamma rays are detected by sensors. The PET-CT (positron emission tomography-computed tomography) approach combines PET scanning with X-ray computed tomography to create sequential, three-dimensional images of brain biochemical activity to form single, superimposed images.

PET scans have identified some people with ADHD as having dopamine-release deficits in the caudate and limbic regions, which can be compensated for through the use of ADHD psychostimulants, particularly dextroamphetamine (Dexedrine), lisdextroamphetamine (Vyvanse), methamphetamine (Desoxyn), and methylphenidate (Ritalin). Some PET scans indicate deficits in the transporter systems, suggesting atomoxetine (Strattera) could be useful in treating the individuals' ADHD.

Single-Photon Emission Computed Tomography

Single-photon emission computed tomography (SPECT) is another neuroimaging approach that uses gamma-ray emitting radioisotopes to generate two- and three-dimensional images of active brain regions. Radioactive isotopes used in SPECT scans have half-lives, making them easier to handle, more widely available, and considered safer than PET scanning.

Other Techniques

Other technologies can be used to study the brains and brain activity of those with ADHD. Electroencephalography (EEG), which measures brain-wave activity, is widely used. Magnetoencephalography (MAG), which produces more detailed images of neuronal activity, may better examine issues relevant to ADHD. A perhaps more relevant technique is quantitative EEG (qEEG) which measures the ratio of slower theta brain waves to faster beta waves, where patterns of underarousal in areas of the cortex, referred to as cortical hypo-arousal, are sometimes used to help confirm an ADHD diagnosis. The qEEG has been used to predict who will likely better respond to psychostimulants.

Additional neuroimaging approaches, either recently developed or about to be, may offer better ways to study the brains of individuals with ADHD, perhaps providing more accurate brain segmentation, enhanced correction of imaging artifacts, and other relevant imaging-derived measures.

FUTURE CHANGES IN MEDICATIONS USED TO TREAT ADHD

The future has yet to be written for changes in how varied medicines may be used to treat ADHD. Promising rays of light are beginning to illuminate how to best address ADHD, including medicines and novel drug-delivery systems, as well as better understanding of how to effectively combine medicines with other treatments. Perhaps we will acquire insights to disentangle the nearly virtual indivisibility presently between ADHD and being prescribed ADHD medicines.

Innovations in fields such as quantum computing and synthetic biology may permit engineering pharmacological products that better treat ADHD with fewer side effects. Scientific endeavors, along with regular, sophisticated genetic screening, will hopefully bring us closer to individualizing treatments, particularly pharmacologically based ones.

There are opportunities to explore ways to reduce and prevent misuse of ADHD medicines through social-media platforms, such as Facebook and Twitter. Social media has the potential to enhance substance-use screening, prevention, and treatment with minimal financing. Social media offers possibilities to better understand areas such as ADHD medicine-use patterns and prevailing attitudes toward medicines in subpopulations.

Use of digital-interactive and certain other forms of electronic social media is increasing rapidly and is already associated with health benefits and risk reduction. In 2016, the American Academy of Pediatrics issued guidelines concerning the benefits and risks of exposure of young children to electronic media. Benefits include early learning, introduction of new ideas and knowledge, increased social contact and support, and availability of appropriate health-related prevention. Risks associated include negative impacts on learning and attention; decreased physical activity and sleep patterns; increased prevalence of health problems such as depression and obesity' threats to personal privacy and confidentiality; and exposure to inaccurate, inappropriate, or unsafe content and contacts. Young children, beginning as young as eighteen months, can learn from high-quality digital programming.

Other fields may yield better knowledge, novel technologies, and other benefits that may prove useful in addressing ADHD. It is impossible to identify beforehand where such innovations may come from. If history teaches anything, it is that new developments can come from the least likely places. We should remain optimistic and open to possibilities for better applications and more informed insights. We can assume current understanding of ADHD will change and be revised.

New Medications

Research into new medicines for ADHD and related conditions is perennial for pharmaceutical companies and others. In the United States, scheduling of drugs and clinical trials for developing and testing medicines is primarily regulated under the CSA. Similar comprehensive legislation pertaining to drugs was passed in other countries. In 1971, the United Kingdom enacted the Misuse of Drugs Act and, in 1966, Canada passed its Controlled Drugs and Substances Act. These and related laws passed help nations comply with treaty commitments under international agreements to help regulate and control development and production and curtail misuse and abuse of existing drugs and of new substances that may help in managing and treating ADHD and related conditions.

Researchers continue evaluating new substances for treating ADHD and related conditions. The potential of cholinergic drugs, such as acetylcholinesterase-inhibitors, including donepezil and tacrine, is being examined. Nicotinic analogues, like ABT-418, are being considered as potential ADHD medicines. Studies are being conducted with NFC1, a glutamatergic agonist, which seems to be safe and effective for ADHD. NFC1 essentially targets glutamatergic pathways that are known to be dysfunctional in some people with ADHD. This type of drug doesn't target the entire brain, as drugs such as methylphenidate (Ritalin) or a combination-amphetamine formulation (Adderall) do. The action of these new drugs is hoped to be more focused with fewer side effects.

Nitric oxide has a very short half-life after release and is involved in neurotransmission modulation and other physiological processes. It is endogenously produced and has potential for varied conditions, perhaps including ADHD. Nitric oxide is created by the action of nitric-oxide synthase, and the resulting nitric oxide acts on several pathophysiological systems, including the cardiovascular system; peripheral nervous system; and, of greatest concern, the central nervous system. Medicines enhancing the production or blocking degradation of nitric-oxide synthase could potentially help influence neuronal transmission, which is central to ADHD.

Another group of drugs that is being considered as potential ADHD medicines is those that raise orexin levels. Orexin-producing cell bodies in the hypothalamus have projections that spread out across the central nervous system. Orexins act primarily as excitatory neurotransmitters. These neuropeptides regulate arousal and promote wakefulness, similar to eugeroic ADHD medicines, such as modafinil and armodafinil, and are being examined for use with ADHD.

These are just a few examples of potential classes of substances that may yield new medicines for ADHD. It is difficult, if not impossible, to predict where the next ADHD drug may come from, but it is worth recognizing that there are efforts to find them. Many medicines that are already developed or that are currently being used for other conditions might be found efficacious for ADHD.

Novel Delivery Systems

Alternative drug-delivery systems are under consideration to offer improved ADHD management. For example, a unique drug-delivery system was created for a methylphenidate-formulation released in 2000 and marketed as Concerta. It consists of a capsule that is coated with small amount of methylphenidate, which is available for immediate use, but as the capsule moves through the gastrointestinal tract, it absorbs water, causing gel in the bottom of the capsule to slowly expand, gradually pushing out more methylphenidate through small openings that were laser-drilled in the capsule. This results in a drug-delivery system that allows therapeutic dosing of methylphenidate lasting approximately twelve hours in normal, healthy individuals. Concerta has low-abuse potential, since the capsule is hard to open, and the contents must be processed by complex extraction processes to access pure methylphenidate.

Transdermal patch delivery systems are available for many ADHD medicines. However, there are disadvantages to this delivery technique. One of the most common disadvantages is a high rate of contact dermatitis. Problems with transdermal-patch adherence are common in humid environments for physically active individuals. For instance, patch replacement is often necessary after swimming or physical exertion. Inconveniences associated with transdermal patches lead to noncompliance. Another novel technique is administering an ADHD medicine via a transdermal delivery system, using microneedles that are attached to an adhesive patch. Tiny needles create micro-meter-sized porous holes through the skin for active ingredients to pass through more easily. Such small needles do not create perceived pain, yet permit easy drug delivery. Drug permeation can be enhanced if the active ingredient is encapsulated in backing-layers, circumventing the premature closure of the micro-needle holes. This drug-delivery system could potentially be used on very young children. It also permits larger dose of active ingredient to be delivered faster, reducing skin irritation.

Development of drug-delivery systems that make abuse harder is important. A need for deterrent systems is indicated by the rising rates of abuse of several ADHD medicines. The National Survey on Drug Use and Health (NSDUH) collects data on substance use and misuse among Americans aged twelve and older, representing over 265 million individuals. Past-year misuse of psychostimulants, like ADHD medicines marketed as Adderall and Ritalin, was reported in the NSDUH of 2015 by 5.3 million Americans. Past-year initiation of psychostimulant abuse in 2015 was reported by 1.3 million. Findings indicate a need for more effective abuse-prevention strategies, of which tamper-resistant drug-delivery systems could be crucial. Many pharmacological abuse-deterrent approaches are under consideration. One approach is the development of altered capsule and tablet formulations that make it more difficult to crush the pharmacologically active contents of capsules or tablets into powders for snorting, swallowing, or injecting. Altered formulations could provide substantial barriers to routes of administration that are often selected by abusers.

No prevention strategy, however, is going to be effective while we socially tolerate the disturbing increases in use of psychostimulants without prescriptions, a direct result of the dramatic increases in use of ADHD psychostimulants, as evidenced by the twenty-one million individuals in the United States, aged twelve or older, who were prescribed such in 2015. This statistic reflects trends developed over time. For example, medication sales data for ADHD medicines from IMS Health's National Disease and Therapeutic Index database for 1998–2005 for adolescents aged thirteen to nineteen indicates a 133 percent increase for amphetamines, such as Adderall; a 52 percent increase for methylphenidate products, such as Ritalin; and an 80 percent increase for both together. Over the same eight-year period, for the same age population, there was a 76 percent increase in number of calls to the American Association of Poison Control Center's National Poison Data System related to intentional abuse or intentional misuse of these drugs.

Rising abuse of ADHD prescription medicines clearly reflects increases in availability. Very strong positive relationships between availability and abuse have been observed time and again with many different substances, including alcohol, tobacco, and opiates, and it is not surprising when looking more closely at ADHD medicines, particularly psychostimulants.

Combining Medications with Other Treatments

Use of ADHD medicines in combination with other treatments can potentially become more important. As effective as any ADHD medicine may or may not be, combined approaches will likely yield enhanced results when administered concurrently with other treatment modalities. Brain neuroplasticity suggests that the use of additional treatment approaches will help individuals with ADHD not only achieve greater brain health but healthier lives.

Research suggests that combining ADHD medicines and lifestyle changes can be the most effective. Conjunction treatments can include simple, but beneficial, lifestyle choices, such as staying properly hydrated, sleeping enough, meditating, and getting regular exercise.

It would be helpful for anyone needing an ADHD medicine to also follow lifestyle choices that contribute to optimal health. Personalized choices would not only promote overall health, but foster scenarios where ADHD medicines would likely attain maximal therapeutic efficacies.

A good night's sleep is important to everyone, including those with ADHD. Those with ADHD generally sleep poorly and less than neuro typicals. As sleep becomes restless, all of experience decreases in attention and ability to concentrate and focus. Mental function is less effective in those not getting normal, restful sleep. Establishing regular sleep routines, such as going to bed and waking up at the same general time each day, helps brains work optimally at any age. The National Sleep Foundation reports that up to 80 percent of adolescents don't get enough sleep. Children who are sleep-deprived typically lack focus and may demonstrate hyperactivity.

Eating large meals or drinking alcohol or caffeinated beverages before bedtime can disrupt sleep patterns. Excessive alcohol use at any time can cause neuronal loss and declining brain volume. Compared with light drinkers, heavy drinkers—those consuming six to nine alcoholic drinks once per week throughout adolescence—have less gray matter in the bilateral anterior cingulate cortex, right orbitofrontal and frontopolar cortices, right insular cortex, and right superior temporal gyrus. This is troubling, as we know that brains continue developing into the mid-twenties and that interfering with normal development by heavy drinking can have serious long-term effects. Smoking tobacco and the use of other substances also accelerate brain-function declines, contributing to memory loss.

Maintaining regular physical activity helps improve brain functioning for everyone, including those with ADHD. Studies indicate that those who exercise regularly have more gray matter in their brains. Regular physical exercise, particularly as we age, helps prevent many illnesses and poor health conditions, such as diabetes, cholesterol, hypertension, obesity, and stroke, that can cause loss of memory and mental agility. Regularly performing complex mental activities, such as word games and puzzles, helps prevent declines in mental function. Maintaining regular physical activity appears to stimulate the release of brain-derived neurotrophic factor (BDNF) that promotes healthy neurons, increasing cognitive factors such as processing time, memory, and attention. Exercising regularly improves the ability to focus and concentrate and stimulates neurogenesis, growth of new brain neurons.

Proper nutrition is important to all, including those with ADHD. Although studies are not conclusive, speculation is that nutritional factors, such as levels of fiber, sugar, and food additives, as well as pesticides, contributes to etiology and maintenance of ADHD. Low-glycemic foods help deliver steady sugar levels, making it easier for someone with ADHD to control behaviors and improve performance.

Use of nutritional supplements may be beneficial. Taking omega-3 fatty acids has been found to decrease inflammation and improve mood, which could help individuals with ADHD; they certainly help improve cognitive skills, such as focus and concentration. Omega-3s, delivered in phospholipid compositions, and specifically formulations in which phosphatidylserine is attached to omega-3s, appear to reduce ADHD symptoms more than triglyceride formulations do. Further, low omega-3 levels are associated with ADHD. Other nutritional supplements may be helpful, such as zinc to reduce hyperactivity and impulsivity or magnesium to aid with relaxation and sleep.

Dehydration is known to affect abilities to concentrate, impairs memory, and is highly associated with fatigue and mood swings. About 55–65 percent of the average human body is water. When you get thirsty, kidneys send less water to the bladder, darkening urine. Body temperature increases as we sweat less, blood thickens and flows sluggishly, and heart rate increases to maintain oxygen levels to brain and other body parts. Keeping properly hydrated and well-nourished is the key to maintaining brain function and health generally, including reducing impacts of ADHD.

Reducing stress levels is a wise health choice for our brains and for allowing ADHD treatments to work optimally. Higher levels of the stress hormone cortisol make it more difficult to retrieve information from memory. Stress-related inflammation, measured by C-reactive protein levels, adversely impacts brain health. Meditating helps many with ADHD concentrate better; they also appear less depressed and anxious. Mindfulness, intentionality, and maintaining positive attitudes are similar approaches that are positively associated with better brain health and less difficulties with ADHD. One study, for example, found that participants in a nine-week mindfulness program had reduced connectivity between posterior cingulate cortex, responsible for self-awareness, and anterior cingulate cortex, involved in impulse control and decision-making. Thus, they tended to have less negative self-talk, which can impair performance.

Many people with ADHD have a distorted sense of time and tend to be out of synchrony with everyday contexts. Desynchronization results in extreme performance deficits. Measuring and defining treatment targets through real contexts and implementing them with appropriate timing details make attaining treatment success more likely.

Since medicine efficacy varies at different times of the day, when to take particular medicines should be carefully considered. Chronotherapy, timing the administration of medications in accord with internal clocks, or circadian rhythms, could enhance therapeutic results for ADHD medicines, with fewer side effects.

Use of digital media is increasing and is associated with both health benefits and risks. Young children, starting at about eighteen months of age, long before they can use ADHD medicines, can begin to learn from digital media and high-quality media programming. The very young, those four to five years old, should only be given ADHD medicines if behavioral therapy was tried and found unsuccessful.

Many alternative therapeutic techniques, such as acupuncture, biofeedback, hypnosis, and massage can be helpful when used in combination with ADHD medicines. Many other techniques have promise and may be found to enhance treatment success. For instance, music therapy has been shown to improve focus and attention, reduce hyperactivity, and strengthen social skills. Transcranial electromagnetic stimulation is a noninvasive technique that has been shown to improve precision of memory recollection, which is problematic for some with ADHD, and may positively augment other treatments.

ADHD medicines make the greatest differences nearly immediately for the majority of those with ADHD. Typically, an individual is introduced to a new medicine via titration, starting at a baseline with the smallest dose and increasing it gradually until a therapeutic response is attained or side effects become undesirable. Physicians generally adjust dosages of ADHD medicines every three to seven days in titration. This is a system of trial and error, as different medicines are introduced and tried. However, other factors play significant roles, such as positive connections individuals have with significant others, including parents, teachers, and health care providers.

Individuals with ADHD often benefit from combination treatments, since they often have comorbidities. For young children, conduct disorders and ODD are more common psychiatric comorbidities. For older children, adolescents, and young adults, antisocial personality disorder, bipolar disorders, depression, and substance-use disorders are the most common. Anxiety, binge eating, premature death, and suicidality are other variables identified as more likely in those with ADHD. Individuals with ADHD benefit from careful, continuous, long-term monitoring and treatment.

ADHD medicines are most effective when not used as stand-alone treatments. When used in combination, many ADHD medicines may be more effective than when they are used alone. Studies indicate that when guanfacine is administered in combination with methylphenidate, the cognitive effects are greater than when either is used alone.

The ways in which behavior is managed at home, school, and elsewhere are important. We must change the ways children with ADHD are taught and regarded.

Social stigma is far more likely if individuals are untreated. Effective treatment helps alleviate both the problem and the associated stigma.

The notion that ADHD and other "disabilities" are socially constructed has been raised in theoretical and practical discussions and supports the understanding of social stigma. Cultural, organizational, and technological factors affecting recognition of ADHD as a disability is part of the larger trend of medicalization of human behaviors. The cultural underpinning of medical models of any disorder assumes that there are recognized normative ranges of behavior. When someone departs from these accepted norms, the medicalization response is typically to define it as a pathology, disease, or disorder, meriting diagnosis and treatment. The history of diagnostic labels for what is now called ADHD supports understanding of ADHD as socially constructed.

The response to prescribe medicine to someone crossing the blurred range between acceptable and unacceptable behaviors is part of medicalizing behaviors. Ever-broadening classes of drugs to medicate ADHD symptoms to encompass more individuals under the ADHD diagnostic umbrella testify to the trends to accommodate apparent incongruities in presenting behaviors of those diagnosed.

An escalation in the numbers of individuals diagnosed with ADHD and prescribed medicines has become a phenomenon globally. This further indicates the social construction of the disorder. Geographical disproportionalities in ADHD prevalence and concomitant prescribing of psychostimulants has been diminishing recently, perhaps attributable to the hegemonic expansion under globalization of diagnostic predispositions to conform to Western medicine and its pharmaceutical tendencies.

This review shows potential from combining the use of ADHD medicines with other treatments. The future of ADHD is difficult to predict, but, if current trends are any indication, we can optimistically look forward to profound developments that revitalize and enhance the lives of individuals with ADHD.

RESEARCH FINDINGS

Research into the possible causes and nature of ADHD and effective management and treatment includes diverse ongoing scientific endeavors that shed light on areas that may offer opportunities to prevent and better treat ADHD. Several factors appear to increase risks for ADHD. For instance, it seems that post-term birth after forty-two weeks of gestation, as compared to the normal forty weeks, substantially increases risks of developing behavioral problems later in life, including ADHD. Poor prenatal nutrition, such as maternal diets containing highly processed foods that are high in fats and sugars, is associated with greater ADHD risk. Paternal, as well as maternal, substance use appears to increase risk. Secondhand smoke exposure is another associated risk factor. Repeated, but not single, anesthesia exposure at young ages also escalates the risk for ADHD. Children experiencing family and other stressors, as well as traumatic experiences, mental illness, poverty, and exposure to violence, are more likely to develop ADHD. Significant genetic influence has been found between childhood trauma and the severity of inhibitory deficits in children with ADHD. It is suspected the male bias of ADHD may be explained somewhat by sexually dimorphic effects in the genes that predispose development of ADHD. These are just a few examples of the areas that recent research implicates as increasing the likelihood of someone developing ADHD.

Research may help clarify if ADHD actually consists of several different disorders, each with unique symptom clusters, as has been suspected. These findings could suggest the need for more varied treatments. Clarification of inherent differences of individuals with ADHD and with respective comorbidities could also lead to more-tailored treatments. ADHD will, no doubt, continue to be redefined, perhaps even renamed. Hopefully, reformulations will yield not only better understanding, but generate more effective strategies to address this complex and intriguing neurodevelopmental disorder.

Policy Research

Policy researchers consider how treatments are authorized and reimbursed by health care plans. Health care plans or state programs, like Medicaid, require prior authorization before medicines can be prescribed. Prior authorization means that the plans or programs must review physician prescription requests before coverage for an ADHD medicine is given. The numbers of children and adults prescribed ADHD medicines has increased dramatically. Many Medicaid programs have prior authorization policies for pediatric and adult use of ADHD medicines. These vary from state to state, as there is no comprehensive federal mandate.

The costs of treating ADHD directly and personal and societal costs associated with it can be substantial. Researchers estimate that the combined annual cost of treating ADHD in the United States is $31.6 billion including health care costs for individuals with ADHD related specifically to diagnosis, health care costs for family members related specifically to the diagnosis of family members, and work absences among adults with ADHD and those of family members. It is unclear how changes, if any, to the Affordable Care Act (ACA) will impact assessment and treatment of ADHD and of substance use and other related issues. It is also too early to evaluate the effects of the Medicare Access and CHIP Reauthorization Act, which functions complementary to ACA and was intended to help move from volume-based to value-based Medicare reimbursement. Better prevention and treatment of individuals with ADHD could produce financial savings and reduce suffering of individuals and families from untreated ADHD and associated problems, including substance use.

The 21st Century Cures Act, signed into law on December 13, 2016, by Barack Obama, is an example of such a measure. Cures Act was intended to improve prescription-drug monitoring programs, implement prevention activities, train health care providers, and expand treatment access. It also amends the Federal Food, Drug, and Cosmetic Act, establishing processes so that the FDA can use patient-experience data to consider risk-benefit assessment of new drugs, including ADHD medicines. It also established Council for 21st Century Cures, a nonprofit corporation that is intended to accelerate the discovery, development, and delivery of innovative cures, treatments, and preventative measures.

Medication Noncompliance

Studies have examined the prevalence, potential causes, and consequences of ADHD medicine nonadherence. As ADHD medicines alleviate many aspects of the disorder and it is well recognized that nonadherence increases the likelihood of subsequent treatment failure, a better understanding of this is important. Research of pharmacy claims and treatment statistics indicate that ADHD medicine discontinuation or nonadherence ranges from 13.2 to 64 percent. The use of immediate-release psychostimulants, like dextroamphetamine, is associated with higher rates of nonadherence than are extended-release formulations of the same medicine. The long-term consequences of ADHD medicine nonadherence is not as well understood, and most studies examined nonadherence in children with ADHD, but few have examined it among adults. There is a need for future research considering a diverse array of issues related to ADHD.

Case Illustrations

Not all individuals with ADHD present with the same set of characteristics, nor will they all have the same experiences. Some individuals with ADHD may exhibit behaviors that are consistent with one subtype, while others may have very different presentations. Some will appear to meet criteria for recognized subtypes, while some will demonstrate less clear patterns. Many will be prescribed particular ADHD medications, and after using these respective medicines, some will experience marked improvement, perhaps within brief periods of time, while others may experience little difference, and some may have mild to severe side effects. If different ADHD treatments, including perhaps another medication, were tried, there might be dramatic differences. Some people with ADHD will try to manage without medication, while many more will use combinations of medication and some of the varied complimentary approaches to help prevent and manage symptoms.

We will briefly consider five case illustrations of individuals with ADHD to explore some of the myriad ways individuals and those around them may be impacted by this condition.

INATTENTIVE CHRISSY

Chrissy G. is a nine-year-old white female in the fourth grade. She was known by teachers and family to be very easily distracted. Chrissy regularly forgot to do many basic activities, such as forgetting chores at home. Her parents commented that Chrissy seemed to wander about with no apparent purpose or direction. Chrissy suffered a traumatic brain injury (TBI) as result of an automobile accident when she was two years old.

At the first parent–teacher night when Chrissy was in the third grade last year, her teacher, Mrs. Tempolski, mentioned to her parents, Mike and Sue

G., that Chrissy routinely didn't pay attention to important details and often made careless mistakes when she was completing schoolwork. Chrissy rarely followed through on instructions. She might start her assignments but rapidly lost focus and became easily sidetracked. The same basic message was repeated at subsequent meetings with teachers, school staff, and administrators over the rest of the year. Mrs. Tempolski recommended that Chrissy be retained in the third grade the next year, even offering to keep her in her classroom and frame it that she was keeping Chrissy as a class helper to assist new third graders, but her parents refused that option. They knew there was something different about Chrissy but felt that with appropriate help, she could progress with her peers to the next grade.

Her parents were well aware that Chrissy generally seemed to have trouble staying focused and keeping on task, even when she was playing. They frequently complained that she regularly appeared to not listen, even when she was spoken directly to. They reported that it was as if "her mind were elsewhere." There were similar reports from teachers, indicating that she was frequently inattentive, even without obvious causes of distraction. It was apparent that Chrissy disliked activities that required focused mental effort, such as matching games. Chrissy reported that facing the day was frightening. She easily became panicked by daily activities and said she would "freeze up." She complained that she had trouble concentrating, was easily distracted, had low energy, had difficulty reading, and had general feelings of being overwhelmed.

The elementary school counselor and principal recommended that Mike and Sue think about having Chrissy evaluated. Her parents brought her to the family pediatrician, who conducted a battery of standard physical examinations and a thorough medical history. The pediatrician then referred them to a local neurologist for specialized evaluation. Mike and Sue completed parent questionnaires and Mrs. Tempolski did one that was designed for teachers. An EEG was taken for Chrissy. She was diagnosed with attention deficit hyperactivity disorder, predominantly inattentive presentation (314.01/ F90.0). The psychiatrist she was seeing conducted a SPECT study, which was performed without her being on any ADHD medication, and this indicated marked reductions in brain activity, particularly in her prefrontal cortex.

Chrissy was prescribed Adderall. After two weeks, her psychiatrist ordered another SPECT image, and this showed substantial overall improvement throughout Chrissy's whole brain, particularly in the prefrontal cortex. Chrissy reported that she was feeling much better, more focused and organized, and now had more brainpower.

Chrissy began exercising more and joined a community soccer team. Her parents paid closer attention to what she was eating. Chrissy lost some of her "baby fat" and took more interest in picking out her clothes each morning. Her parents' post-behavioral checklists on the refrigerator listed important reminders, such as walking the dog and finishing homework. At school, a 504 plan was established, granting her accommodations, such as getting regular prompts from teachers and aides to keep on-task. She is now more focused and has enhanced self-esteem.

Analysis

The fact that Chrissy has ADHD may not be surprising. The CDC estimates that 13–20 percent of U.S. children aged eighteen years of age or younger have some form of mental disorder, of which ADHD is one of the most common. Further incidence and prevalence data is presented in chapter 1. She is somewhat older than the typical age at which most children are diagnosed with ADHD.

The fact that Chrissy had a TBI is a risk factor that is associated with subsequent ADHD development. Research indicates TBI among children, even mild injuries, is strongly associated with increased risk for incident ADHD as well as for suicide.

The predominantly inattentive presentation is not what most individuals imagine when they think about someone with ADHD. Children with predominantly inattentive presentation are usually less disruptive and less active than those with predominantly hyperactive/impulsive presentation or with combined presentation. They are more often overlooked and less likely to be diagnosed. Predominantly inattentive presentation was only added to DSM in 1994. Chrissy demonstrated many signs that are indicative of predominantly inattentive presentation, such as having trouble paying attention to others, and remembering important things, or managing time well.

Most professionals feel predominantly inattentive presentation is the most common ADHD subtype. At any rate, it is currently more commonly diagnosed among females than males.

LONELY PETER

Peter is an eight-year-old Hispanic male in third grade. Near the end of the second grade, Peter had been diagnosed with unspecified attention deficit hyperactivity disorder (314.01/ F90.9). This category applies to individuals in which the predominant characteristic symptoms of ADHD cause impairment in social, vocational, or other major areas of life functioning. An individualized educational plan (IEP) was constructed for Peter, which focused primarily on his educational accommodations and services.

Peter was a nice enough kid but had few friends, and classmates didn't generally like to play with him. He earnestly tried to get other kids to like him, frequently becoming the class clown. However, Peter was rather lonely and knew full well that other children in his class and those in his neighborhood didn't like to hang out with him. This lack of friends, of course, made Peter somewhat sad.

The characteristic self-focused pattern applies to Peter. He routinely jumped into conversations he wasn't part of. Peter also frequently interrupted games or other activities other children were playing or engaged in. He had particularly difficult times waiting for his turn, whether in classroom activities or when playing games with other children. Unfortunately, his behavior also led to his being ostracized and scapegoated.

Rachel, Peter's mother, wanted to have an extraspecial ninth birthday party for Peter, hoping this might help him develop some friendships with classmates. Rachel, a single mother, scheduled an elaborate birthday party at a local funplex center she had heard was one of the most popular places for such events. She had special invitation cards printed and gave them to Ms. Castillo, Peter's teacher, to distribute to his classmates. However, Rachel was getting concerned as the deadline to RSVP passed, and the families of only four students had replied. Two sent their regrets saying they had prior commitments at weekend soccer games. Only two other students said they would be coming. This troubled Rachel, as there was a twenty-person minimum for holding parties at the funplex, and she had already put down a sizeable deposit to reserve the event. Then to make matters worse, she got notes from the mother of one of the two children who had initially replied affirmatively that they had an unforeseen conflicting commitment with a family member in the neighboring state and would no longer be able to attend. When Rachel asked Peter about this, he explained that kids in his class had gotten together and agreed to not attend his party. Rachel, although somewhat heartbroken that Peter had to go through this emotional turmoil, regrouped, called several of Peter's cousins, and held a pleasant enough birthday party for Peter.

At Rachel's meeting with the child study team to update Peter's IEP, she requested that his classroom teachers implement a behavioral plan to help him refocus and to keep on task. She had already initiated a similar strategy at home after learning about this approach at a parent-training seminar she attended and felt it would be helpful. The school counselor also recommended that Peter be taught mindfulness strategies, such as deep breathing and guided meditation, which could provide additional support and help reduce feelings of anxiety.

Analysis

The unspecified attention deficit hyperactivity disorder subtype that Peter was diagnosed with applies to individuals in whom the characteristic symptoms of ADHD that cause impairment in social, vocational, or other major areas of life functioning predominate. It is a new diagnostic category that was introduced as part of DSM-5, as discussed in chapter 2. This is a somewhat rarely used category that is reserved for those who don't quite meet the full criteria for any of the other accepted subtypes and for whom clinicians choose not to specify the reasons the full criteria aren't met and making a more specific diagnosis isn't possible. Peter's behavioral repertoire, as described in the preceding narrative, is congruent with the unspecified presentation.

Not all individuals with ADHD present with the same symptoms, nor do all experience the condition the same. Some who appear to have ADHD don't fit neatly into one of the three standard subtypes, hence the need for the unspecified attention deficit hyperactivity disorder category. Clinicians are sometimes unclear which particular DSM-5 diagnostic category to place a particular individual in, and the unspecified option helps to at least partially resolve this dilemma.

A characteristic feature that is commonly observed among individuals with ADHD is what can appear to be the inability to recognize the desires and needs of other individuals. This apparent self-focused behavior can make it more difficult for individuals with ADHD, particularly children, to form friendships and other meaningful relationships. An individual with a brain that is racing along can find it very difficult not to interrupt others while they are talking or engaging in other behaviors, such as playing a game or completing a class assignment. This deficit tends to impair the ability to make and maintain meaningful friendships, as discussed in chapter 7.

Some refer to the emotional response to rejection or criticism, real or imagined, by those around them as rejection-sensitive dysphoria (RSD). If internalized, this can erupt in angry outbursts. For example, around half of those placed into court-mandated anger-management programs have previously undiagnosed ADHD. Guanfacine and clonidine used together has been found to provide relief for about one-third of those with RSD.

The mindfulness techniques Peter learned, as discussed in chapter 8, have been found to be helpful for individuals with ADHD. Mindfulness is a helpful ingredient for attaining success. Research indicates that children with ADHD who practice mindfulness have better outcomes and are more resilient.

PRESCHOOL PAUL

Paul is a four-year-old biracial male who is attending full-day preschool. Paul's father, Ron, is white, and his mother, Oluwanishola, whom everyone calls Shula, is from Nigeria. Paul was premature, and Shula reported that it had been a difficult pregnancy. Shula admitted that she smoked cigarettes daily and drank alcoholic beverages at least three days a week while she was pregnant.

Paul was a precocious and highly active child. His parents, from his earliest days, realized that there was something different with him. Paul's mother said she remembered that he was extremely active, even in the womb, kicking for extended periods of time and rolling over and over as though he were doing somersaults. She says he was a demanding baby and very active. To complicate matters, Paul had evident sibling rivalry, as he had an eight-year-old brother, Terrell, who had always been a model son and student.

Paul was placed in full-day preschool at age two, and his mother returned to full-time work. Paul's transition to preschool wasn't smooth. After only one month, the preschool director sent home a note detailing some of Paul's unacceptable behaviors. Particularly alarming was his lack of personal self-control. Even under teacher supervision, he hit other children for no apparent reason, jumped off chairs, and rolled around on the floor. Paul also made "ugly" facial grimaces at teachers and talked incessantly. He had extreme difficulty sitting still, even during "quiet time," and squirmed, played with buttons on his clothes, and relentlessly fidgeted. Paul also seemed to reject efforts by other children to become friends. Most of his preschool teachers complained about Paul's behavior—that he frequently got out of his seat, repeatedly burped or cracked his knuckles, and such. Paul's overanimated actions were much more pronounced and severe than could be explained by a short attention span. It got so bad that the director gave an ultimatum to take Paul for psychological evaluation and treatment or he would be expelled.

Ron, Shula, Terrell, and Paul all met with a child psychologist, who was well acquainted with ADHD. After the initial meeting, the psychologist had a strong impression that despite his young age, Paul probably had ADHD. The psychologist asked Ron and Shula to have their pediatrician complete a thorough medical evaluation. They also had to complete parental assessment forms and had a comparable instrument completed by staff at the preschool. The child psychologist determined that Paul had attention deficit hyperactivity combined presentation (314.01/ F90.2).

Ron and Shula enthusiastically participated in a series of parent-training workshops conducted at a local child-development center that taught them to apply behavioral strategies at home. The preschool, however, was unfamiliar with and unwilling to implement the behavioral-management classroom-management techniques available to create a supportive, reinforcing environment. Although Paul started to show some major improvements at home, his performance at preschool only slightly improved.

An unexpected side effect of Paul's improved behaviors at home was the recognition of behavioral problems in his older brother Terrell. What is equally likely to have happened is that as Paul's obvious problems were getting better, Terrell's minor difficulties became more evident. Ron and Shula disciplined Terrell for small digressions, and he resisted and began fighting with them and with Paul. When the child psychologist suggested that they lower their excessively high expectations of Terrell, the family successfully readjusted.

At the urging of the child psychologist, Paul was moved to another preschool that was familiar with the behavioral techniques that have been shown to help with ADHD. However, after two months at the second preschool, complaints about Paul's behavior and lack of academic success were sent home again. In frustration, Ron and Shula asked the child psychologist for help. Working in collaboration with Paul's pediatrician, a 10 mg once per day dose of extended-release formulation of methylphenidate (Ritalin LA) was prescribed to be taken with breakfast. There was also an intentional reduction of sugary foods from his diet. There were marked improvements in Paul's behavior at school, and he made progress in other arenas as well.

Analysis

The fact that Paul's mother smoked cigarettes and drank alcoholic beverages while she was pregnant weren't healthy lifestyle choices. These sorts of poor maternal choices, as discussed in chapter 3, are recognized to be related to significantly increased risk for those children to later be diagnosed with ADHD.

The younger a child is, the more a diagnosis for ADHD must be based upon physical behaviors. Most preschoolers cannot sustain focused attention for very long. Accordingly, the younger a child is, the shorter his or her attention span generally is.

The American Psychological Association and the American Academy of Pediatrics both recommend that for relatively young children from two to five years of age, such as Paul, the first line of treatment should consist of behavioral therapeutic techniques. The parent-training activities that Paul's parents participated in are in accord with this. The collaborative team approach used for diagnosing and treating Paul's ADHD has been found to be the most effective. Different professionals, such as child psychologists, pediatricians, and educators, have different areas of expertise that, collectively, can yield better results.

Family therapists have recognized the phenomenon of a family member becoming impaired as another starts to improve. This is usually attributed to attempts to maintain a family balance. It is speculated that as one member of a family no longer presents the extreme level of neediness, another member may develop declines in psychological adjustment to try to maintain balance. This was demonstrated by the behavioral changes in Terrell, Paul's older brother.

Another feature demonstrated by Paul that is commonly observed in ADHD was his inability to handle intense emotions. Due largely to deficits of working memory and the neural pathways controlling emotional regulation, what for most neurotypicals might be a transitory emotion can become too intense for people with ADHD if they get stuck on it. Research has found that ADHD can raise acute difficulties in handling emotions such as impatience, frustration, and excitability.

OPPOSITIONAL BRAD

Brad was first seen by a psychiatrist when he was in the ninth grade, at the age of fourteen. His parents wanted him to see a psychiatrist due to ongoing difficulties and being unsuccessfully treated at a clinic for children with behavioral problems. Brad's parents were concerned about his bad school performance, continuing since kindergarten. His parents told the psychiatrist, "His attitude is generally negative or else just indifferent." Teachers reported that he was insolent or arrogantly disrespectful.

Brad's early life was typical of many with ADHD. He was a very active child who demonstrated rapid motor-developmental milestones. He walked at less than one year of age. Brad was described as always being on the go as a youngster.

Brad was the middle of three children born to Alan and Elaine. Brad's siblings, two girls, had done poorly academically despite having superior intelligence scores. Brad's younger sister, eight-year-old Melissa, had a full-scale IQ score of 149, which placed her well above the 99.9 percentile, but she was getting low B grades in school. His older sister, eighteen-year-old Tanya, was a freshman in college who got mostly Cs and Bs in high school, despite also having a high IQ. Brad placed above the 99th percentile on a verbal scholastic aptitude test and in the 88th percentile on the nonverbal portion. Yet Brad was getting Ds and Cs in all academic subjects in the ninth grade. Alan and Elaine were vocally disappointed with his lack of academic success.

Brad's family offered an interesting background. His father, Alan, was a bright, driven, self-made man who grew up in rural Kentucky and was presently an executive in a high-tech company. Alan's own academic performance had been highly variable, some of which he later attributed to his probably having ADHD. At any rate, Alan had excelled in computer science classes, where he was hyperfocused. Elaine was a first-generation immigrant from Ecuador who experienced chronic depression for many years. Their marital adjustment was poor, and they regularly avoided interacting with each other. Alan routinely took extended business trips, and Elaine consistently stayed at home. Her large extended and close-knit family was in South America, and she had few close friends in the United States.

Brad's psychiatrist eventually diagnosed Brad as having both attention deficit hyperactivity combined presentation (314.01/ F90.2) and oppositional defiant disorder (313.81/ F91.3). Brad was initially prescribed a 20 mg dose of methylphenidate (Ritalin) to be administered twice daily, but this made him even more hostile, and he had difficulty sleeping. He was next switched to a three-times per day dosage regimen, but that didn't help much. Then he was given a lower 15 mg dose, and then a 10 mg dose, but his hyperactivity and inattention symptoms worsened at the 10 mg level. Brad's prescription was then changed to a twice per day dosage for an intermediate-acting methylphenidate formulation (Metadate ER) at 20 mg. While this helped reduced his characteristic ADHD symptoms, he again had trouble getting to sleep. A low dose of clonidine (Kapvay) was added at bedtime, and he experienced both good resolution of ADHD symptoms and was able to get a good night's sleep.

Brad also entered into long-term behavioral therapy with a counseling psychologist to work on his aggression and mood issues. Brad's parents found he was calmer when he took omega-3 fish-oil supplements with breakfast. He was also given a high-protein and low-carbohydrate diet and plenty of sports activities, particularly track and swimming, as these non-team sports are typically more compatible with the needs of individuals with ADHD. He was able to be more settled and better focused and enjoyed a positive response to treatment. He is doing much better in school and is continuing to work on other issues. His parents are also involved in couples counseling with a marriage and family therapist.

Analysis

It is estimated, as discussed in chapter 5, that somewhere around one-third to one-half of all males with ADHD also have ODD. It is somewhat less common among females prior to adolescence. With respect to ADHD subtypes, it is thought that ODD co-occurs in about one-half of children with the combined presentation and around one-quarter of those with the predominantly inattentive presentation. Prevalence of ODD in the general population ranges from 1 to 11 percent, with an average prevalence estimate of 3.3 percent. Individuals with ODD tend to be defiant, noncompliant, and stubborn. They often have temper outbursts and may become belligerent.

They typically have angry and irritable moods and can be very vindictive, holding on to grudges for months. Children with ODD usually argue with adults, and they generally refuse to obey authority figures. Brad certainly fit this general profile, and, like many with ODD, he routinely blamed others for his own mistakes and misbehaviors. In addition, individuals such as Brad often deliberately annoy those around them and have troubling tendencies to be rather vindictive. These sorts of traits are, unfortunately, rather common among individuals with ODD.

Symptoms of ODD can appear to some extent in individuals without the disorder. It is the frequency and persistence of symptoms that exceed what is typical for an individual's age, gender, and culture that suggest ODD. Since many young children with ADHD exhibit patterns of problematic interactions with others, it is the frequency and persistence of symptoms that must be evaluated in considering ODD. Many young children might occasionally have temper tantrums, but only if they did so on most days for at least the preceding six months would that be considered indicative of ODD.

Use of omega-3 fish oil supplements has been found to be beneficial in managing ADHD, as mentioned in chapter 3. Several studies have indicated that many people with ADHD have lower omega-3 fatty-acid levels compared to neurotypicals. Further, omega-3s have also demonstrated other significant benefits, including, at least for EPA, antioxidant and anti-inflammatory effects.

HYPERFOCUSED HENRY

Henry is a sixty-eight-year-old African American male who is lonely and unhappy. He has been married and divorced twice and has two children from relationships with two other women. He did not have any children during his first marriage, but he did have one, a daughter, with his second wife. Although he has three children, none of his children are speaking with him; however, he has managed to maintain a strained relationship with a grandson, Andre. Although Henry, a taxation accountant, has enjoyed reasonable success in his career, he doesn't experience much joy in his personal or social life.

Henry tended to be somewhat argumentative and decidedly negative; he also worried constantly. Individuals who knew him recognized that he held onto his opinions and generally would not listen to others. While Henry was somewhat rigid and oppositional, he sincerely disliked being alone. Nevertheless, he was typically unpleasant whenever he was around others. Further, if things did not go his way, he frequently exploded with an exuberant emotional outburst, which, to say the least, could be rather difficult for others to accept.

Henry first encountered a psychiatrist during a family review for his grandson Andre. Andre was fiercely negative and argumentative, not unlike his grandfather, and he had a history of throwing loud tantrums when he couldn't get his way. Andre, not surprisingly, didn't cooperate with teachers and, consequently, did poorly in school. He also didn't get along with other students. Henry had been called in for a meeting with his daughter Zinaha to help construct a family strategy to assist Andre.

The psychiatrist asked Henry to meet separately with her, and he agreed to be evaluated as well. It was determined that Henry exhibited many of the characteristics of an individual with ADHD who was hyperfocused, such as having extreme trouble shifting attention from one subject to another, having difficulty in seeing options in most situations, and generally being unpleasant when around others. Henry had a reputation both at home and at work for needing to have things done in just a certain way or else he became very upset. The ability to hyperfocus on a project he found interesting and stimulating, which is one of the benefits often cited by individuals with ADHD, has served him well as an accountant. Further, his sharp observational skills and his exceptional memory for certain facts, both of which are frequently reported as positive attributes of someone with ADHD, served him well professionally.

The psychiatrist ordered a positron emission tomography-computed tomography (PET-CT) test for Henry, which she explained indicated that he had substantially reduced prefrontal cortex activity when engaged with concentration tasks, as well as pronounced increased activity in his cingulate, both at rest and during concentration. She diagnosed him with attention deficit hyperactivity disorder, predominantly inattentive presentation (314.01/ F90.0) and initiated treatment with medication, exercise, and a stricter diet. Since Henry was hypertensive, his psychiatrist prescribed the nonstimulant ADHD medication atomoxetine (Strattera). His exercise program began with increasing the amount of walking he did until he got up to an hour of continuous walking at a brisk pace, which he usually did in a local park at least four days each week. A nutritionist recommended saffron and 5-HTP supplementation. This, along with his higher protein and lower carbohydrate diet, not only helped to improve his mood but also helped lower his blood pressure. Henry got better at letting go of grudges, and he was able to reestablish a relationship with his daughter and improve his relationship with his grandson.

Analysis

About 4–5 percent of U.S. adults, approximately ten million individuals, have ADHD, as discussed in chapter 1. It is estimated from population surveys that about 2.5 percent of adults worldwide have ADHD. Differences are largely attributable to the use of differing diagnostic criteria. However, ADHD, as presented in chapter 2, was formerly thought to be a disorder of only children and not one that adults could even have. There had briefly been a diagnostic category of "Residual Type" ADHD, introduced in 1980 with DSM-III, to cover adults, when necessary, but it was removed in DSM-III-R in 1987. Finally, with DSM-5, released in 2013, there is recognition that adults can have ADHD as well as children.

The fact that Henry was first diagnosed with ADHD after coming in to help deal with issues his grandson was having shouldn't be that surprising. This phenomenon has been found to be rather common among individuals Henry's age. When Henry recalled his own dysfunctional family history, he revealed many characteristics that suggested both his father and mother, Zinaha's paternal grandparents, probably also had ADHD (although it was not recognized as such back then, as discussed in chapter 2). The fact that Henry's grandson has ADHD and both of his parents also probably had it shouldn't be surprising, as ADHD tends to run in families, and, accordingly, it has a high probability of being passed on genetically, as reviewed in chapter 3. There is about a 15–20 percent chance that parents of affected children will also have ADHD. Many adults are only now being diagnosed after learning that their children, or, in this case grandchildren, have the disorder. Furthermore, we now know that untreated ADHD, which was true of Henry for most of his life, is associated with greater risks for dementia and Alzheimer's disease.

Glossary

Abuse
Intentional continued consumption of any drug despite recognition of the harmful consequences of such problems.

Action potential
Rapid change in electrical potential between the inside and outside of a neuron, which, when attained, results in depolarization, with electrical impulse transmitted down the axon; it is an all-or-nothing process, resulting in activation or not firing at all.

Adrenergic
Related to the activation of the neurons and organs that are controlled by epinephrine or similar substances, such as norepinephrine.

Agonist
The substance that binds to a receptor site and activates it by mimicking the action of other substances that also bind there.

Alternative therapies
Various modalities of promoting health, also referred to as complementary, integrative, or holistic medicine.

Amine
Any of a broad class of organic compounds containing a nitrogen atom, including catecholamine neurotransmitters; amino acids; and many medicines, such as TCAs, amphetamines, and opiates.

Amygdala
Part of the limbic system of the brain, located in the temporal lobe of the cerebral hemisphere. It functions in generating feelings of pleasure, pain, and fear.

Antagonist
A substance that binds to a receptor site and blocks its action, preventing drugs or neurotransmitters from activating it.

175

Aromatherapy
Use of essential oils, employing sense of smell to promote relaxation and heighten concentration.

Art therapy
Alternative therapeutic modality using nonverbal self-expression to enhance self-awareness.

Autogenic training
Alternative therapeutic modality in which individuals give conscious messages to respective parts of their body.

Autonomic nervous system
The part of the peripheral nervous system that regulates internal organs and glands.

Axon
Fibrous structure that transmits neuronal impulses away from cell body to neurons or other structures, such as glands or muscles.

Basal ganglia
Groups of neurons, located at the base of the cerebrum, that control complex learned movements, mainly motor activities such as walking or riding a bike.

Behavioral therapy
Therapeutic approach based on principles of classical and operant conditioning to help individuals change problematic or self-defeating behaviors.

Bioavailabilty
The extent of the availability of a particular drug after oral administration, expressed as a percentage of dose taken.

Biofeedback
Alternative therapeutic modality using equipment to monitor and amplify body signals so that someone can alter their intensity.

Biogenic amines
Internally produced organic substances that are critical to brain functioning. They can be subdivided into catecholamines and indolamines.

Biotransformation
The processes by which the body, usually the liver, alters the chemical structure of a substance so that it can be eliminated, typically by excretion through urine.

Brain stem
The part of the brain closest to the spinal cord, through which signals are transmitted. Most basic natural functions are controlled here, such as respiration and heart rate. It consists of the medulla, pons, and midbrain.

Catecholamines
Group of biogenic amines, derived from phenylalanine, that contain a catechol nucleus, such as dopamine, epinephrine, and norepinephrine.

Caudate nucleus
Part of the corpus striatum, shaped with a long extension, like a tail.

Central nervous system
The brain and spinal cord. It serves to centrally process information from sensory systems and to select appropriate responses.

Cerebellum
Part of the human brain, located below the posterior part of cerebrum. It is the part most responsible for balance, movement, and muscular coordination.

Cerebrum
The largest and most complex part of human brain, divided into two hemispheres. It is responsible for control of thought and learning, including imagining, thinking, planning, and remembering.

Chi
Asian concept of a universal life force that is said to surround and permeate everything.

Cholinergic
Neurons and neural pathways related to activation that are controlled by acetylcholine, particularly parasympathetic nerve fibers.

Clinical trial
Experimental study designed to determine if a medicine or other medical intervention is safe and effective.

Cognitive behavioral therapy
Treatment that helps individuals change the way they think and behave by changing their ways of thinking.

Corpus striatum
Part of the human brain, situated at the base of each cerebral hemisphere.

Cortisol
Hormone released by the adrenal glands that helps prepare a response to stressful events by increasing the release of glucose and lipids into the circulatory system for rapid energy metabolism.

Dendrite
Fibrous structure that transmits neuronal impulses toward cell bodies. One neuron can have many hundreds of dendrites, each of which can potentially receive signals from adjacent neurons.

Depolarization
Increase in action potential across neuronal membrane, accompanied by a build-up of positive charges inside a cell, reversing its charge or polarity.

Distress
Negative interpretation of a real or imagined event as being unfavorable or threatening and prompting feelings of anger or fear.

Dopamine
Catecholamine neurotransmitter and precursor of epinephrine and norepinephrine that is involved in feelings of arousal and pleasure.

Dopaminergic
Related to cells that are stimulated by the neurotransmitter dopamine.

Downregulation
Process by which the number of receptor sites on a neuron is reduced, decreasing sensitivity to stimulation.

Enzyme
Protein that affects a specific molecule to accelerate the rate of a chemical reaction in the body.

Epinephrine
Catecholamine neurotransmitter that, among other functions, elevates blood pressure and heart rate.

Eustress
Term introduced by Hans Selye to designate a positive, life-enhancing form of stress.

Extrapyramidal symptoms
Signs of dysfunction of the extrapyramidal system, frequently associated with side effects of drugs. These include drooling, involuntary postures, motor inertia, muscular rigidity, restlessness, shuffling gait, and tremors.

Gate control theory
Theory suggesting a gate along the spinal cord either allows signals to transmit to the brain or blocks them.

Indolamines
Biogenic amines that have both an indole ring and an amine-group chemical structure, such as serotonin and tryptophan.

Limbic system
Interconnected brain structures that control emotions and motivation, includes the amygdala, hypothalamus, and septum.

MAOIs
Monoamine oxidase inhibitors are medicines that inhibit the enzymes that break down neurotransmitters, such as dopamine and serotonin, thereby increasing their levels.

Massage
Alternative therapeutic modality based on the manipulation of skin, muscles, and soft tissues.

Meditation
Alternative therapeutic modality based on focused concentration of internal stimuli to attain a state of greater focused attention and awareness.

Meridians
Pathways of subtle energy that are said to flow throughout the body, with hundreds of points along them used in techniques such as acupuncture and shiatsu.

Mesolimbic system
Interconnected brain system controlled by dopamine and running from the ventral tegmental to the nucleus accumbens and responsible for reward.

Misuse
Consumption of any drug in any manner or for any purpose other than that which has been recommended or prescribed by a health care professional.

Myelin sheath
Fatty, white lipid and protein protective covering of axons. It provides white matter for the brain and spinal cord and helps accelerate the transmission of neural impulses.

Neuron
A nerve cell in the brain and nervous system that transmits chemical and electrical impulses.

Neurotransmitter
Chemical substance that enables signal transmission between neurons and related structures, such as norepinephrine, dopamine, and serotonin.

Norepinephrine
Catecholamine neurotransmitter, also referred to as noradrenalin, that, among other things, prepares for a fight-or-flight stress response.

Physical dependence
Physiological state of adaptation resulting from chronic use of a drug, where tolerance is generally developed, and in which withdrawal symptoms typically manifest when use is dramatically reduced or ceased. It can occur with any type of chronic use, either appropriate or inappropriate use, of a drug.

Plasma protein binding
The affinity of a drug to chemically bind to proteins in blood, particularly albumin.

Polydrug abuse
Abuse of two or more drugs at the same general time.

Pons
Part of the brain stem, situated between the medulla and midbrain, serving as a bridge between the right and left halves of the cerebellum.

Postsynaptic potential
Change in the potential of a neuron's membrane that received transmission signal from another neuron.

Prescription abuse
Use of a drug without a prescription, or use in any way other than prescribed. Used interchangeably with nonmedical use.

Psychostimulant
Any substance that, when administered, increases arousal, blood pressure, heart rate, respiration, and so forth.

Putamen
Large, lateral part of the lenticular nucleus of the corpus striatum.

Rational emotive therapy
Psychotherapeutic approach developed by Albert Ellis as a way to help individuals change their perceptions of stressors.

Receptor site
Structure on a neuronal surface that allows specific neurotransmitters or other substances, such as psychoactive drugs, to fit into it and, thereby, activate it to create action potential.

Serotonin
Indolamine neurotransmitter that serves as a vasoconstrictor. Important in neurotransmission, sensory perception, and sleep.

Stress
Nonspecific response to a real or imagined threat or challenge.

Striatum
Part of the corpus striatum, consisting of the caudate nucleus and putamen.

Substantia nigra
Large nucleus located in the midbrain and containing dark melanin-pigmented cells, responsible for motor functions.

Substitution
Practice of administering any substance with the intent of replacing it for misuse or abuse of any drug.

Synapse
Minute space at the junction between two or more adjacent neurons, where neurotransmission or inhibition of chemical signals occurs.

Thalamus
Inner part of the cerebrum, responsible for integrative and sensory functions.

Tolerance
Situation of adaptation where increasingly greater amounts of a substance are required to produce a similar effect to that experienced during earlier use with less.

Use
Consumption of any drug, whether by legal or illegal means.

Vesicle
The small saclike structure of a neuron, containing a neurotransmitter or precursor substances.

Withdrawal
Unpleasant physical and psychological effects that appear when chronic use of substance one was habituated to is abruptly reduced or stopped. Symptoms might include abdominal pain, convulsions, delirium, tremors, and vomiting.

Yoga
Alternative therapeutic systems from India intended to unite the mind, body, and soul. The term "yoga" is derived from Sanskrit, meaning union.

Directory of Resources

BOOKS

Brown, T. E. (2013). *A new understanding of ADHD in children and adults: Executive function impairments.* New York: Routledge.

Hallowell, E. M., & Ratey, J. J. (2006). *Delivered from distraction: Getting the most out of life with attention deficit disorder.* New York: Ballantine Books.

Hallowell, E. M., & Ratey, J. J. (2011). *Driven to distraction: Recognizing and coping with attention deficit disorder.* New York: Random House.

Shankman, P. (2017). *Faster than normal: Turbocharge your focus, productivity, and success with the secrets of the ADHD brain.* New York: TarcherPerigee/Penguin Random House.

Stolberg, V. B. (2017). *ADHD medications: History, science, and issues.* Santa Barbara, CA: ABC-CLIO.

Wedge, M. (2015). *A disease called childhood: Why ADHD became an American epidemic.* New York: Penguin.

WEBSITES AND ORGANIZATIONS

A.D.D. Warehouse

The A.D.D. Warehouse is a secure electronic web resource center for the understanding and treatment of ADHD and related developmental disorders. It makes available books, assessment products, and training programs, including Continuing Medical Education (CME) on ADHD.

www.addwarehouse.org

ADHD Coaches Organization (ACO)

ACO is a not-for-profit worldwide professional membership organization for ADHD coaches. ACO provides a community where ADHD coaches can come together to develop and excel professionally and where those with ADHD can easily find a coach to match their needs. ACO is also committed to advocating for the profession and educating those interested in learning more about ADHD coaching.

www.adhdcoaches.org

American Professional Society of ADHD and Related Disorders (APSARD)

APSARD is a society for diverse mental health professionals working to improve the quality of care for those with ADHD through the advancement and dissemination of evidence-based practices and research. APSARD works with government, patient care, and media organizations to advocate for advancing scientific research and dissemination to benefit those with ADHD.

https://apsard.org

Association of Higher Education and Disability (AHEAD)

AHEAD, formerly known as the Association on Handicapped Student Service Programs in Postsecondary Education, is an international, multicultural volunteer professional organization. AHEAD provides communication, education, leadership, and professional development related to participation in higher education for individuals with disabilities, including ADHD.

www.ahead.org

Attention Deficit Disorder Association (ADDA)

ADDA is an international nonprofit, tax-exempt [501(c)(3)], entirely volunteer-run organization that provides information, networking opportunities, and resources to support adults with ADHD.

www.add.org

Attention Deficit Information Network (ADIN)

ADIN is a nonprofit volunteer organization providing information to families of children with ADHD, adults with ADHD, and professionals.

www.flandershealth.us

Children and Adults with Attention-Deficit/Hyperactivity Disorder (CHADD)

CHADD is a national nonprofit, tax-exempt [501(c)(3)] organization that provides advocacy, education, and support for individuals with ADHD.

www.chadd.org

National Resource Center on ADHD (NRC)

The NRC is a national clearinghouse for evidence-based information on ADHD. It is funded through the Centers for Disease Control and Prevention (CDC) National Center on Birth Defects and Developmental Disabilities (NCBDDD) and operates as a program of CHADD.

www.help4adhd.org

References

Amen, D. G. (1995). *Windows into the A.D.D. mind: Understanding and treating attention deficit disorders in the everyday lives of children, adolescents and adults.* Fairfield, CA: Mind Works Press.

Amen, D. G. (2013). *Healing ADD: The breakthrough program that allows you to see and heal the seven types of attention deficit disorder.* New York: Penguin Random House.

American Psychiatric Association. (2013). *Diagnostic and statistical manual of mental disorders* (DSM-5). Washington, D.C.: Author.

Barkley, R. A., & Peters, H. (2012). The earliest reference to ADHD in the medical literature? Melchior Adam Weikard's description in 1775 of attention deficit (*Mangel der Aufmerksamkeit, Attentio Volubilis*). *Journal of Attention Disorders* 16(8), 623–630.

Beard, G. (1869). Neurasthenia, or nervous exhaustion. *Boston Medical and Surgical Journal* 3, 217–221.

Berger, M. (1981). Remediating hyperkinetic behavior with impulse Control procedures. *School Psychology Review* 10(3), 405–407.

Conners, C. K., & Delamater, A. (1980). Visual-Motor tracking by hyperkinetic children. *Perceptual and Motor Skills* 51(2), 487–497.

Crichton, Alexander. (1798). *An inquiry into the nature and origin of mental derangement: Comprehending a concise system of the physiology and pathology of the human mind. And a history of the passions and their effects.* Vol. 2. London: T. Cadwell, Junior, and W. Davies.

Freeman, R. D. (1976). Minimal brain dysfunction, hyperactivity, and learning disorders: Epidemic or episode? *School Review* 85(1), 5–30.

Hoffmann, H. (2015). *Struwwelpeter 2000.* Translated by C. Blyth. Kingston, Ontario: Iolair Publishing.

James, William. (1890). *The principles of psychology.* New York: Henry Holt & Co.

Kellogg, J. H. (1915). *Neurasthenia: Or, nervous exhaustion.* Battle Creek, MI: Good Health Publishing Co.

Knights, R. M., & Hinton, G. G. (2004). Minimal brain dysfunction: Clinical and psychological test characteristics. *Intervention in School and Clinic* 4(4), 265–273.

Laufer, M. W., Denhoff, E., & Solomons, G. (1957). Hyperkinetic impulse disorder in children's behavior problems. *Psychosomatic Medicine* 19(1), 38–49.

Shaywitz, S. E., Cohen, D. J., & Shaywitz, S. E. (1978). The biochemical basis of minimal brain dysfunction. *Journal of Pediatrics* 92(2), 179–187.

Still, G. F. (1902). The Goulstonian lectures: On some abnormal physical conditions in children. *Lancet* 159(4102), 1008–1013.

Index

About the Author

Victor B. Stolberg, EdM, MA, MS, MA, MSEd, MAT, MAH, MALS, MA, is an assistant professor and counselor at Essex County College, Newark, New Jersey, where he previously directed both the Office of Disability Support Services and the Office of the Substance Abuse Coordinator. He is the author of Greenwood's *Painkillers: History, Science, and Issues* and *ADHD Medications: History, Science, and Issues*. He has authored or coauthored 49 scholarly articles, 87 encyclopedia articles, 6 chapters and contributed papers, and 63 miscellaneous other publications. He has delivered hundreds of professional presentations in over twenty states, including papers, workshops, and panel discussions at state, national, and international venues. He serves on the editorial board of the *Journal of Ethnicity in Substance Abuse*. In addition to his substance abuse and disability experience, he is a trained archaeologist and historian.

About the Author